Egypt and the Politics
of U.S. Economic Aid

D1521790

About the Book and Author

The massive U.S. economic aid program for Egypt initiated in 1975 resulted in a bilateral aid relationship shaped by the interaction of political and development goals. In this study of the program's origins and consequences, Professor Weinbaum describes its scope and identifies the constraints that delayed and limited program implementation. The author discusses the modest U.S. leverage designed to encourage economic reforms and argues that far-reaching reforms could only be attained through a major change in Egypt's political structure. He finds that, despite its failure to make Egypt more economically self-reliant, U.S. assistance has enabled the country to attain a level of consumption and development planning possible with no other alternative. The profit to the United States results from the regime's moderate foreign policies and compatible views on strategic threats to the region. Despite the mutual benefits of this aid program, Professor Weinbaum concludes that the United States must display greater sensitivity to Egypt's political and economic problems if the "special relationship" is to survive through the 1980s.

Marvin G. Weinbaum is director of the program in South and West Asian Studies and professor of political science at the University of Illinois, Urbana-Champaign. His most recent book is *Food, Development, and Politics in the Middle East* (Westview, 1982).

For Peter, Meg, and Ted

Egypt and the Politics
of U.S. Economic Aid

Marvin G. Weinbaum

Westview Press / Boulder and London

HC
830
.W45
1986

This Westview softcover edition was manufactured on our own premises using equipment and methods that allow us to keep even specialized books in stock. It is printed on acid-free paper and bound in softcovers that carry the highest rating of the National Association of State Textbook Administrators, in consultation with the Association of American Publishers and the Book Manufacturers' Institute.

All rights reserved. No part of this publication may be reproduced or transmitted in any form or by any means, electronic or mechanical, including photocopy, recording, or any information storage and retrieval system, without permission in writing from the publisher.

Copyright © 1986 by Westview Press, Inc.

Published in 1986 in the United States of America by Westview Press, Inc.; Frederick A. Praeger, Publisher; 5500 Central Avenue, Boulder, Colorado 80301

Library of Congress Cataloging-in-Publication Data
Weinbaum, Marvin G., 1935–
   Egypt and the politics of U.S. economic aid.
   (Westview special studies on the Middle East)
   Bibliography: p.
   Includes index.
   1. Economic assistance, American—Egypt. 2. Egypt—
Foreign relations—United States. 3. United States—
Foreign relations—Egypt. 4. Egypt—Economic policy.
I. Title. II. Series.
HC830.W45 1986   338.91'73'062   86-1662
ISBN 0-8133-7124-4 (soft: alk. paper)

Composition for this book was provided by the author.

Printed and bound in the United States of America

The paper used in this publication meets the minimum requirements of the American National Standard for Permanence of Paper for Printed Library Materials Z39.48-1984.

6   5   4   3   2   1

Contents

Tables and Figures

Acknowledgments

The research for this book was made possible by a Fulbright research grant that enabled me to study in Egypt in 1981-82. Subsequent travel awards by the Research Board of the University of Illinois at Urbana-Champaign were also invaluable. I profited greatly from my discussions with faculty members in the Political Science Department at Cairo University, where I was affiliated. I particularly wish to acknowledge the valued comments of Hassan Nafaar, Abdul Al-Mashat, Mustafar Kamel, and Ali Dessouki. Although we did not always agree, their informed views challenged me to strengthen my arguments. I must thank Professors Gouda Abdel-Khalek, Heba Handussa, Galal Amin, Tim Sullivan, and Elias Tuma at the American University in Cairo for sharing their thoughts about the Egyptian economy and contemporary politics. The observations, in part based on personal experiences with the U.S. aid program, of Andy Korvall of Catholic Relief Services, Ronald Wolf of AMIDEAST, and Michael Albin with the Library of Congress were highly instructive and insightful.

I also interviewed many Egyptians, mainly ministry officials and journalists, in connection with this study, and although I have chosen not to identify them directly, they helped to shape many of my conclusions about the bilateral aid relationship. Most of all, I am indebted to the several members of the AID mission in Cairo who were able to stand back from their activities and take a hard, often scholarly look at their own agency. Although none is responsible for any errors of fact or judgment, John Blackton, Owen Cylke, Graham Kerr, Ray Fort, Vann McKutchen, Bob Mitchell, Frank Moore, John Roberts, Bill Rucker, and Jerry Zarr, among others, contributed greatly to the final product. Nancy Cylke and Silvia Mitchell, who at different times headed the mission's Information Center, were untiring in their efforts to help me collect data and were always good company during the long hours I pored over materials in their reading room. My research was also facilitated by the staff of the American Educational Commission in Cairo. Their professionalism in helping me and my family adjust to life in Cairo and their timely introductions went a long way toward enabling me to complete my work. The several papers and articles that have preceded this book have elicited useful comments from readers. Although most of these critiques are anonymous, I can gratefully acknowledge the comments and corrections in one article by former ambassador to Egypt Hermann Eilts and former AID director in Cairo Don Brown. The sound advice of my editors at Westview Press, Kathy Streckfus and Janice Murray, must also be acknowledged. At Illinois the endurance and word processing skills of Eileen Yoder and Stephany Howard have been critical to this enterprise.

I also want to thank my wife, Francine, who, as an informal editor and travel companion, helped to form many of my thoughts about U.S.-Egyptian relations and to express them on these pages. And to my children, Peter, Meg, and Ted, to whom this book is dedicated, my appreciation is long overdue for their forbearance of a father who has so often over the years asked them to leave behind friends and school for another year abroad.

Marvin G. Weinbaum

Introduction

Western democratic models and accompanying strategies for economic growth and development were traditionally carried to the Middle East by elites who came into direct contact with the governments and economic systems in the West. Formal education and travel provided the inspiration and examples for leaders of government and business who succeeded in importing institutions and ideas to their countries, usually to see them superficially implanted and disappointingly practiced. Later, whole cultures became exposed to Western aspirations and values through the reach of the electronic media. Although this penetration has unalterably changed these societies, events in the Middle East have also made us acutely aware of the potentially adverse popular reactions to aspects of Westernization that threaten earlier authority patterns and values and leave unfulfilled high expectations. A more subtle pressure steering domestic policies and processes toward Western concepts of development is the activity of foreign consultants, technicians, and other resident advisors. The vehicle for much of this influence and direction is foreign aid programs, whose valued resources can provide strong incentives for liberalizing economies and inducing political changes.

Foreign aid is sought by policymakers in low-income countries in the Middle East as elsewhere in the belief that external support is necessary to overcome the constraints of insufficient capital investment resulting from limited savings and foreign exchange. The resource gap, as it is called, is to be filled by financial and technological assistance that creates the conditions needed for self-sustaining economic growth. Profound economic problems predictably force a lengthy gestation period prior to any "takeoff." Yet, with a reliable flow of foreign aid to guide and stimulate a country's own efforts and to encourage an appropriate domestic environment, economic growth and productivity are expected to register short-term improvement that affects the lives of most citizens. Not incidentally, the initiative and released enterprise of an expanded private sector is presumed by most Western economists—and by many in the developing countries as well—to provide an unrivaled means of spurring economic growth. The gains are, in turn, thought to promote political stability and, through this, close ties and favorable attitudes toward the aid donors and their economic systems.

1

More than a decade of U.S. economic assistance to Egypt gives us ample reason to question some of these premises and projections. Substantial aid transfers have indeed been one way for Egypt, with its limited export potential and modest prospects for capital mobilization from domestic sources, to improve the growth rate of its Gross National Product (GNP). Dependency on foreign aid may be an unavoidable, rational policy where national goals and political imperatives call for simultaneously raising levels of mass consumption and investment in development. U.S. bilateral aid to Egypt, including commodity and technology transfers, has probably been indispensable for meeting immediate resource needs and the infrastructural requirements of industry. Few, if any, good alternatives may exist to an aid-based development strategy and a strong U.S. role. Whatever the asymmetries between Egypt and its major donor, the relationship can serve mutual economic and political goals.

Still, the discussions in this book raise doubts about whether generous foreign assistance has always been constructive in bringing the kinds of development that ensure a capacity for sustained economic expansion. The evidence suggests that foreign aid has at times substituted for domestic effort and that too much of it has come in a form that stimulated consumption, often luxury, at the expense of development. High levels of assistance often seem to be inversely related to Egypt's ability to use the aid effectively or wisely. Foreign support appears also to have contributed to unbalanced sectoral growth and created new inequities in the society. Modern sector private enterprise in Egypt has been more difficult to generate and the public sector more entrenched than many U.S. advisors had supposed. It remains at issue whether assured flows of assistance have acted more to put off than to induce needed domestic policy reforms. Even more uncertain is the anticipated positive impact of aid on Egypt's political order.

Egypt possesses many attributes not ordinarily associated with a developing country. It can boast of a highly productive agricultural system and energy self-sufficiency. In terms of education and skills, the country retains a strong human resource base. Egypt gains substantial foreign exchange earnings from oil exports, remittances from workers abroad, Suez Canal tolls, and tourism. Balance-of-payments surpluses occurred with some regularity in recent years. Economic growth since 1977 has averaged about 8 percent, up from a rate of less than 3 percent annually between 1967 and 1974. The expanded economy reflects a remarkable upsurge in public and private investment, totaling between 25 and 30 percent of GNP.

Yet the basic structure of Egypt's economy in the mid-1980s is weak and hardly self-sustaining. The more than $2 billion received annually from the West in foreign grants and loans, military aid aside, are needed to cope with the government's deep budget deficits, to feed its citizens, and to augment available capital and technology for industry, agriculture, and social services. Egypt is still relatively poor with an annual per capita income of $690 and, on a very limited arable land base, a yearly rate of population increase averaging close to 3 percent. The Egyptian government also shares with most of the Third World difficulty in mobilizing and managing effectively its available domestic resources.

The economic liberalization-cum-political strategy embarked upon by President Anwar Sadat in 1974 assumed that the advanced Western countries and the United States in particular would become Egypt's major sources of aid and investment. By fall 1985, U.S. economic assistance programs had committed more than $10.8 billion for Egypt. The yearly aid package since 1975 far surpasses assistance by the United States to any other country except Israel. These two countries receive more than one-third of all U.S. economic aid. Had Egypt been just another friendly country in the developing world, the level of overall economic assistance from the United States would probably not have exceeded $150 to $200 million yearly. Successive U.S. administrations concluded, however, that strategic objectives, namely, an ending of Egypt's confrontation with Israel and the securing of U.S. interests in a wider regional political stability, were directly served by generous economic aid. Egypt's cooperation was to be gained through a tangible and positive expression of the U.S. commitment to an expanding Egyptian economy. The foreign policies, Western-oriented economics, and democratization plans of Sadat and his successor, Hosni Mubarak, were considered by U.S. leaders to rest on the government's ability to realize popular demands for economic improvement. A continuity of government policies and, very probably, the survival of a friendly regime depended, in the U.S. view, on the satisfaction of economic expectations among key supporting segments in the society. In few countries, then, were the political motives in aid more prominent and the recipient's economic needs or assessments of its capacity to absorb funds for development given less weight in deciding the magnitude of aid.

The very size of the aid effort set it apart in the sense that whatever lessons were learned in Egypt would not necessarily be applicable to the sixty or so other countries receiving various forms of U.S. economic assistance. Nevertheless, Egypt's visibility in the Middle East and Third World and the depth of its problems made the country a prime testing ground for development ideas and strategies. The level of funding also assured that approaches and programs that could be implemented only in part elsewhere would have a fuller application to Egypt. From the outset, the U.S. development assistance has been multifaceted and wide ranging. It involves commodity transfers of consumables, raw materials, and finished goods as well as development aid for large capital projects and technical assistance. The program touches every sector of the Egyptian economy—industry, commerce and agriculture—but also basic human services and local government financing. Of the roughly $1 billion authorized for Egypt in annual economic aid through the mid-1980s, about $450 million was slated directly for development projects, another $300 million for commodity aid, and the rest for sales under the Public Law 480, Food for Peace Program. Long-term concessional credits, approximately $250 million yearly, available mainly for wheat and wheat flour, made Egypt by far the largest recipient of the U.S. food aid program. Additionally, $1.2 billion was earmarked in 1984-85 for military sales to Egypt, a level of assistance that has risen sharply during the 1980s.

It fell to the U.S. Agency for International Development (AID) to lead the efforts to salvage a very sick Egyptian economy in the mid-1970s and to provide the resources needed to pursue economic expansion and also sustain adequate consumption levels. In time AID/Cairo became the largest overseas U.S. aid mission. Its projects carried not only the weight of development but the burden of trying to spearhead effective policy reform in the country. The AID program that has emerged bears the constraints imposed by the larger official U.S. community in Egypt, AID's Washington bureaucracy, and the U.S. Congress as well as AID's interactions with Egyptian policymakers. Most of all, the programs exhibit the heavy baggage of development ideas, procedures, and regulations acquired in a generation of giving aid to poorer countries.

The direction and tone of U.S. economic aid to Egypt has been governed by several goals and norms. The most important of these assumes that economic growth and development will be most fully realized through Egypt's integration with the West's market economies. The aid programs do give expression to many of the interests and priorities of Egyptian policymakers, and their government ministries are normally expected to assume responsibility for contracting for imports, engaging technical services, and distributing loans. The United States is also mindful of Egypt's deeply ingrained desire for social equity. Nevertheless, the assistance program essentially conforms to strategies of capital accumulation devised in the West and the development experiences of the United States, other Western donor countries, and international aid agencies.

To the extent that the U.S. program has followed a development model for Egypt, it is one that, put briefly, envisions a more export-oriented industrial society, supplemented by a highly productive agricultural sector. The implicit model foregoes national self-sufficiency in order to maximize Egypt's supposed comparative advantage in both industry and agriculture. Declining rates of growth are anticipated from most current revenue sources, including foreign assistance, to be gradually replaced by more effective domestic taxation and new sources of foreign exchange. Domestic policies that constrain free market activities, protectionist policies, and interventions in prices and labor markets are expected to give way to those that effectively encourage productivity and economic growth. Built into the model are constraints that acknowledge a normative consensus that the benefits of economic growth and stability not be too disproportionately shared and a floor for consumer buying power and basic services be assured. However, the economic course also presupposes a larger, vigorous private sector along with a stabilized and improved public sector and a greater decentralization of development decisions. Aid plans envision an Egypt that is an even more highly congested urban society with adequate, if minimal, public services and relatively low real income, but a country that has learned to use its natural assets and human resources to greater benefit.

The following chapters describe and analyze the motives, means, and consequences of this broadly gauged approach to economic assistance to Egypt. They offer an excellent opportunity to observe geopolitical, development, and humanitarian objectives in the Egyptian situation and to better understand how their intertwining forms the U.S. program. Above all, the study raises the question of whether an aid effort that during its history has been based more on political considerations than careful attention to economic needs and capacities is likely to serve Egypt's interests or, for that matter, contribute in the long run to assuring a regime able to serve U.S. designs for peace and stability in the Middle East.

Chapter One surveys the changes in direction and funding for U.S. economic assistance to the developing world. It describes in particular the influence in the 1980s of the strong free market philosophy promoted by the Reagan administration. The major objectives in present U.S. aid programs are discussed as a prerequisite for understanding how assistance to Egypt has conformed to the general thrust in U.S. aid policy and has also been permitted to deviate because of Egypt's special political role. Chapter Two surveys the close relationship between U.S. aid and Egypt's liberalizing economic policies. After examining the pre-1974 foreign aid experiences in the context of a quasi-socialist economy, the discussion points out the motives in opening Egypt economically and politically to the West. The discussion considers the consequences of the revised policies for growth and equity in Egypt's economy. The chapter stresses the facilitating role of U.S. aid and how, in turn, disappointments with the more liberal economic policies have colored Egypt's attitudes toward U.S. aid activities.

Chapter Three weighs arguments that the United States and other foreign aid donors have created production disincentives and distortions in the Egyptian economy. The chapter evaluates whether Egypt's dependent economic relations with the industrial West and the United States in particular are an unavoidable price for economic growth and stability. It also notes how politically motivated aid, for all its obligations on the recipient, carries some notable advantages. The chapter does not find aid to Egypt to be a good case study in classic dependency theory. The Egyptian turn to the West is seen as a calculated decision by a nationalist-minded government that perceived Western aid as the most promising course for a country faced with immediate economic and political crises. Multinational firms, the familiar *bete noire* in the dependency perspective, are found to have played a relatively small role relative to the investment in Egypt of bilateral and multilateral aid donors. Despite its association with Egypt's liberalized economy, the United States has had only limited success in promoting policy reforms or in imparting its development values to the Egyptians. Failure to date of massive U.S. aid to show much progress in building a more productive, self-sustaining economy in Egypt comes not as a result, it is argued, of a U.S. effort to keep Egypt economically weak and exploitable, but largely as a consequence of the size of the task, AID's own institutional impediments, and the inability of the Egyptians themselves to manage more successfully new resources and technologies.

Chapter Four describes the key features and the specific content of the current AID program in several economic sectors. The lengthy delays in competing projects are underscored and the obstacles identified. Particular attention is given in this chapter to agricultural development strategies adopted by AID and its financial assistance to decentralization plans and rural development. Cooperation and competition by the United States with other aid donors are also described. In a conclusion, the alternatives to the present dominant project mode of aid delivery are explored along with the arguments for and against change.

Chapter Five examines the character of the U.S. AID mission, the private U.S. contractors it finances, and their interaction with Egyptian ministries and agencies involved in development activities. On one side is what appears to be a rationally oriented foreign aid donor, encouraging the use of objective economic analyses in the formation and evaluation of programs and insisting on the application of adequate economic incentives to ensure their implementation. On the other side is an Egyptian bureaucracy, both patrimonial and socialized, ostensibly hostile to classic concepts of economic efficiency and rationality. In fact, it is not simply a study of contrasts. As this chapter shows, the AID mission in Cairo often lacks the flexibility and autonomy necessary for adequate response to Egypt's development needs. The Egyptian bureaucracy, in its attitudes, politics, and procedures, may be largely rational in pursuit of those national goals it deems primary. Sometimes conflicting development priorities of the donor and recipient go far toward explaining the only limited progress to date of the U.S. aid effort. But a fuller appreciation of the problems also necessitates a study of the goal-setting and implementation process formed of the interactions between the U.S. and Egyptian bureaucracies. The discussions in this chapter posit the view that bureaucracy per se accounts for much of the delays and the derailment of aid, and normative contrasts between the two bureaucracies largely explain the often difficult donor/recipient relationship.

Chapter Six focuses on Egypt's system of food and energy subsidies. Pressures for reform as well as maintenance of these policies provide a picture of those contemporary political forces, domestic and foreign, that help to shape the country's economic choices and its development values. The origins of government pricing and subsidy policies are examined and their impact on equity/redistributive goals weighed. The chapter describes the pressures for policy changes by the United States and other aid donors and points out their only limited leverage over Egypt's policy makers. It also suggests some ways in which the U.S. and other aid donors have in fact helped to perpetuate the system of subsidies and the role foreign aid might play in easing the transition to a domestic price structure closer to world prices. Two broad conclusions are reached in the chapter. The first asserts that international pressures that so often try to instigate a more market-oriented, decentralized economy, when accompanied by generous, politically motivated foreign aid, in fact lessen the probability of domestic economic reform by reducing the urgency for change and relieving authorities from having to make politically difficult choices. The second is that for reform to be implemented successfully, the government must either employ more political repression than it is capable of mounting or introduce greater democratization than it seems willing to risk. Lacking either the power to ignore popular interests and feelings, or the instruments that could enable it to mobilize popular consent for change the Mubarak government is unable to move quickly on vigorous, meaningful policy reform.

Chapter Seven examines recent political events in the Middle East for their bearing on the U.S.-Egyptian aid relationship. The increased suspicions and unfavorable images growing out of U.S. policies in the region and its program in Egypt are found among both Egyptian elites and broader publics. The chapter describes the efforts of Egypt's leaders to redefine aspects of the U.S. programs and, in particular, their attempts to gain greater control over the terms and uses of aid. Meanwhile, increased doctrinal approaches to aid from Washington and pressures on the Cairo government for economic reforms put additional strains on relations. Although mutual political and economic interests continue to be a strong basis for cooperation and few attractive alternatives to U.S. aid are identified, the study concludes that the United States will have to exercise greater sensitivity to Egypt's mounting political and economic dilemmas if the "special relationship" is to survive through the 1980s.

1

Directions and Strategies
in U.S. Foreign Aid

Bilateral assistance programs have remained prime instruments of U.S. economic and security policy throughout the postwar years. U.S. foreign aid first to Europe and then the developing countries laid the basis for strong dependent and interdependent relationships, commercial, political, and military. During the four decades since the end of World War II, U.S. economic aid has taken various forms and directions in accordance with changing global needs and the short- and long-term objectives of the U.S. government. The aims and content of U.S. assistance have also reflected the rise and decline of development ideas. Throughout this period, economic aid has involved transfers of capital, technology, and commodities, especially food. It has focused on broad programs and country strategies as well as on specific projects. Progress in overcoming many problems of the developing countries continues to hinge on the adequacy and appropriateness of this external aid. But it also is thought to depend on the absorptive capacity of the recipient country as determined by its physical and human stock and, above all, a political will expressed through domestic policies.

To its advocates, U.S. and other Western aid transfers, both bilateral and multilateral, supplement a recipient country's resources and help stabilize weak economies. In the long run, aid improves conditions for high levels of output and employment, in part by stimulating the recipient country's ability to mobilize its own resources. Aid rarely escapes controversy, however. In the absence of good theories or agreed guidelines to indicate how much and what kind of aid are optimal for realizing stated economic and development objectives, differences regularly arise about the content of programs and whether aid is being allocated in the most desirable form. There is little empirical evidence, moreover, that demonstrates cross-nationally the relative effectiveness of official aid programs compared with private investment strategies and commercial loans or, for that matter, the alternative to external aid in policies of national self-sufficiency.[1] But much of the debate is essentially subjective, often moral. Opposing views rest on ideologically inspired judgments about Western economic institutions and values. Detractors focus on the alleged tendency of aid to inhibit recipient countries' own productive efforts and to waste resources. In contrast to the view that assumes the indispensability of foreign exchange for development and the gains from integration into a global market system, many critics stress the tethering of developing countries to Western industrial economies and an inherently unequal distribution of the proceeds of aid. Differing doctrinal approaches also variously prescribe aid as a means to sustain a status quo, to improve or reform economic and social conditions, or, in a more radical vein, to help mobilize the poor, facilitating their efforts to organize against those who hold power.

Differences appear even when similar economic philosophies and political goals prevail. Policy-makers within the United States and other Western donor countries are not always in agreement about the purposes of aid. Some emphasize economic efficiency in choosing development programs; others give greater weight to their presumed impact. Disagreements frequently pit those anxious to use aid to promote economic growth and stability as a means to political ends against those more committed to development assistance for its own sake. Politically allied countries receiving assistance complain about the levels and terms of support and frequently decry explicit economic conditionality in aid and implicit political obligations. These governments often question their own ability to help shape assistance programs. They perceive unwarranted interventions in their domestic affairs and protest that programs too often reflect the priorities and development experiences of the donors rather than the real needs of the recipients. Almost inevitably there arise resentments growing out of the extended economic and technological dependency and financial indebtedness incurred by low-income, less developed countries.

This study concedes the primacy of politically motivated aid and the importance of commercial and trade interests in prompting U.S. budgetary and development assistance to much of the Third World. No state can, after all, be expected for any extended period to slight foreign policy objectives or ignore the implications of aid for its own economic well-being. Indeed, aid-giving that repeatedly fails to recognize domestic self-interest may be difficult to sustain in a democracy. Aid policies plainly involve mixed motives and can serve several purposes at the same time. Thus, concessional food sales meet humanitarian needs even as they are used to reduce grain surpluses and help stimulate long-term commercial markets for farm exports. Food shipments that succeed in coping with problems of hunger and malnutrition may contribute, not incidentally, to the political viability of a friendly regime. The same assistance that finances development project contracts and creates commodity dependencies is also likely to relieve host governments from having to draw on their limited reserves for critical imports and to increase available resources for social investment.

At issue in politicized and commercially self-serving aid is the extent to which such aid distorts or denies the full value of assistance. Aid strongly colored by a donor's economic philosophy may be particularly inappropriate, even if incrementally beneficial to the recipient. It is argued here that the United States in its economic assistance programs has simultaneously and sincerely tried to pursue political and commercial as well as developmental and humanitarian objectives, but that contradictions do arise in so broad a strategy. Much as U.S. political aims and domestic economic interests do not always run parallel in foreign aid, both at times are incompatible with the development needs of recipient countries. It may be unfair to conclude, as some do, that when politics predominates in aid the poor cannot be served. Yet it is probably valid to say that politically motivated aid tends to strengthen the status quo. The failure of the United States and its aid agency to come to terms with incompatibilities in aid objectives often results in unrealized expectations and bitter frustrations with foreign aid.

Evolving Approaches to Aid Policy

The recent history of U.S. economic assistance began with the massive lend lease program undertaken to bolster the war efforts of allies during World War II. Between 1941 and 1946, a total of $50 billion was spent, four-fifths of which went to British Commonwealth countries and the Soviet Union. But the major precursor to present-day programs was the postwar effort to rebuild war-shattered economies of Western Europe. The Marshall Plan's economic and technical assistance from 1947 to 1952 met acute shortages of commodities, revived an industrial capacity, created markets for U.S. goods, and assured a united front in the emerging Cold War with the Soviets. By the early 1950s, with the reconstruction of Europe assured, the United States found itself with resources and skills that could be employed to assist a greatly expanded number of newly independent countries. The appropriateness of Western technological and development goals was largely taken for granted. As in the Marshall Plan, the purpose of the U.S. aid was to provide the resources and know-how that would launch these new states on the road to self-sustaining development.[2] U.S. aid to developing countries was spurred by a post-Stalin era challenge from the Soviets who were now ready with aid agreements to help Third World governments sever ties with the West and adopt a Soviet development model. In the competition with the Soviets, much of the U.S. economic aid beginning in the mid-1950s shifted from aid to countries allied to the West to those that had, at least publicly, accepted the principles of non-alignment. As such, the political obligations in taking economic and food aid became more implicit and the effectiveness of this aid as an instrument of U.S. foreign policy diminished.

To implement assistance to the less developed countries, President Harry Truman in 1950 inaugurated the Point Four Program. Its Technical Cooperation Administration was soon replaced by an Economic Cooperation Administration and still later by the Mutual Security Agency (MSA). Increasingly, the programs undertook economic as well as technical assistance and military aid under MSA. In 1961, Congress consolidated several nonmilitary programs in authorizing the Agency for International Development (AID) as an independent unit in the Department of State. Created by an idealistic and security-minded Kennedy presidency, the new agency coincided with a policy of accelerating economic growth in the less developed countries. AID and its immediate predecessor spent roughly $2 billion annually to aid countries in Asia, Africa, and Latin America (compared with the $15 billion distributed to a few European countries during the four years of the Marshall Plan).[3] The Vietnam War and then the costs of meeting requests of aid clients in the Middle East later raised expenditures to approximately $4 billion annually. By 1985, AID was directly responsible for disbursing about $6 billion in economic and development assistance. Another $800 million to $1 billion has been allocated yearly since the mid-1950s to finance the sale of agricultural surpluses under Title I, Public Law 480, a program of highly concessional loans administered by the U.S. Department of Agriculture. Each year, an additional $100 million or more are also spent for humanitarian emergency aid to needy countries.

Early in the postwar period, the United States held the conviction, which was reinforced by the European aid experience, that developing countries could best realize economic growth through domestic capital accumulated in expanded trade in a liberalized world economy. Rather than external capital inflows, trade and a suitable domestic policy environment would be sufficient to stimulate domestic investment and attract private foreign funds. Where loans were necessary from international sources, they should be made available on strictly commercial terms. By the mid-1950s, however, serious doubts had arisen whether trade could serve as the primary and most effective means to promote growth in the less developed countries. A revised view saw development in these countries constrained by insufficient expansion of capital stock created by shortages of local savings and foreign exchange as well as by the need for technological assistance. Aid strategists concluded that foreign financial assistance would have to supply more of the investment for capital goods production and guide the efficient allocation of resources.[4] This aid was expected to serve U.S. foreign policy interests by increasing chances for political stability and encouraging the democratic processes believed necessary to stave off communist penetration. The United States was also behind the World Bank's expansion of its lending capacity in the late 1950s and the founding of the International Development Association (IDA), an affiliate institution of the bank created to offer softer development loans to the lowest income countries.

The development approach that dominated U.S. policy during the 1950s and 1960s focused on increasing aggregate production and macrolevel planning in recipient countries. Gains were registered through new agricultural techniques, but industralization was generally viewed as the fastest path to rapid development in low-income countries. This strategy assumed that mass poverty in recipient countries would eventually be solved by expanded employment in a more rationalized and productive economy. Serious maldistributions of the benefits of growth were deemed a necessary price to pay in order to assure high investment rates. The model expected better mobilization of local capital through domestic taxation and restraints on government consumption expenditures. Foreign assistance was supposed to facilitiate large-scale infrastructural improvements, the purchases of Western equipment and technologies, institutional building, and opportunities for useful education and training.[5] Once they could overcome various resource constraints, the economies of developing countries would be ready for a "takeoff" stage that would graduate them from the need for further external aid.

Doubts about this development model increased during the 1960s. The approach that emerged in the 1970s to replace it addressed a different set of problems, namely, the creation of aid programs more relevant to the poorest countries and to the least well-off members of their populations. Economic growth was a legitimate goal but only if it was instrumental in alleviating poverty and allowing investment aimed at strengthening "human capital." The task was somehow to increase the incomes and productivity of the urban jobless, the tenant farmers, and the landless laborers, the bottom 40 percent of the Third World's population, enabling them to make a contribution to national economic prosperity through their savings, investment, and, ultimately, consumption. In place of gross economic indicators, improved opportunities for employment and gains in living standards would measure progress. The prescriptions allowed, moreover, that foreign aid might be an appropriate tool in bringing about administrative decentralization and, where required, major social and economic reforms in recipient countries. There was ample evidence that the earlier strategies that largely ignored distributive consequences, such as the application of technological advances registered by the Green Revolution in agriculture, had created greater income disparities while increasing overall production.

The New Directions, as the revised approach to foreign aid came to be called, was taken up not only by the United States but by other donor countries and international agencies, most notably the World Bank. In the United States this approach could not be entirely separated from much of the post-Vietnam questioning in the Congress and elsewhere about a legitimate and appropriate U.S. role in the Third World and how to best correct the economic and social conditions thought to lead to totalitarian regimes. More directly, advocates in Washington believed it imperative that the United States help people in recipient countries to participate in a manner that would assure more responsible, successful government. Changes in the directions of development aid were also a token of the disillusionment felt by many Third World leaders with their country's slow progress in gaining economic growth and the worsening terms of trade with the developed countries. Sensitivities increased with mounting external indebtedness and the seeming loss of economic independence in the face of rising populist, often radical, domestic pressures.

The new mandate in U.S. foreign aid gave special emphasis to agricultural development and the basic needs of rural populations. Planners argued that, after all, the majority of the poor are still concentrated in the rural areas and their economic hardship pushes so many of the unemployed into overcrowded cities. But interest extended beyond modernizing agricultural technology and raising crop yields. Attention was to be given to the access of small farmers to productive assets through programs such as agricultural credit and equitable land tenure arrangements. There would be special concern for the landless and their plight. In programs to support integrated rural development, alternative means were designed to provide income for the landless and underemployed as well as to assure the delivery of basic social services.

Inevitably, there has been an adverse reaction to the New Directions philosophy. In stressing project aid and the delivery of services to the poor, the difficulties of implementation were often badly underestimated. Health, nutrition, housing, and education needs were always larger and more complex than had been conceived by planners, and specific projects to implement improvements were frequently stymied in the recipient countries by shortages of skilled managers and, in general, a weak institutional capacity. Few foreign experts fully appreciated the determination of local elites to resist change and the relative powerlessness of the poor. There were unrealistic expectations about how quickly various strategies, including broadened credit facilities and employment generating programs, would have economic payoffs. Critics often expressed doubts about the cost-effectiveness of many new initiatives and whether adequate attention was given to domestic policy constraints and workers' incentives. In the concern for income transfers, resources, including savings, were not always adequately mobilized by aided countries. Need for a better balance was stressed by the critics, one that recognized long-term returns for social welfare in capital investments, technological innovations, training, and managerial improvements. They questioned whether infrastructural requirements and the industrial sector's needs were now being slighted just as agriculture had been earlier. The stress on equity and popular participation seemed to some no less a fad in development thinking than had been the prior preoccupation with economic growth.

Funding Foreign Aid

During forty years of aid programs, the United States has offered some form of economic assistance at some level to virtually every country outside the Soviet orbit and several within it. The grand total spent for foreign aid since World War II comes to more than $250 billion, almost 60 percent of which went for economic assistance. More than $35 billion was contributed as food aid since the enactment of P.L. 480 in 1954. Excluding Vietnam, the principal recipients of economic and military assistance have been Israel, India, South Korea, Egypt, Britain, France, and Pakistan. Aid has taken the form of both grants and loans, with the former comprising about 70 percent of economic aid to date. During the period 1968–1972, while the war in Vietnam was in progress, economic aid to all countries ran only slightly ahead of military assistance. By 1973–1977, the military segment of bilateral foreign aid had slipped to 43 percent, and between 1978 and 1982 the yearly average fell to just 33 percent. In fiscal year 1984, however, it had climbed back to 42 percent of expenditures. A record $12.8 billion was approved for foreign aid by the U.S. Congress for each of two fiscal years beginning October 1985 with military assistance claiming 49 percent of the authorization.[6]

Judged by the level of development aid prescribed by the United Nations for developed countries—0.70 percent of GNP—the U.S. yearly average contribution had declined to 0.20 percent by the early 1980s; this compared with 0.43 percent of GNP in other aid-giving industrial countries and ranked the United States fifteenth among seventeen major Western donors. (The United States, however, with the world's largest economy, was the single greatest source of economic assistance for developing countries, running far ahead of the USSR in both absolute terms and percentage of GNP.) U.S. aid had also fallen off when measured as a percentage of budgetary expenditures, from 3 percent in 1960 to 1.6 percent in 1970 and to 1.1 percent in 1982.[7]

The mid-1970s marked a clear geographical redirection of U.S. foreign aid. Although much of the aid had been siphoned off for Southeast Asia (a total of $17 billion) from 1968 though 1973, assistance to the Middle East dominated the second half of the 1970s and continued into the 1980s. Israel and Egypt were treated most generously, and the almost sixty other recipients were left to share the rest. Aid to the two countries was accounted for in a separate category of economic assistance, known first as Security Supporting Assistance (SSA) and, beginning in 1978, as the Economic Support Fund (ESF); in either case it was acknowledged to be aid primarily linked to foreign policy objectives. Although U.S. officials were encouraged by legislation to seek out economically worth-while projects and, where possible, to promote development goals, allocations under ESF were less restricted by the New Directions mandate. ESF also justified a disproportionately large share of the foreign aid to just a few countries (see Table 1.1 for countries with substantial programs). Of all the countries with ESF programs in fiscal 1984, nine of them in the Middle East, Israel and Egypt alone took more than one-half of the $3.4 billion authorized.[8] Several of the ESF recipients were, like Israel, relatively high-income countries. Moreover, the $750 million in ESF that went to Egypt in 1983-84 was many times larger than economic assistance slated by the United States for countries with lower incomes and far greater populations. Notwithstanding official rhetoric, the poorest coun-tries are not strong claimants of U.S. aid dollars. Wide recognition of this lack of congruence between U.S. aid and the needs of low-income states often leads those who covet U.S. support to stress and sometimes exaggerate their security requirements and the U.S. stake in their economic well-being. Willingness to agree to U.S. bases on their territory is for many countries the best guarantee of generous treatment in U.S. foreign aid legislation.[9]

At the same time that a very few countries have done exceedingly well in attracting huge sums of U.S. foreign aid, domestic support for aid programs in the United States has withered. What was once a solid pro-aid coalition of legislators and public groups has nearly disappeared under the weight of shocks and disappointments. The misuse and manipulation of economic assistance in Vietnam, including food financing, badly tarnished the once largely pristine image of aid and resulted in tightened postwar controls on aid by Congress. A decade of high inflation, economic recession, and then massive budget deficits has focused attention and given priority to domestic needs. In recent years, the split in Congress focuses on those who advocate reserving aid mainly for security objectives and those who continue to promote funding for

TABLE 1.1
Economic Support Fund (ESF) Programs, Fiscal Years
1984 and 1985 (in millions of dollars)

Country	Fiscal 1984, Final[a]	Fiscal 1985, Preliminary[b]
Egypt	750	815
Israel	910	1,200
Jordan	20	20
Lebanon	0	5
Pakistan	225	200
Turkey	138.5	175
Cyprus	15	15
Spain	12	12
Portugal	40	80
Philippines	50	140
Tunisia	1.5	20
Somalia	35	30
Morocco	7	15
Sudan	120	114
Zaire	10	10
Costa Rica	130	160
El Salvador	210.5	195
Guatemala	0	12.5
Honduras	112.5	75

[a]Includes regular and supplemental requests and amounts appropriated by Congress in continuing resolution and supplemental bills.

[b]Amounts allocated under a continuing resolution signed into law October 12, 1984.

Source: *Congressional Quarterly*, November 24, 1984, p. 3003.

development. Although some find, at best, a weak link between assistance programs and U.S. core interests, others perceive aid as a blatant foreign policy tool, used, in particular, to prop up unpopular regimes. Contributions to multilateral development agencies whose loans assist countries that oppose most U.S. policies furnish a common complaint. Congressional critics also find reason to reduce funding where evidence exists of corruption in large-scale projects and where doubts are raised about the effectiveness of programs. The once supportive U.S. labor movement has turned against foreign aid in its preoccupation with halting the flight of industrial investment and protecting jobs against foreign competition. Even U.S. farmers who profit from the export markets provided by U.S. concessional food commodity sales have turned on foreign assistance programs as allegedly transferring the technical know-how that builds aid recipient producers into competitors for the world's commercial markets.

In the absence of a broad, reliable foreign aid constituency, the program remained alive through the mid-1980s only through continuing appropriations resolutions in Congress and through supplemental bills.[10] At a roughly constant level for most development and food aid country programs, this funding represents a real loss in the purchasing power of economic aid dollars. Yet the total foreign aid outlays during the Reagan administration increased steadily. This reflected no sense of urgency about economic and social issues but the need to keep arms flowing to the Middle East and elsewhere.[11] The unpopularity of foreign aid was more than counterbalanced by support in Congress for Israel and, as a proxy, for Egypt. Those aid categories considered "security assistance," namely, the Economic Support Fund and military sales and assistance programs, were the recipients of the bulk of the increases, with the most dramatic gains in grants for countries to buy U.S.-made weapons. Major military aid programs went from $3.2 billion in the last Carter administration budget to $6.3 billion authorized for 1985-86.[12]

Reordering Priorities

The Reagan administration inherited a development aid program worldwide that it could not immediately alter or undo. Much of the financial assistance was based on long-term commitments to projects in progress. Any abrupt halt or sharp reduction in programs could send unfriendly signals to countries in the Third World that were expected to cooperate with U.S. policy. At the same time, additional funds for creating new initiatives were not available. The New Directions mandate of the 1970s, although seen by administration officials as seriously flawed, could be disavowed outright only at the cost of seeming insensitivity to humanitarian concerns. All the same, by 1982, new criteria for determining U.S. aid investments and for evaluating recipient government policies were apparent. A country's observance of human rights as a criterion for qualifying for economic assistance was, most noticeably, jettisoned. AID in Washington stressed increased attention to more effective management of the U.S. aid dollar, accelerated improved technology and skills, and institution building. As much as possible, self-help would replace resource transfers. In a larger sense, U.S. officials sought to restore a pre-1973 philosophy aimed at facilitating economic growth among those already more productive sectors and groups in the aided economy. Foreign aid in the 1980s was, above all, expected to make its contribution toward building a strategic consensus against communism and help recipient countries assume their role in the market global economy. Although most aid programs continued to be justified on development grounds, there were fewer excuses made for the overt use of aid in diplomatic and political strategy and for more determination in assuring the visibility of U.S. aid programs.

A zeal in selling its economic philosophy at home was soon infused into the administration's aid program. Economic assistance offered the opportunity to exhibit the correctness and strength of the free market as a means to solve economic problems in the less developed countries. Encouraging the transfer of funds to the private sector was expected to help rectify the inefficiencies, if not cure the evils, of the dominant public sector economies in these countries. Much of the current aid going through government channels for basic needs was judged to be, in effect, welfare payments that were ineffectual and degrading to the poor. Private sector activity was conceived as the more efficient way to deliver services and stimulate production. The private sector would assume a large role in all except investment in larger physical infrastructural improvement. Market strategies were designed to replace the earlier mandate's perceived orientation toward administrative solutions and its supposed anti-market biases. The U.S. private sector was envisioned as playing a facilitating role. Need for major income transfers and other radical policies would be obviated in the poorest countries through sound programs to encourage income generation and mobilization of local resources. It would be necessary as well to gain recipient government's cooperation in discarding policies such as subsidies and price controls that worked against free markets and were thought to defeat or undermine aid programs.

The Reagan administration's use of foreign aid as an instrument to extend private investment probably saved the bilateral nonmilitary aid program from deep funding cuts in the early 1980s, even if it did not lead to any new generosity. There was already, to be sure, a strong connection in U.S. aid programs with U.S. private sector promotion. In the three fiscal years preceding July 1981, for example, more than one-half of all U.S. aid disbursements involved expenditures in the U.S. private sector.[13] U.S. firms were used to implement projects and provide needed commodities. Though seeming to come full circle in the renewed stress on economic growth, the free market policies of the 1980s were distinguishable in their greater emphasis on stimulating a broad-based, productive economy that was, not incidentally, supposed to achieve higher standards of living for the less well-off. Ten countries whose economies were viewed as amenable to private sector strengthening, including Egypt, were singled out as demonstration cases. Almost none, it must be noted, could be called a truly poor country. The Reagan administration repeatedly pointed to South Korea, Singapore, Taiwan, and, for a time, Brazil, as countries that had succeeded in reviving market forces and private initiative to create superior economic performances.[14]

Moral values coupled with capitalist doctrine became a prominent issue in U.S. foreign aid policy during the mid-1980s. U.S. law enacted during the Reagan tenure had already banned the use of funds to finance forced or coerced abortions in other countries. In response to anti-abortion lobbyists, administration officials threatened to deny U.S. support for population control programs that sanctioned abortion as a method of family planning. At least $100 million of the nearly $300 million in AID funds designated to go to government and private organizations were at stake. Consistent with its economic philosophy, the Reagan administration explained that overpopulation could be most successfully dealt with through the willingness of governments to lift oppressive economic policies that threatened the free market.[15] The best way to curb population increases, Reagan officials contended, was through higher incomes obtained by economic growth. U.S. officials ignored the complaints of Third World governments and family planning groups who insisted that the poorer countries did not have the luxury of waiting for decades, as in the West, for a possible decline in population growth rates and improvements in living standards. To protest support by the UN Fund for Population Activities to China, where abortions are encouraged to slow population growth, the Reagan Administration withheld in 1985 a payment of $10 million pledged to the UN Fund.

The strongest test in allocating aid funds throughout the Reagan years has remained a political one. Programs designed to assist economic growth or encourage self-help in recipient countries are expected to meet foreign policy requirements reflecting U.S. economic and security interests. Desired diplomatic advantage has been behind Washington's attempt to de-emphasize multilateral aid in favor of bilateral assistance. Administration efforts to scuttle funds to some World Bank affiliates, including the International Fund for Agricultural Development, were ignored in congressional appropriations in 1984. The U.S. commitment of $2.5 billion to the bank's International Development Association was, however, one-third lower than the United States had previously pledged.[16]

The view that economic aid must be linked with national security gained new credibility with the 1983 report of a commission created by Secretary of State George P. Schultz to review foreign assistance programs and to recommend improvements, including ways to increase public support. The bipartisan panel of businessmen, labor leaders, and congressmen, with Frank Carlucci, a former deputy secretary of defense as chairman, recommended the abolition of AID and the creation of a new agency that, as in the 1950s, would administer both economic/development and military aid programs. The commission argued that the close integration of the two was the surest way to increase public understanding for foreign aid. Although critics of the report welcomed its request for additional foreign aid funding, they argued that the real purpose of the recommendations was to accelerate the trend away from economic development toward assistance exclusively for strategic and political allies. Some contended that the administration was already using economic development aid to the Middle East and Central America as a means of allowing legislators to clear their consciences in approving requests for increased military assistance. Whatever the final disposition of the commission report, Third World development, like so much else in the 1980s, had become increasingly politicized, drawn ever more into the vortex of an East-West struggle of ideologies and geopolitical interests.

Policy Objectives

The orientation in the 1980s toward economic growth and productivity gains notwithstanding, U.S. aid policy did not revert to an underwriting of the kind of sectoral biases that had characterized many countries' earlier policies. Agriculture and rural development, the focus of much global attention in the 1970s after two decades of relative neglect in planning decisions, continued to be seen as an essential contribution to balanced national development. The rural sector, not unimportantly, offered a promising setting for applying free-market policies. Indeed, the independent farmer was for many the quintessential small enterpreneur of the Third World. It was believed that liberating the farmer to make market-based decisions could, if also given the capacity for self-help, begin to undo many social and economic problems of the countryside along with helping to meet food and employment needs in the cities. As a result, aid policy toward agriculture and the rural areas underwent fewer changes in the Reagan administration than those applied to other aided economic sectors.

To realize broad U.S. objectives, AID has proposed four elements as the basis for an interrelated strategy. The first is the belief in a need for a policy dialogue and reform. The United States is committed to the view that possibilities for long-term growth depend on the policy climate created by recipient country governments. Economic assistance is considered ineffective unless host governments are persuaded to remove the key constraints to food production and marketing in prevailing policies. Interventions in setting food prices and influencing agricultural output cost are roundly attacked. Specifically, recipient governments are expected to realize that holding prices paid to farmers artifically low is discriminatory and acts as a disincentive to increased production.[17] Policymakers are prodded to create incentives through freer markets for farmers as well as for other private sector entrepreneurs. Policy changes at the macroeconomic level, including exchange rates, interest and wage rates, tariffs, and taxes, are additionally prescribed to get people to produce, employ, save, and invest. AID is also willing to assist countries to improve their policy analyses and planning capacity.

AID often threatens to withdraw its assistance from those countries unprepared to adopt what it considers appropriate, rational policies. In practice the agency is willing to accept evidence of policy improvements and shows considerable patience, especially when political calculations have weighed heavily in the aid program. U.S. officials clearly prefer the leverage that comes with bilateral agreements and put less stock in multilateral approaches as a means to effect policy concessions. As often presented, host governments have a moral responsibility to reform so that they may realize the kind of economic changes conducive to growth. But lest the United States be accused of neglecting equity concerns, AID argues that the same policies that distort economies and impede agriculture and industry are also hurting the poor by excluding them from access to productive resources and employment.[18] Government regulation and other misguided policies, more than private privilege, are accused of denying most rural dwellers equitable access to land, water, and credits.

The second element in the U.S. strategy, greater use of the private sector, is already prominent in the above discussions. In the agricultural sphere this strategy presupposes efforts to get indigenous private sector participation in such activities as the distribution of agricultural inputs and, for the rural areas in particular, the manufacture and marketing of products for health and population programs.[19] Aid is interested in identifying private sector institutions, including banks and trade and marketing associations, as the channels for the effective transfer of technical and financial assistance to private enterprises. U.S. agribusinesses, in direct or joint ventures, are slated to play a major role in strengthening local entrepreneurs in food and agricultural development. Labor-intensive, small-scale rural enterprises are expected to be the sources of substantial new employment. U.S. private voluntary organizations normally identified with emergency food relief are also considered valuable for their contribution to developing rural institutions. The flexibility and commitment of the private voluntary groups in organizing local energies and improving social services and productive activities are emphasized.[20] In general, U.S. aid officials are convinced that there are many aspects of agricultural and rural development activities that centralized public bureaucracies cannot do very well and that the private sector, given supportive policies, can perform at lower costs and with higher efficiency.

A third element serving as the cornerstone of the AID approach is institutional development. In the rural areas it aims at such programs as building agricultural extension systems and improving health care delivery. More effectiveness in maintaining and operating rural infrastructures, delivering farm inputs and credits, and processing, storing and marketing farm products is also envisioned. A stated commitment also exists to raise institutional capacity for food and agricultural planning and policy analysis. The agency accepts the obligation to train professional, technical staffs, and farmers in-country, in the United States, and in other countries. Commitment to long-term institutional development is, of course, not a new thrust in U.S. aid policy, but in the 1980s this commitment bears directly on improving non-government institutions. Again, the United States stresses the limitations of public bureaucracies and the superiority of the private sector in, for example, distributing medicines, contraceptives, and other social needs, along with training and production techniques.[21] AID has been willing at times to assist countries in strengthening public institutions where their activities are essential or unavoidable, especially if such aid promises to increase food production. But in assuming the ineffectiveness of national institutions, AID carries over from the 1970s a desire for greater decentralized participation in development planning and execution.

A fourth and related basis for policy recognizes the need for technological development and transfers. AID proposes to lead in the introduction of new technologies in such areas as agriculture and family planning. Dynamic breakthroughs are sought as presumably the best way to overcome the scarce resources in low-income countries and the inability of external aid alone to alleviate endemic economic and social problems. As in AID's promotion of an oral dehydration program, which offers a dramatic way of reducing infant and childhood mortality, the aim is to find inexpensive approaches that can be easily disseminated. Renewed emphasis is given to research into new farm practices and crop varieties able to withstand the usually adverse soils, climatic conditions, insects, and diseases found in most aid recipient countries. Policy continues to stress the need to link research to institutions capable of adopting and applying technologies. AID also insists that successful science and technology generation and transfers require a domestic economic policy environment that expresses market economic forces. This offers, it is argued, the greatest likelihood that improved agriculture and other advances will be appropriate and acceptable to farmers. Access to land and more secure land tenure arrangements are conceded as necessary to assure that small producers benefit from the improved methods. Yet these concerns are in fact seldom at the forefront of current AID planning and policy for rural areas.

Programmatic implications obviously follow from these several policy orientations. Funded programs have had to take into account AID's limited staff, far fewer than in the 1960s, and relatively less resources for economic development than in the 1970s. In the 1980s, there is thus a premium put on identifying more focused strategies for AID missions in recipient countries. Approaches are encouraged that share more of the burden of program initiation with host countries and their private as well as public institutions.[22] Because of the acknowledged limited administrative capacity in most recipient countries, the United States is anxious to identify rural development projects that are smaller and less complex. In planning and designing programs, AID is resigned to thinking of longer-term perspectives, even as, in its concern for early political dividends, Washington also insists on higher visibility projects. The United States seeks to employ various modes of assistance that combine technical, capital, commodity, and food aid in agricultural and rural development, though the mix may vary greatly for individual countries. There is generally a desire to increase support for those areas of development where the United States is demonstrably best, notably agriculture, education, population control, health, and rural electrification. To address economic inequities, programs that support mass consumption industries, including agribusinesses, are intended to replace redistributive policies of the past. In all, the programs of the 1980s are expected to foster broad growth, new technologies, and more efficient management and, wherever possible, advance market strategies in place of administrative solutions. How well these programs have succeeded in their objectives is probably best revealed in the aid experience in Egypt since 1975.

The Egyptian case can help to determine, moreover, whether economic assistance from the United States and other Western donors improves, as it is often claimed, chances for political stability, anti-communism, and the emergence of democratic forces in recipient countries. Aid that promotes economic activities and allows developing countries to meet severe resource deficits is also likely to relieve governments from making hard economic choices and better enable them to satisfy immediate material demands. But aid that also leads to rising incomes and unrealistic expectations, that helps breed greater inequities, and that appears to compromise national sovereignty, hardly contributes to building stable, popular government. The argument is often made that economic growth with its accompanying social fragmentations is probably a more proximate cause of political disorder than are chronic conditions of poverty. Economic growth per se may in many instances progress faster in the absence of democratic institutions and under conditions of arbitrary rule and inequalities. Generous foreign assistance can even help to perpetuate authoritarian institutions by enabling regimes to satisfy key groups and strengthen instruments of coercion.

Notes

1. See discussion in John A. White, *The Politics of Foreign Aid* (New York: St. Martin's Press, 1974), pp. 190–194.

2. Elliott R. Morss and Victoria A. Morss, *U.S. Foreign Aid: An Assessment of New and Traditional Development Strategies* (Boulder, Colo.: Westview Press, 1982), p. 22.

3. Ernst A. Lewin, "Foreign Aid: Paying the Pittance," *Washington Quarterly* (Winter 1981): 189.

4. A good overview on the uses of aid is found in Joan E. Spero, *The Politics of International Economic Relations*, 2nd Edition (New York: St. Martin's Press, 1981), pp. 144–155.

5. Morss, *U.S. Foreign Aid*, pp. 22–23.

6. *Congressional Quarterly*, July 27, 1985, p. 1475. The amount approved was exclusive of $1.5 billion in emergency economic assistance to Israel and $500 million to Egypt.

7. *The New York Times*, June 28, 1981. Lewin, p. 190.

8. *Congressional Quarterly*, November 24, 1984, p. 3003. Israel and Egypt alone accounted for about 45 percent of all U.S. foreign aid in 1984.

9. That the bulk of U.S. economic aid goes to military clients and many middle-income countries is a broader pattern. The World Bank (or International Bank for Reconstruction and Development [IBRD]) estimates that of the $17 billion in development aid from all donor countries in 1980, only $6 billion went to the poorest countries. *The New York Times*, June 28, 1981. The Bank also admits that only 30 percent of its IBRD/IDA lending is specifically focused on the poor. Keith Marden and Alan Roe, "The Political Economy of Foreign Aid," in Pradip K. Ghosh (ed.), *Foreign Aid and Third World Development* (Westport, Conn.: Greenwood Press, 1984), p. 135. The U.S. Congress did succeed in 1983, over the objections and lobbying efforts of the Reagan administration, AID, and others to require through legislation that AID devote at least 40 percent of its budget directly to those countries classified as "absolute poor" by the World Bank.

10. In recent years, only in 1981 and 1985 has Congress succeeded in enacting full-scale foreign aid authorization bills.

11. William Sommers, "Rescuing AID," *Foreign Service Journal* (May 1982): 15.

12. *Congressional Quarterly*, August 3, 1985, p. 1543.

13. U.S. General Accounting Office, "Report to the Chairman of the Committee on Foreign Affairs, House of Representatives, on Private Sector Involvement in the Agency for International Development's Programs," August 26, 1983, p. 1.

14. To promote private development in aided countries, a Bureau of Private Enterprise was established within AID in 1981.

15. *The New York Times*, June 18, 1984.

16. *Congressional Quarterly,* October 20, 1984, p. 2742.

17. Peter McPherson, "Administrator's Message to Employees of the Agency for International Development, State of the Agency," March 2, 1984, p. 2.

18. U.S. Agency for International Development, Bureau for Program and Policy Coordination, "AID Policy Paper: Food and Agricultural Development," May 1982, p. 3.

19. Peter McPherson, "Statement by the Administrator of the Agency for International Development: Background Briefing on AID Budget," February 1, 1984, p. 3.

20. AID Policy Paper, p. 6.

21. McPherson, "Administrator's Message to Employees," March 2, 1984, p. 3.

22. AID Policy Paper, p. 8.

2

Aid and Egypt's *Infitah*

Almost as dramatic and consequential as Egypt's crossing the Suez Canal in October 1973 and President Anwar Sadat's surprise journey to Jerusalem in 1977 was his announced intention in October 1974 to restructure and reorient Egypt's economic relations. In place of the government-managed economy inherited from Gamal Abdul Nasser, Sadat proposed a system that would rely more on private initiatives and investment, domestic and foreign. Egypt would evolve from an inwardly geared economy to one more broadly based on export-oriented industries that would reintegrate the country with the economies of the world's developed market economies. This *Infitah* or Open Door policy, the outcome of both domestic socio-economic forces and foreign pressures, was conceived to enable Sadat's Egypt to realize political objectives unattainable through military means and to attract the external assistance needed to cope with an immediate economic crisis. By realigning its regional and global economic ties, Egypt willingly forfeited its close links to the East. A partially liberalized economy paved the way for a more consumption-oriented society, exploitable by domestic interests, and subject to the vicissitudes of international trade and the influences of Western creditors and aid donors. Plainly, much had changed since the Nasser era.[1]

Nasser's Closed Door

The Free Officers who seized power in Egypt's July 1952 Revolution were intent on ridding the country of foreign domination and reducing the economic power of a wealthy landowning class. They held no economic philosophy other than that contained in a nationalism anxious for economic prosperity and committed to improving social and economic justice for Egypt's masses. Aside from early agrarian reforms, a cautious and usually pragmatic leadership at first retained an essentially liberal economic strategy that saw a strong business community as instrumental to economic expansion and the realization of comparative advantages for Egypt's exports in world markets. With the nationalization of the Suez Canal in 1956, however, British and French property was seized, and overall government intervention in the economy increased, particularly through financial controls. By the beginning of the 1960s, policies ideologically more consistent with Egypt's now closer ties to the communist bloc economies, together with domestic political motives, led to the virtual elimination of the country's merchant-capitalist class. All private industries with twenty-five or more employees were nationalized between 1960 and 1963. A wide array of public sector, ministry-directed companies was created for such activities as mining, utilities, communications, finance, manufacturing, and transportation. In the transformation to a quasi-socialist state, the economy became relatively closed as a result of domestic regulations and controls and policies that sharply constrained Egypt's relations with the West.

The movement of private capital in and out of the country was severely curtailed, and foreign investment could enter Egypt only under highly restrictive terms. The Central Bank acquired comprehensive control for the state over foreign exchange and import policies and was able to monopolize foreign trade. Most market features of the economy were replaced by centralized, government planning, and all investment capital was allocated through the Ministry of Finance and publicly owned banks.[2] The often-described "inward looking" economy, with its heavy industry orientation, followed where possible autarkic import substitution policies. Agriculture alone among the major sectors remained dominated by private interests. However, a far-reaching land redistribution began in 1961, and a strengthened cooperative system ensured, among other objectives, the meeting of government production quotas.

Additional redistributions of assets through nationalizations, new educational opportunities, and state subsidies represented substantial strides toward an egalitarian society and implemented the leadership's populist convictions. The rural poor increased their share of national income. Benefits in the form of public education, new health services, and employee rights and benefits improved the well-being of the urban population and opened avenues of social mobility in the context of planned socioeconomic development. Higher wages increased consumption for workers in industry and civil service, and the public sector provided guaranteed employment to university graduates. Thousands of farmers with new titles to land could avail themselves of subsidized agricultural inputs and government loans. Most important for future budgets, the regime made available to all economic groups subsidies for a wide range of basic commodities as a shelter against international inflation and protection against domestic price increases.

Equity gains, however, were generally costly when judged in terms of efficiency and long-term economic growth. After expenditures on social programs and economically doubtful land reclamation projects, little was left for improvements for a deteriorating urban and rural infrastructure. Public ownership had the effect over time of creating serious overemployment and stimulating corruption and poor management. Strongly centralized decisionmaking contributed to the stifling of initiative among public employees and the lowering of incentives in the productive sectors. The nationalizations and formation of cooperatives ensured state control over relative prices that, along with open, indirect, and hidden consumer subsidies, often prevented rational investment choices. Tariffs and exchange controls to protect domestic production that relieved planners of the need for careful assessment of Egypt's comparative advantages also weakened cost-effectiveness as a significant factor in industrial decisions.

Throughout the 1960s, Egypt's industry, sustained by Soviet aid, expanded by an annual rate of 5.4 percent. The important agricultural sector managed only a 2.9 percent average growth during the decade, despite the Green Revolution in technology and agriculture's still relatively good claim on public investment.[3] These sectoral figures are depressed by the serious stagnation in the general economy after 1966 as defense expenditures assumed a large share of the country's resources and attention. Real per capita GNP growth averaged roughly 1 percent between 1966 and 1973. The bill for government consumer subsidies was increasingly burdensome, and urbanization brought a steady rise in demands for public services and benefits. Even so, social gains made earlier showed signs of eroding.[4] With a balance-of-payments crisis building, Egypt's financial and political indebtedness to the Soviet Union increased conspicuously.

Egypt had obviously not been transformed into a self-sustaining economy. Agricultural exports remained the prime source of foreign exchange. From 1957 to 1964, trade as a proportion of national income ranged between 36 and 43 percent, and the country had accrued an external debt of more than $2 billion.[5] Ten years later, the civilian debt to the socialist countries alone was calculated by the International Monetary Fund (IMF) at $725 million and the military debt at more than $4 billion; unofficial estimates were much higher.[6] The major change during the Nasser period, paralleling Egypt's foreign policies, was the diminishing of Egypt's traditional trade and aid relations with the West in favor of the planned economies, notably the Soviet Union's. Six separate aid loan agreements with Moscow, carrying highly attractive terms for Egypt, were signed through 1971. More than one-third of all economic assistance from Moscow went for construction of the Aswan

High Dam, which a Western consortium led by the United States had reneged on financing in July 1956. Of the remaining $950 million in Soviet non-military aid, the bulk was targeted for building up Egypt's heavy industry, especially iron, steel, and aluminum, and was paid for by exports to the USSR of cotton, rice, and the products of small-scale labor-intensive industries. Urban workers profited as expected from the jobs created by Soviet-aided industrial projects, and a broad urban population, including many in the middle class, benefited from the final products of these industries.[7]

Soviet aid programs showed sensitivity to Egypt's nationalist fervor. That the Soviet Union appreciated the political and strategic importance of Egypt is clear in comparisons with per capita assistance it gave other client states during the same period.[8] Still, no explicit political or military attachments were sought by the Soviets, and their project assistance was unconditioned by demands for changes in Egypt's broad economic policies. Soviet technicians were numerous on many projects but seldom obtrusive. Following the disastrous June 1967 War with Israel and the subsequent war of attrition, however, Egypt's security concerns prompted greater reliance on the Soviet Union. With the arrival of new military equipment came thousands of additional Soviet advisors. As Ibrahim observes, "The presence of so many Russians in Egypt after 1967 was a reminder of the regime's failures and proof of its dependence."[9] Tensions with the Egyptian bureaucracy and military establishment increased as the Soviet role in the Egyptian economy and interference in domestic politics grew. Many Egyptians also became convinced that the Soviets were in Egypt as elsewhere in the Middle East not out of any desire to assist in the struggle against Israel but rather to establish military bases and form alliances as bargaining chips to be traded away in negotiations with the United States on various political and economic issues.[10]

U.S. economic aid through the Nasser era had been closely tied to the ups and downs of U.S.-Egyptian relations. A technical cooperation agreement had been signed with the Royal Government in 1951. The United States agreed to provide Egypt with technical advisors, equipment, and materials and to train Egyptian personnel in the United States. This accord served as the basis for an agreement with the new Revolutionary Government in May 1953 and as a framework for a specific project named the Egyptian-American Rural Improvement Service (EARIS) aimed at community development and rural rehabilitation in two provinces.[11] The change in U.S. administrations in 1953 and the determination by officials in Washington to politicize assistance in this Cold War era made the EARIS project and promises of further development funding part of the effort to woo the military regime in Cairo. The decision by the Eisenhower administration to immediately make available a $10 million lump sum, upfront cash payment on EARIS left little doubt of the serious political motivation behind the aid. Although the shift in emphasis in U.S. aid policy did not have an immediate impact on the Egyptian project, resistance by the Nasser government to Western pressures to join the Middle East Defense Organization (Baghdad Pact) brought a deterioration in relations and aggravated differences between U.S. technicans and Egyptian personnel assigned to EARIS. The U.S. decision against financing the Aswan High Dam and subsequent nationalization of the Suez Canal set the stage for the Suez War of 1956 that halted U.S. participation in the project as well as U.S. shipments of wheat that Egypt had been receiving on concessional terms.

When relations improved during 1959 and 1960, P.L. 480 food shipments were renewed, and U.S. participation in EARIS was slowly reactivated.[12] In an agreement signed in March 1960, $32.5 million in U.S. aid was earmarked for economic development, a purpose also served by the loaning back to the Egyptian government at low interest rates local currency taken in payment for food shipments. The creation of a new aid bureaucracy in Washington and the appointment of an AID director in Cairo armed with the macro-economic development strategies introduced by the Kennedy administration had limited impact in Egypt where ideological differences held U.S. assistance to largely stopgap efforts. Aid authorization fell off sharply when relations again cooled in 1965 and 1966.[13] Although Nasser continued to request food shipments and a less sympathetic Johnson administration still hoped to use its aid as a means of moderating Egypt's foreign policies, the increasingly divergent directions of the two countries were impossible to ignore. To match U.S. policies he perceived as increasingly pro-Israel, Nasser strengthened Egypt's ties to Moscow. The U.S. government protested Egypt's role in the Cyprus and the Congo conflicts, and the Egyptian president irritated U.S. officials and congressmen with his handling of anti-U.S. riots in Cairo and his criticism of U.S. involvement in Vietnam. Only the fear that a failure to support the Egyptian economy might lead to a chaotic or communist Egypt kept U.S. policymakers intent for so long on salvaging the U.S.-Egyptian relationship. Loans and grants that had totaled $94.5 million between 1962 and 1965 dropped off to only $1.5 million for fiscal year (FY) 1966 and to roughly one-half that amount before ceasing entirely early in 1967. By appearing to reject political conditions for U.S.-financed food aid, Nasser received wide popular backing at home. All the same, urban dwellers had become accustomed to, and domestic peace contingent on, abundant, low-priced imported wheat and flour. Nasser had no alternative but to seek other sources for food grains that in the early 1970s his successor, Anwar Sadat, was unable even to find or finance.

The War and *Infitah*

Whether by design or opportunistic afterthought, President Sadat counted on the restoration of Egypt's self-respect in the October 1973 War and the switch in foreign alignments to attract the kind of financial assistance from wealthy Arab regimes and Western investors needed to restructure the economy. From the outset, U.S. officials appreciated Sadat's dire economic predicament and his political vulnerability at home. Egypt would require immediate, tangible evidence of U.S. support, enough to enable Sadat to improve domestic economic conditions sufficiently to allow him to accept political risks in the disengagement of Egyptian and Israeli forces and participation in a more comprehensive regional peace.

The evidence came quickly, coinciding with the January 1974 separation of forces accord between Egypt and Israel. The United States announced the commitment of $8.5 million for an initial program to help clear the Suez Canal of war debris and to begin the reconstruction of the canal cities. The Nixon administration on March 1 asked Congress for a total of $250 million for FY 1975 and programmed an additional $50 million to Egypt as it prepared the 1976 budget.[14] By mid-May 1974, however, U.S. Ambassador in Cairo Hermann Eilts reported to Washington that higher levels of aid were needed, especially shipments of commodities and spare parts that could help Egypt immediately to conserve its meager foreign exchange. Ambassador Eilts was concerned, however, that the level of aid not be viewed by the Egyptians as the principal basis on which improved relations would rest, for the amount promised was far lower than U.S. commitments to Israel of economic aid, not to mention military support.[15]

In fact, this is essentially what President Sadat had in mind—economic aid that, even if packaged differently, would give Egypt rough parity with Israel. Sadat found opportunity to press his case directly in March 1975 during the Kissinger shuttle diplomacy that led to the second Sinai disengagement agreement. Kissinger had already approved raising assistance to Egypt to $500 million, of which $300 million was to be for commodities. But during the March talks the figure of $750 million emerged, not by chance an amount close to what Israel was receiving from the United States for economic objectives. An additional $200 million was set aside for P.L. 480 Title I food aid.

Although primarily a political decision for both parties, the level of funding was not, despite the meetings of joint working groups, based

on any careful assessment of Egypt's budgetary and development ḥ₋₋₋₋
or, for that matter, on what it could absorb successfully. The aid needed
to be substantial enough to address Egypt's grim economic circumstances
and reward Egypt for its plans to reorient its economy. Beyond this the
aid would go far to ensure that the Soviet Union did not regain its
economic and political foothold in Egypt. Investments in the clearing
of the Suez Canal and the reconstruction of Egypt's war-torn cities were
also psychologically important both in demonstrating U.S. confidence
that the peace with Israel would hold and in reassuring the Israelis of
future Egyptian intentions. Because the FY 1976 dollar amount symbolized
an evenhandedness in U.S. economic aid policy between Egypt and
Israel, it set the essential parameters of U.S. programs in subsequent
years, providing a continuing test of Washington's commitment to Egypt.
Any reduction would be interpreted by the Egyptian government as a
softening of U.S. backing for the regime or a changed expectation about
Egypt's role in keeping the region's peace.

Sadat's *Infitah* promised marked changes from many of the statist
economic policies in force. It would revive and expand the private sector,
relying far more on market forces to determine investment decisions.[16]
The economic incentives created were designed to attract private foreign
capital in joint ventures. Loans and tax policies would create a favorable
climate as well for domestic entrepreneurs and allow them reentrance
into foreign trade. The Open Door policies, basically structured in Egypt's
Law 43, enacted in June 1974 and amended in 1977, waived for foreign
firms the usual tariffs on imported equipment. Those investing in
agricultural projects and food production, among other sectors, gained
tax advantages and were promised easy repatriation of profits and
protection against nationalization. Having gained the IMF's blessings,
the new policies helped to improve Egypt's credit worthiness in world
markets.

The economic redirection was a natural response to Egypt's immediate
predicament. In 1974, the country's budget deficit had stood at LE 530
million (ca. $1.3 billion), up more than five-fold in just one year,
representing 18 percent of the state budget.[17] At the same time that
economic growth was sluggish, inflation had reached nearly 24 percent,
and Egypt's international credit plummeted as its balance-of-payments
gap widened. Rapprochement with the West promised, aside from
diplomatic and direct aid benefits, the possibility of lowering military
expenditures and attracting new investments by making Egypt less risky
for foreign private capital. An end to hostilities with Israel was also
calculated to enhance the state's coffers from canal fees, increased tourism,
and, of course, from revenues after the return of Sinai oil fields. Egypt
hoped additionally to obtain preferential treatment in regional and

Western markets for its exports. Above all, the Sadat government encouraged the belief that peace meant prosperity for the average Egyptian.

Sadat's economic and political strategies have to be viewed in the
context of the Middle East's newly acquired oil wealth. For its war effort
and losses, Egypt felt it had earned direct financial assistance from the
now more affluent conservative Arab states. The Cairo government had
earlier won their plaudits in 1971 in jailing local communists and, in
July 1972, by ordering 25,000 Soviet military advisors out of the country.
Despite some assistance during the October 1973 War, Sadat further
distanced himself from the Russians by accepting U.S. help in saving
his trapped army and in keeping alive negotiations with Israel. Egypt's
limited oil reserves denied it a place among Arab oil exporting giants;
yet the country expected to share in the region's economic growth with
its pool of exportable skilled manpower, large market, and central
location. In a more economically assertive Arab world, Egypt could play
its traditional leadership role, conceivably showing the way for moderate
Arab governments to obtain territorial concessions from the Israelis.

A convincing argument is also made that Sadat's actions leading to
Infitah were prompted by the course of East-West détente. Realizing
that the United States was unmovable in its support for Israel and the
Soviet Union had chosen to give priority to improving economic and
political relations with the West, Sadat concluded that Egypt would have
to act more autonomously on the field of battle and elsewhere. Egypt
would try to diversify its military purchases, reassert its Arab role, and
assume a more prominent position in Third World and non-aligned
forums. Sadat's plans for revitalizing Egypt's economy envisioned Arab
capital in concert with the West's technology. Implied in these policy
changes was a strategy that opened Egypt to foreign investment and
world market-oriented policies.[18]

The neoclassic formulas proposed for economic growth were not
intended to turn back the clock to pre-1952. The break with the past
contemplated in *Infitah's* expected reordering of priorities in the economy
was by no means complete. Nasser's socialist legacy, for all its economic
shortcomings, embodied a popular consensus on maintaining the social
achievements of the revolution. Elites who might prosper in the new
economy would presumably make their fortunes by attracting outside
capital rather than in grabbing off a larger share of the public domain.[19]
There was some anticipation of Sadat's policies in Nasser's waning years.
Although Nasser was reluctant to accept the advice of those who
counseled reopening the economy to Western financing and technology,
the government had taken modest steps to reinvigorate the private sector
in order to obtain additional hard currencies to cover Egypt's mounting
debt.[20] Despite official statements in 1974 and later about allowing the

market to allocate resources and set prices, the state was never expected to withdraw from regulating and planning the economy. At most, the socialized industries would face competition for the first time. A continuing reliance on economic and technical aid from foreign governments and international agencies also ensured the bureaucracy an active and preeminent role in the economy.

U.S. Patronage

The United States had much at stake in the success or failure of President Sadat's economic policies. Popular approval or at least acquiescence in Egypt's political realignment could not be sustained without measurable progress in reversing economic trends and in achieving broad gains in employment, income, and consumption. *Infitah's* affinity with Western economic principles and practices and the obvious expectations of massive Western aid and investment ensured that the United States, above all, would be perceived as patron of Egypt's economic liberalization. Whatever the actual U.S. influence in setting the direction and pace of *Infitah*, the policy's acceptance and the U.S. welcome would be inextricably bound together.

Assistance to Egypt, beginning so shortly after the U.S. experience in Vietnam, naturally carried that war's supposed lessons. U.S. policymakers could not quickly forget how food aid had been deliberately used by the Nixon administration to compensate for the denial by Congress of other forms of assistance to the Saigon government and that development aid had failed to reach those for whom it was targeted. In accordance with the New Directions philosophy, aid to Egypt would be expected to reach the poor majorities and, in effect exchange an earlier "trickle down" strategy for a "percolate up" one. Funds would raise the productivity of Egypt's peasant farmers by giving them better access to available resources and control over decisions affecting them (see Chapter Four). Despite Egypt's security-oriented aid classification, Congress designated that a substantial portion—roughly one-half of the $750 million—go for projects that could be justified on developmental grounds. However, the large sums set aside required a heavy portfolio of projects, most of them small or medium scale, if the new mandate were to be implemented. The Cairo AID mission was thus strained, with its initially small staff, in trying to identify worthy projects and figure out ways to spend quickly vast amounts of money.

AID had scant knowledge of Egypt's economic problems or reliable technical data on which to base its analyses. Without these, little attention went to how much Egypt could in fact absorb or what the impact of aid might be on the domestic economy. AID had much to learn, moreover, about the most effective, powerful units and individuals in the Egyptian bureaucracy and the relevant cultural and political constraints. Most importantly, the mission received a shopping list of possible projects from the Egyptian government. Aside from agreeing to broad priorities, the Egyptians offered very little guidance, even after their government's multi-year plans were articulated. The mission found itself with virtually no choice but to earmark development funds for large-scale, expensive war reconstruction projects and to eliminate bottlenecks in the economy. Members of the U.S. Congress who were otherwise strong advocates of aid for basic needs, especially for agricultural development, rural health, and employment, deferred to their colleagues and AID administrators who argued the logic of first addressing Egypt's problems of economic instability and infrastructural deterioration. Although Egypt's leadership generally deferred to AID's allocation decisions, government officials, accustomed to massive Soviet turnkey projects and a centralized style of decisionmaking, were often less comprehending of an U.S. aid strategy that avoided concentrating funds in a few highly visible "monuments" and required participation and coordination among the ministries in implementing the project aid.

U.S. officials charged with formulating the aid projects had to juggle objectives. Along with the efforts needed to bolster Egypt's short-term economic stability, they hoped to set in motion programs for long-term economic growth and productivity. These goals were somehow to be pursued while AID managed to avoid doing great violence to earlier achievements in social and economic equity. Inevitably, differences about program priorities emerged, even within the official U.S. community, including disagreements between the politically sensitive diplomats and the more development-oriented AID professionals. More serious for Egyptian-U.S. relations, however, were the perceived incompatibilities between U.S. development ideas and the many structures and practices carried over from the Nasser years. AID officials discreetly but persistently reminded their Egyptian counterparts that the over-centralized state-managed economy, the rigidities of the financial system, and the reluctance in some quarters to expand the private sector would undermine the planned development.

Particularly objectionable for AID's liberal economists (and many similarly minded Egyptians) was the commingling of welfare and economic policies best expressed in the country's food and energy subsidies. Unless Egypt's sheltered price structure was adjusted to world market levels, domestic prices would, it was argued, be unable to guide employment and investment to sectors of comparative advantage (see Chapter Six). The U.S. approach to development, stressing export-oriented industries, did not rule out import substitution or public sector enterprises.

The value of transitional policies and the role of Egypt's sizable internal market were conceded. But U.S. advisors insisted that the proper yardstick for investment decisions in the public and private sectors alike should be the classic criteria of efficiency, productivity, and reasonable financial return.

The U.S. aid programs that started up in 1975 evolved in several phases. Until 1977, the top priority was the serious foreign exchange shortage, dealt with mainly through the financing of food, industrial raw materials, and spare parts. The commodity program assured, for example, the availability of tallow so that Egypt's domestic soap industry could return to full capacity. Along with the relatively effective balance of payments support, funds were set aside for the reconstruction of the Suez Canal and its immediate area. With the AID mission unprepared to present many suitable development projects, the funding of large, expensive infrastructural projects was attractive to planners because these projects were easily identified. War rehabilitation projects such as the reconstruction of the canal cities were thought ideal for their relatively unsophisticated designs and promise of rapid completion. Both the budgetary and construction priorities, whatever their economic imperatives, were also plainly political. The United States and Egypt sought to have the aid make an early and demonstrable impact on the economy.

Political factors figured prominently in aid to Egypt between 1977 and 1979. To show support for the shaken regime following food riots that occurred in January 1977, the United States acted immediately to shift $190 million in already committed capital development funds to commodities that would enter the economy quickly. Later, as a reward for signing accords with Israel at Camp David, the U.S. Congress agreed to supplement Egypt's aid with a $300 million "peace dividend" during a three year period, adding such programs as a Peace Fellowship for development-related studies in the United States for up to 1,900 Egyptians. The aid carrot also included establishing a military assistance program that promised $1.5 billion in supplemental aid during a three-year period. The new generosity was expected to bolster Sadat at a time when he needed to solidify support for his regime in the armed forces and enhance his stature in regional politics.[21]

U.S. officials felt some obligation to try offsetting the decline and then cut-off of assistance from Arab governments, assistance that between 1974 and 1977 had officially reached more than $7 billion.[22] Led by Saudi Arabia and Kuwait, several Arab countries had begun economic aid to Egypt for reconstruction after the 1967 War. Aid for development as well as defense to compensate Egypt for its losses was much welcomed as balance-of-payments support; this aid was greatly increased in the aftermath of the 1973 War. Egypt's desire for increased funding from

Arab countries flush with oil dollars and Arab concern that much of their aid was being used to finance consumption soon put strains on the aid relationship.[23] But it took Sadat's overtures to the Israelis beginning in 1977 to bring about the ostracism of Egypt economically and politically by most of the Arab world. Significantly, aside from Libya, few of the income-remitting Egypt workers in Arab oil-exporting countries were repatriated. Arab businessmen also continued investing in real estate, construction, and other economic activities in Egypt. The move toward normalization with Israel, not incidently, contributed to the jump in Egypt's foreign exchange earnings, an outcome no doubt anticipated by Sadat. Handsome gains in oil, Suez Canal, tourism, and other government revenues had by the late 1970s eased Egypt's liquidity crisis.

Meanwhile, the AID mission extended its concern for infrastructural upgrading, and major contracts were signed to expand power generation across the country, improve port facilities in Alexandria, raise grain storage capacity, modernize communication systems, and undertake water and sewerage construction in Cairo and Alexandria. Not until 1978 did the basic human needs mandate begin to figure more prominently in U.S. assistance; sizable programs were arranged with the government for small farmers, health services, and family planning.[24] AID also moved ahead with plans to strengthen industry, both to raise exports and improve productivity, and to help Egypt expand employment. Funds provided to the regime were expected to reach the private as well as the public sectors. By 1980, the United States had given more per capita aid to Egypt than it had spent in post-war Europe during the Marshall Plan.

The United States was not of course Egypt's only Western aid benefactor during this period. Donor assistance flows from all sources, which had stood at $800 million in 1973, moved up sharply but erratically to a peak of nearly $2.9 billion in 1977. The structure of foreign assistance altered considerably by the late 1970s, however, with the drying up of official Arab assistance. Meanwhile, aid disbursements from Western donors, aside from the United States, grew from $540 million in 1976 to $1.1 billion by 1979. The largest financial contributors, mainly in the form of development projects, were the World Bank, West Germany, and Japan. Together with the United States, the total aid commitments (not actual disbursements) from Western donors during the early 1980s averaged about $2.1 billion annually. Additionally, Egypt received by 1979 some $500 million in direct private investment from Western sources, at least one-half of it from foreign oil companies.[25] The flexibility of most bilateral aid was in some contrast to earlier lending practices by the IMF, which had pressured Egypt to accept IMF recommendations on monetary and fiscal reform, including reduced consumer subsidies.

In finally giving in to IMF demands as a concession to international creditors, including Saudi Arabia, Egypt paid a high political price. The economic stabilization agreement worked out with the IMF raised prices on food and energy and thereby sparked the 1977 urban riots that very nearly toppled Sadat's regime before the increases were rescinded (see Chapter Six).[26]

Infitah's Gains and Losses

Overall, *Infitah's* record is impressive if measured by most gross indices. Average annual Gross Domestic Product (GDP) growth in constant prices for a six-year period after 1977 rose by more than 8 percent. The deficit in goods and services fell off steadily to $1.5 billion in 1979 from $2.5 billion in 1975. Also, by 1979, Egypt was showing a small surplus of $700 million in its balance of payments. In 1980, oil exports provided nearly $3 billion in revenues, canal fees upward of $1 billion, remittances $2.7 billion, and tourism and agriculture exports approximately $600 million each. Domestic public investment between 1973 and 1980 gained by roughly 26 percent and private investment by 78 percent. New foreign private (nonoil) investment, though still below expectations, climbed to more than $400 million yearly by 1980, up from just $100 million three years earlier.[27] Egypt's debt servicing became for the time more manageable with the steep rise in foreign exchange earnings and a continued influx of foreign economic assistance. By the time of Sadat's death, Egypt's per capita GNP had risen to $630.

In addition to the apparent gains from *Infitah*, Egypt also became economically more exposed. Integration into the global arena, the subject of the next chapter, meant that changes in world prices for Egypt's exports and imports registered sharply on the domestic economy. Indeed, all of Egypt's principal sources of foreign exchange were closely tied to economic conditions abroad, likely to rise or fall with demand in the major industrial countries, and contingent on the continued high incomes and economic expansion of the Middle East's major oil-exporting countries. One early manifestation of Egypt's heavy external interdependence was a spiraling inflation rate. By 1977, consumer prices were by various estimates rising, even with many key consumer items price-controlled, at an annual rate of more than 30 percent. The repressed level of inflation for urban residents held at about 25 percent through the mid-1980s.[28]

In retrospect, too many of the investment priorities of the Open Door approach were misplaced and too many plans miscalculated. The government and its media oversold the probable benefits of change to the Egyptian people much as they understated the structural problems blocking rapid economic progress. The *Infitah* policies that were expected to overhaul prices, management, marketing, employment, and investment in Egypt's industry were never implemented. Unlike the agricultural and service sectors, which were predominantly in private hands, industrial output came largely from public enterprises that employed more than 1 million workers. Although the share of output by the private sector rose from approximately 20 percent in 1974 to about one-third a decade later, Egypt's private industry remained small scale and technologically backward.[29]

The impact of the liberalized economy on well-entrenched interests in the public sector was not impressive. Industry continued to be burdened by excessive employment levels, insufficient capitalization, price controls, and inappropriate wage structures. Industry did not take the lead, as planned, in the country's economic expansion; much of the rapid growth of GDP came in the banking and service sectors. Private capital, as a rule, shunned long-term investment. Foreign firms, provided with tax holidays and other incentives, steered clear of the projected joint ventures in labor-intensive basic industries and agribusinesses.[30] Aside from oil exploration, investor attention was focused on banking, pharmaceuticals, construction, and tourism. More than 60 percent of all foreign investment went into the service sector.[31]

In trying to attract foreign capital while still uncertain about the role of the private sector in economic development, the government often sent out inconsistent and confusing policy signals that led prospective foreign investors to question its attitude and commitment. Bureaucratic proscrastination in investment approval procedures and various forms of interference and corruption also did their part to scare off potential investors, and foreign businessmen were frequently turned away by Cairo's deteriorating services and the country's poor infrastructure. Caution among U.S. and other private investors reflected as well doubts about Egypt's long-term economic prospects, which in the late 1970s and early 1980s were clouded by continuing Arab economic sanctions and uncertain world economic conditions.

Throughout this period merchandized exports fell even as the overall economy was growing. Egypt's industry proved increasingly uncompetitive in the face of higher quality foreign goods. The country, which had been viewed by Western businessmen as a huge market for durable goods, saw its limited foreign exchange earnings severely drained for imports, much of it for luxury items. A large share of U.S.-supplied low interest business loans found their way to Egyptian importers, many of whom were unnecessary middlemen, reselling the goods they purchased to the Egyptian government. Others in the reborn private sector failed to take advantage of AID-channeled funds because they could not understand or were frightened off by complicated U.S. government-imposed regulations and procedures. The *Infitah*-assisted domestic industries, expected through export earnings to create new sources of foreign exchange, instead catered to the consumption demands of the middle-class and did little to create the expected new jobs. With so much of the government's budget focused on the urban-industrial sector, agriculture lost out in medium and longer term investment, a reality reflected in declining productivity in the Nile Delta and steep rises in food imports. To make economic policies more politically palatable by meeting equity concerns, comprehensive consumer food and energy subsidies were permitted to grow rapidly.

Liberal agricultural policies together with renewed efforts in desert land development were supposed to spearhead increased national food security. Land reclaimed by the state earlier was sold or otherwise distributed to individuals or firms in hopes of raising production as well as lowering government expenditures.[32] Publicly-financed low-interest loans were designed to attract private enterprise to such businesses as dairy, poultry, and fisheries. But again, the level of private investment was disappointing as higher rates of return were normally found elsewhere. More important in the strategy, a loosening of many of the restrictions on farmers, allowing them to respond more effectively to market signals, was designed to increase the incentives for production. In fact, agriculture through most of the 1970s received a far lower share of the public investment budget than in the previous decade, and agricultural policies in the 1970s were in many cases self-defeating. Overall crop production, which had been virtually stagnant between 1970 and 1977 at a growth rate of less than 1.5 percent annually, grew at a better than 3 percent rate in 1978–1980 and fell only slightly through 1982. A decline was recorded, however, in Egypt's principal export crop, cotton. Although the regime raised the procurement price on cotton and other major crops and eliminated farmers' wheat quotas, prices were still depressed relative to the world market. Understandably, farmers shifted much of their cultivation to uncontrolled fruits, vegetables, and berseem (a clover to feed animals), often at the expense of cotton. In freeing the farmers from obligations to cooperatives, the government also succeeded in further weakening a major institutional link with the rural masses.

The distributive effects of the economic liberalization were instrumental in promoting class divisions and tensions. The gap between Egypt's rich and poor widened. Although the lowest 20 percent of the population held 6.6 percent of national income in 1960 and had improved their share to 7.0 percent in 1965, that percentage dropped to 5.1 percent by the late 1970s. By comparison, the income of the highest 5 percent dipped slightly to 17.4 percent from 17.5 percent between 1960 and 1965 but increased markedly to 22 percent after several years of Sadat's policies.[33] Between 1978 and 1981, gains were in fact made in the real incomes of workers in the modern private sector and in those of less skilled government employees; the daily wages of farm laborers also improved.[34] But an entrepreneurial class spawned by *Infitah* and supported by foreign capital enriched itself in the economic expansion. Speculators, middle-men, and merchants, the *ottat suman*, literally "fat cats," became highly visible examples of the wealth accruing through contracts and kickbacks to some in the private sector. Recruitment to the new business community included, along with former landowners and the older private bourgeoisie, members of a public sector elite created during the Nasser era. Under Sadat, elites with a stake in *Infitah* became increasingly indistinguishable from the new, more unified upper class.[35] The country's widening income inequalities most adversely affected Egyptians without family members working abroad, those tied to fixed incomes, and the small rural landowners. Resentment against Sadat's policies and the new rich also came from managerial-level civil servants, intellectuals, and the many employed in the traditional economic sectors who shared in very little of the economic liberalization and whose real incomes eroded in the accompanying inflation. The regime's political opponents argued that the new economic program had strayed from ideals of equity at home and solidarity with the Arab World.

The United States could not easily disassociate itself from *Infitah's* policy errors and unfulfilled promises. Blame for the rising cost of living, laid by many Egyptians on Sadat's liberalizing policies, also unavoidably tainted those perceived to have sponsored him. The *Infitah* class benefited specifically from U.S. aid loans and from the associated advantages created in the improved climate for private investment. Accumulated evidence of profiteering, corruption, and waste in private sector activities reflected directly on the U.S. role. Socialists blamed foreign economic penetration for Egypt's difficulties in solving most of its development and financial problems. Sadat's critics, left and right, refused to separate U.S. aid from the increased political repression that marked his final year and especially his last months in power.

Washington and then the Cairo government stood accused by a vocal minority, in time a popular majority, of having induced Egypt to pursue a separate peace with Israel in exchange for territory and vague promises of Palestinian autonomy. The United States could not escape responsibility as broker for the fast-rising dissatisfaction about Israel's failure to follow through on its Camp David agreements. Left-wing opponents of the regime found confirmation of their view that efforts to have Egypt normalize relations with Israel were calculated to distract Egypt from meeting its political and moral obligations to the Palestinians. In its agreement with the West's geopolitical views, the Sadat regime was also said to have subordinated Egypt's national interests to become a proxy for U.S. military strategists.

No assessment of *Infitah* and its U.S. connection can be complete without weighing its psychological impact. In response to the visual evidence of accumulated wealth and luxury consumption by urban elites and a government withdrawing its paternalistic presence in the economy, there has emerged a feeling by rural and urban masses alike of being "left out," i.e., that a contractual agreement between the people and government established during the Nasser era was broken. Many better educated Egyptians, observing the intrusion of Western values and the dependence on foreign consultants and capital, again appear to have lost confidence in themselves and their country. This is reflected in the revival of fears that foreign aid activities are intended to divert the country's energies and resources and that foreign agents use Egyptians to obtain information that can undermine national security. The weakened influence of Egypt politically and inspirationally in the Arab world together with the sense of guilt, if also relief, in the U.S.-orchestrated normalization with Israel has reinforced these feelings of inadequacy. For many upwardly mobile young people, denied alternative political outlets, an increasingly familiar means to overcome this weakened self-identity and helplessness has been to find solace and solutions in fundamentalist Islam.

Reassessments of *Infitah*

An Egypt in transition from a largely closed socialist economy constructed in the late 1950s and 1960s offered what appeared to be one of several test cases for a U.S.-assisted reorientation toward private enterprise. The country could serve as a model for other developing states attempting to alter their public-sector-dominated economies. The expansion of private industry was supposed to coincide with other policies in using the market system for allocating resources and setting domestic priorities. Private U.S. firms and other investors would join in helping to turn the Egyptian economy around. But Egypt's laboratory proved contaminated, and the example it set was discouraging. Several U.S. administrations underestimated the structural obstacles in the Egyptian economy much as they did the public's commitment to retaining the social achievements since the 1952 Revolution. The will and capacity for change by the Cairo government was meanwhile overestimated. The 1977 food riots indelibly marked off the limits of policy reform tolerable to the urban masses.

Some reassessment of *Infitah* was also inevitable after the sudden exit of President Sadat. Well before October 1981, the Egyptian leadership raised complaints about the kinds of foreign private investments entering the economy. Sadat was particularly disappointed by the legally favored foreign companies that had concentrated their investments in consumption-oriented industries rather than basic productive enterprises that would employ large numbers of Egyptian workers. As evidence of corruption mounted and as it became clear that many of Sadat's close relatives and associates were accumulating fortunes, the regime came under attack. Hosni Mubarak soon after assuming office expressed new doubts about the consequences of economic liberalization and the need to rethink some programs. Informed observers doubted that he would emulate Sadat's decisional style or feel bound by domestic or foreign policy decisions in which he had little direct role. Mubarak would thus not necessarily feel a personal stake in the success of *Infitah* or the U.S. connection. As an early expression of dissatisfaction with previous policies, Mubarak replaced Dr. Abdel Razzak Abdel Meguid, the economic czar responsible for guiding the liberalization. The new president assured the country that he would resist investments, foreign or domestic, not directed toward expanding Egypt's productive capacity. Mubarak instructed his economic advisors, moreover, to explore ways of reducing the heavy burden on the national budget of consumer subsidies, a move welcomed by Egypt's Western creditors.

The post-Sadat leadership let it be known that ideally they would rather not have to choose between a U.S. or Soviet economic development model. Experiences to date with the Open Door policies are enough to suggest that laissez faire economics, however theoretically sound, is unable to serve Egypt's concern for development with social justice. In the popular disappointment with *Infitah*, the values and goals of Egypt's socialism are romanticized by some, including the belief that Nasser was on the right development path, ready to make the necessary corrections, before being thrown off course by foreign policy distractions and externally imposed constraints. Yet there has emerged no broad demand to return to the heavy-handed policies of the Nasser era, with their economic distortions, inefficiencies, and stagnation. Many Egyptian economists insist that they are seeking a set of politically and socially viable economic policies that combine planning and market forces. Freedom for private capital and the individual is expected to be exercised more in accordance with the national interest. Planners in the government speak of striking a better balance between growth/productivity and equity goals.[36]

Subsequent chapters show, however, that although the official rhetoric has changed in some respects under Mubarak, the state's basic economic policies underwent little modification during the 1981–85 period, and Egypt's dependence on the United States never waivered. Even though *Infitah* lost much of its luster and Mubarak imposed a number of deliberalizing measures affecting imports, he refused to disavow the principles of *Infitah*.[37] The restrictions were not designed to decrease economic penetration through increased self-sufficiency. Rather, the high duties laid on some key imports were intended to stimulate local production by means of joint ventures with foreign investors. Egypt had after 1974, then, committed itself to international market solutions that cannot be easily discarded. In the belief that prosperity within the global economy is predicated on comparative advantage and an acceptance of interdependency, Egypt has made a heavy political and economic investment.

Notes

1. An earlier version of this chapter appears in Marvin G. Weinbaum, Egypt's *Infitah* and the Politics of U.S. Economic Assistance, *Middle Eastern Studies*, Vol. 21, no. 2 (April 1985): 206–222.

2. A fuller description of these characteristics is provided by John Waterbury, "The Implications for U.S.-Egyptian Relations of Egypt's Turn to the West," a paper delivered at a conference on "Politics and Strategies of USAID in Egypt," at the Middle East Center, University of Pennsylvania, January 18–20, 1978.

3. World Bank, *World Development Report 1980* (New York: Oxford University Press, 1980), p. 112. For a discussion and comparative analysis, see Marvin G. Weinbaum, *Food, Development, and Politics in the Middle East* (Boulder, Colo.: Westview Press, 1982), pp. 26–33.

4. Although Egypt by the early 1970s had realized a physical quality of life index of 43, an impressive level for a low-income country, its disparity reduction ratio had dropped to 1.2 percent, suggesting that progress in improving quality of life had at best slowed. U.S. Agency for International Development, "Egypt: Country Development Strategy Statement, FY 1983" (Washington, D.C., January 1981), p. 10.

5. See discussion in Gouda Abdel-Khalek, "Looking Outside or Turning Northwest? On the Meaning and External Dimensions of Egypt's *Infitah*," *Social Problems*, Vol. 28, no. 4 (April 1981): 394–409. Also, Joe Stork, "Egypt's Debt Problem," *MERIP Reports*, no. 107 (July-August 1982): 12.

6. John Waterbury, *The Egypt of Nasser and Sadat: The Political Economy of Two Regimes* (Princeton: Princeton University Press, 1983), p. 398.

7. Saad Eddin Ibrahim, "Superpowers in the Arab World," *The Washington Quarterly* (Summer 1981): 86.

8. See discussion in Mohamed Heikal, *Autumn of Fury: The Assassination of Sadat* (London: Andre Deutsch, 1984), pp. 77–78.

9. Ibrahim, "Superpowers," p. 87.

10. Galal Ahmad Amin, "External Factors in the Reorientation of Egypt's Economic Policy," Malcolm H. Kerr and El Sayed Yassin (eds.), *Rich and Poor States in the Middle East* (Boulder, Colo.: Westview Press, 1982), p. 303.

11. The Egyptian-American Rural Improvement Service (EARIS) had among its objectives land reclamation, the settlement of landless families, improved housing and community aid, water management, and assistance to farm cooperatives.

12. Former Ambassador John S. Badeau recalls that the decision to consider a multi-year P.L. 480 program was brought about by the Kennedy adminstration's desire to ameliorate Egyptian-Israeli tensions through negotiations for food aid with Nasser's government that paralleled those under way in Israel. *The Middle East Remembered* (Washington, D.C.: The Middle East Institute, 1983), p. 192.

13. EARIS was phased out at the end of 1964. Its total cost reached $42.5 million.

14. U.S. General Accounting Office, "Report on Egypt's Capacity to Absorb and Use Economic Assistance Effectively" (Washington, D.C., September 15, 1977), p. 3.

In all, during the twenty years prior to 1967, the United States supplied about $930 million in assistance to Egypt, 70 percent of it under the food aid program and the remainder for infrastructural improvements and small-scale projects. During the hiatus in U.S. government aid between 1967 and 1975, private development aid to Egypt continued, albeit on a modest scale. The Ford Foundation and Catholic Relief Services (CRS) maintained offices in Cairo and made allocations for various projects. CRS was able to function through private donations and EEC contributions, though its total budget was less than $1 million yearly. In Washington, CRS lobbied for a restoration of U.S. assistance, at least for emergency relief purposes, but found it a political step the Nixon administration was not as yet prepared to undertake.

15. U.S. General Accounting Office, "Egypt's Capacity to Absorb and Use Economic Assistance Effectively," p. 4.

16. For a useful discussion see Donald S. Brown, "Egypt and the United States: Collaborators in Economic Development," *The Middle East Journal*, Vol. 35, no. 1 (Winter 1981): 4. Also, Ellen B. Laipson, "Egypt and the United States" (Washington, D.C.: Congressional Research Service, The Library of Congress, June 4, 1981), p. 18.

17. *Middle East News, Economic Weekly*, Cairo, May 14, 1982, p. 3. The current accounts deficit in 1974 stood at 13 percent of GDP and rose to 20 percent the next year. U.S. Agency for International Development, "Country Development Strategy Statement, FY 1985, Annex D," Washington, D.C., January 1983, p. 4.

18. See Waterbury, "The Implications of U.S.-Egyptian Relations," pp. 7–8.

19. Alan W. Horton, "Egypt Revisited," *American University Field Staff Reports*, no. 23, African Series, 1981, p. 3. See also World Bank, "Arab Republic of Egypt's Domestic Resource Mobilization and Growth Prospects for the 1980s," Report no. 3123–EGT, December 10, 1980, p. 2.

20. Waterbury, "The Implications of U.S.-Egyptian Relations," p. 5.

21. William J. Burns, *Economic Aid and American Policy Toward Egypt, 1955–1981* (Albany: State University of New York Press, 1985), p. 192.

22. The actual amount of assistance from Arab governments is not clear. Mohamad Heikal quotes a former Ministry of Finance official who put the figure at $14 billion for the period from 1971 to 1977; other sources claim it ran as high as $17 or even $22 billion. There are obvious discrepencies in accounting, depending on whether the money was deposited in the Central Bank. Contributions to Egypt's defense were most likely to have escaped detection in ordinary accounts. Heikal, *Autumn of Fury*, 79–80.

23. Waterbury, *The Egypt of Nasser and Sadat*, pp. 416–417.

24. Donald S. Brown, *Economic Development in Egypt—An American's Perspective* (Cairo: U.S. International Communications Agency, March 1982), p. 8.

25. U.S. Agency for International Development, "Egypt: Country Development Strategy Statement, FY 83," p. 27.

26. See discussion in Weinbaum, *Food, Development, and Politics*, pp. 160–162.

27. World Bank, "Arab Republic of Egypt's Domestic Resources Mobilization and Growth Prospects for the 1980s," Report No. 3123–EGT, p. 3. Nonoil U.S. direct investment totaled less than $100 million through 1980. *The Journal of Commerce*, October 7, 1981. The U.S. contributed merely 2.4 percent of the $1.4 billion investment in all joint projects through 1981–1982. Arab private investors provided the bulk of the capital. *The Christian Science Monitor*, February 10, 1983.

28. Comptroller General of the United States, "Egypt's Capacity to Absorb and Use Economic Assistance Effectively," p. 13. U.S. Embassy, Cairo, "Economic Trends Report: Egypt," April 15, 1985, p. 23.

29. U.S. Embassy, Cairo, "Economic Trends Report: Egypt," April 17, 1984, p. 9. Roger Owen, "Sadat's Legacy, Mubarak's Dilemma," *MERIP Reports*, no. 117 (September 18, 1983): p. 18. See also Arab Republic of Egypt, Ministry of Agriculture and the USAID, "Strategies for Accelerating Agricultural Development: A Report of the Presidential Mission on Agricultural Development," July 1982, p. 37.

30. The benefits accorded foreign investors under Law 43 were later extended in Law 159 to private Egyptian investors. Even so, the regime had little success in attracting the expanded capital of Egypt's resurgent middle and upper classes into productive investment. Alan Richards, "Egypt's Agriculture in Trouble," *MERIP Reports*, no. 84 (January 1980): 12.

31. Arab Republic of Egypt, *Egypt's Five Year Plan, 1982/83–1986/87*, December 1982, Part 1, Chapter 1, p. 14.

32. Robert Springborg, "Infitah, Agarian Transformation, and Elite Consolidation in Contemporary Iraq," paper presented at the World Congress of the International Political Science Association in Paris, France, July 15–20, 1985. A fuller discussion is found in his "Patrimonialism and Policy Making in Egypt: Nasser and Sadat and the Tenure Policy for Reclaimed Lands," *Middle Eastern Studies*, Vol. 15, no. 1 (January 1979): 49–69.

33. World Bank, *World Bank Tables 1980* (Washington, D.C.: Johns Hopkins University Press, 1980), p. 463. The most recent statistics are calculated on a somewhat different population base, and comparisons with those from the 1960s

must therefore be considered tentative. For an extensive treatment of income inequality see articles in Gouda Abdel-Khalek and Robert L. Tigner (eds.), *The Political Economy of Income Distribution in Egypt* (New York: Holmes and Meier, 1982). Real per capita increases in income that across the economy rose rapidly in the late 1970s slowed to an approximately 2 percent growth after 1980. U.S. Agency for International Development, "Congressional Presentation, FY 1986," Washington, April 1985, p. 28.

34. Statistics on increases in annual rates for farm workers, less skilled civil servants, and employees in the modern private sector are found in U.S. Agency for International Development, "Egypt: Country Development Strategy Statement, FY 1984, Annex: Benefits of Growth," Washington, D.C., February 1982, p. 13. Open unemployment in the early 1980s was generally estimated at between only 5 and 7 percent, although underemployment was an acknowledged problem. Public employment in ministries and economic authorities numbers 3 million workers. Another 1 million work in public sector companies, and 500,000 are in active military service. U.S. Embassy, "Economic Trends Report, 1985," p. 13.

35. Raymond A. Hinnebusch, "From Nasser to Sadat: Elite Transformation in Egypt," *Journal of South Asian and Middle Eastern Studies*, Vol. 8, no. 1 (Fall 1983): 46.

36. See *Middle East News, Economic Weekly*, Cairo, February 5, 1982, pp. 2–3.

37. See discussion in Marie-Christine Aulas, "Sadat's Egypt: A Balance Sheet," *MERIP Reports*, no. 107 (July-August 1982): 15. Also Jim Paul, "Foreign Investment in Egypt," ibid., p. 17.

3

Dependent Development

Egypt is firmly ensconced in the ranks of the Third World's more dependent, financially troubled economies. The country's outstanding foreign debt, less than $3 billion in 1973, grew to $16 billion by 1979. By the end of 1982, the external debt was estimated at nearly $22 billion, and in fall 1985 at $32.5 billion, with the servicing of obligations absorbing more than one-third of export earnings.[1] The terms of trade were also moving against Egypt as its major exports lost value. A trade deficit, registered largely with the European Economic Community (EEC) countries and the United States, stood at the equivalent of $5 billion in 1984-85. In the same fiscal year, the current account deficit reached more than $1.7 billion.[2] In the absence of government budget surpluses and adequate local savings, Egypt has adopted a development strategy for which continuous flows of imported capital, commodities, and technology are indispensable. External financing contributes as much as 80 percent of public investment. Most importantly, all the principal sources of income for the country, namely, its oil revenues, remittances from workers abroad, Suez Canal tolls, tourism, cotton exports, and foreign aid, are closely linked to uncertain world economic conditions.[3]

Nowhere are the financial burdens and vulnerability of Egypt's economy more apparent than in the food sector. The costs of imports are staggering, having risen in value to almost $4.4 billion in 1981 before declining, up from only $427 million in 1973.[4] Egypt, which purchased abroad only 7 percent of its foodstuffs in 1961, saw its imports increase to one-fifth of national requirements a decade later. As late as 1974 the country maintained a favorable net agricultural trade balance; but by 1983, imports of agricultural products from all foreign sources accounted for one-half of the total domestic food consumption. International markets supply, on various terms, about 75 percent of internal consumption of wheat, Egypt's most important food staple. Egypt ranked in 1983 as the world's third largest importer of U.S. wheat and wheat flour.[5] Although less than 20 percent of Egypt's total food bill comes in trade with the United States, the U.S. P.L. 480 program has supplied most of the wheat bought by Egypt on concessional terms and, as is often pointed out, accounts for about a one-third of the bread sold in Cairo.[6] Indeed, for some years Egypt has been the world's largest beneficiary of the P.L. 480 credits and is second only to India since the food program began in 1955.

More than one-half of all foreign economic assistance committed yearly to Egypt is provided by the United States. A significant part of the impressive 27 percent of GNP that Egypt devotes to public investment comes from official U.S. grants and loans, more than $10.8 obligated through 1985. Direct private investment in Egypt by U.S. citizens and corporations added roughly $1.4 billion more, mostly in petroleum and related industries.[7] Military assistance from the United States has risen sharply in recent years, totaling $4.5 billion in loans and grants allocated by 1984.[8]

The bounty of aid saddles Egypt with an outstanding debt to the United States of more than $8.5 billion, making the United States Egypt's major creditor. Although project aid and military sales have more recently been financed by outright grants, Egypt's obligations from earlier U.S. loans, the bulk in interest due on military purchases negotiated at commercial rates, left the country at the beginning of 1985 with a debt service of $726 million.[9] Carrying a burden almost equal to the dollars committed yearly by the United States for all economic and development aid, the Egyptians fell seriously behind on debt repayments. Unable to secure debt forgiveness or rescheduling, they turned to Washington in 1985 for increased assistance and received $500 million in emergency economic aid.

Disincentives and Distortions

Two highly disparate views are commonly aired about the impact of aid on Egypt's domestic economy and especially its production functions and policy outcomes. The issues raised are obviously applicable to most donor/recipient exchanges in the Third World and involve the most fundamental questions about whether aid is beneficial economically and acceptable politically. The positive view contends that aid is supplemental. In the form of goods and technical services it furnishes assistance that is otherwise beyond the reach of the recipient country or alleviates the need for purchases that require drawing off scarce foreign exchange. By covering a portion of a country's consumption, for example, U.S. commodity assistance increases the recipient's investment budget and helps to expand its expenditures for development purposes. In the Egyptian case, these flows of financial assistance and imports were intended to enable the country to modernize its infrastructure, strengthen its productive capacity, and improve management skills as well as meet consumption requirements. Not incidentally, they would also be expected to improve chances for political stability. There is little doubt that U.S. financial aid in the mid-1970s, as already described, assured critical inputs for Egypt's industry and helped the country to overcome its pressing foreign currency reserve problems. Although it is harder to demonstrate how far the dollar assistance, technical skills, and Western economic analyses contributed to the efficiency and performance of the Egyptian economy, on balance, foreign aid is seen, in this view, as favorable to development. It allowed Egypt to effectively mobilize its resources and spared the country from having to make politically distasteful economic choices.[10]

A displacement explanation of aid, or negative view, insists that programs of aid to Egypt have the important effect of discouraging domestic production and are responsible for imposing alien values and patterns on Egyptian society. The recipient country is kept from realizing the full potential of its industry and is induced to aggravate tendencies toward a dual economy. Even with the best of intentions by donors (something usually not assumed by critics), the aid sets in motion domestic policies that are considered detrimental to hopes of bringing more self-generated processes of change. Further, there is the belief that the availability of U.S. programs and a large bureaucracy to implement them determines the priorities for Egypt's decisionmakers, thereby denying the country the opportunity to make the most advantageous choices and fully utilize its own talents.

One does not have to accept the displacement view entirely to recognize that U.S. aid helps to shape Egypt's development strategies and channel its investment budget. The country is indisputably hooked on external finances and cannot forego foreign equipment and technical services. President Sadat's economic liberalization policies, by stimulating consumer demand, left Egypt unable to compete in quality and sometimes even in price with many imported goods. To aggravate the problem, U.S. aid programs normally stipulate that concessional financing be tied to U.S.-made products, regardless of more competitive prices elsewhere and irrespective of Egypt's ability to produce the same items. Indeed, in order for Egypt to obtain certain critical imports from the United States, it may also have to accept an entire procurement package. Because U.S. financing is frequently available only for the purchase of capital equipment and higher technologies, investment decisions may be made without full assessment of opportunity costs and may be at times inappropriate to Egypt's development needs and capabilities. Very seldom, for example, are projects designed to optimize the kind of labor-intensive approaches that can offer solutions to Egypt's serious urban employment problems. At the same time, the country is also forced by aid agreements into hiring high-priced foreign experts whose handsome salaries and other benefits are resented by their Egyptian counterparts. U.S. regulations are often considered inflexible because they fail to increase the use of Egyptian consultants and contractors.

Foreign aid's disincentive effects are most often identified in Egypt's agricultural sector. Considerable food imports on easy terms could account for some of the sluggish growth in output and the disappointing levels of public and private investment in the rural areas. Commodity aid as well as externally funded agricultural projects frequently stand accused of having enabled authorities during most of the 1970s to divert resources away from the agricultural sector. Plainly, Egypt is relieved of some pressures to increase its efforts to feed itself as long as food aid, especially wheat, is readily available and, for the most part, affordable. U.S. shipments assure that a good portion of the wheat deficit is covered and, as general budgetary support, help the Egyptian government to meet its large commercial food bills in world markets. The extensive imports until 1983 of poultry and its sale at subsidized prices no doubt brought the steady decline in the production of poultry and eggs. With demand increasing, U.S. assistance for livestock production led to an increase in planting of berseem on land previously given over to growing food for human consumption. The availability of aid has not, as in some countries, induced consumers on a large scale to change food preferences and shift away from domestically grown crops to imported ones. Yet, in helping to free up land for fodder crops and making it easier for the country to import feed grains, the United States has done little to discourage the luxury of higher meat consumption.

By making food available on concessional terms, farmers are discouraged from boosting the production of certain crops. U.S. sales facilitate, for example, the unrestricted availability of government-subsidized flour that sets a low ceiling on the value of domestic wheat in private markets. With grain prices so depressed, locally grown wheat is sometimes more valuable as animal feed and is considered a by-product of straw used to make bricks. U.S. law requires the secretary of agriculture to affirm that food shipments under the Food for Peace (P.L. 480) legislation do not cause a substantial disincentive to farmers. But AID officials in Cairo admit privately and their analyses show that food aid has a negative impact on domestic wheat production.

Aid programs are also credited in part for budgetary burdens resulting from the government's considerable food and energy subsidies for urban consumers. Together these subsidies, directly and indirectly, cost more than $7 billion in 1984 and accounted for slightly under one-third of the government budget. The responsibility of the United States and

other donors stems from the fact that a large portion of the funds
needed to sustain low-cost food comes from the savings to the public
treasury made through purchase of concessional wheat and other commodity aid programs (see Chapter Six). Moreover, nearly all of the wheat
imported yearly through P.L. 480 agreements goes directly into the
urban subsidy distribution system. Rural dwellers, more than 50 percent
of the population, are outside this system and benefit far less from state
subsidized food prices. Indeed, because the high cost of the consumer
subsidies is a principal reason for the depressed prices paid to farmers
for state-procured crops, government policy supports the adverse terms
of trade between urban and rural areas.

Even within urban areas, the food aid and related subsidies are not
well targeted. The benefits of subsidies on wheat and other controlled
food items are shared unequally by economic groups. Although for the
urban middle class these subsidies make up a smaller part of their
disposable income than for the lower class, the higher rates of per capita
consumption of the better off give them a disproportionate share of the
benefits (as described in Chapter Six). The U.S. loans and grants for
U.S.-made tractors, trucks, industrial spare parts, and raw materials are
no more redistributive. Whether these commodities and credits are
channeled to private enterprises or farmers, they are absorbed, not
surprisingly, by the already established businessmen and, in the countryside, by the large- and middle-sized, more prosperous landholders.

Without disputing that the United States and others have facilitated
a policy framework that confronts Egypt with its current pricing and
subsidy dilemmas, it is another matter whether these and other problems
would improve without external assistance. For one, government's planners are unlikely to direct greater investment into the agricultural sector
in the absence of foreign aid. It is altogether likely that agriculture
would continue to be biased against both as a consequence of prevailing
concepts of development and the political muscle of urban groups. If
anything, it can be argued that in recent years the programs of foreign
donors have stimulated domestic interest in rural development. Project
aid has captured a larger portion of the national budget in local cost
financing for agriculture than would otherwise be allocated. At their
best, projects have created a stronger consciousness of planning, organization, and evaluation in the Egyptian bureaucracy, and agricultural
research and training have probably received more attention because
of outside advisors.[11] Food aid, whatever its disincentive effects, has
very little to do with Egypt's basic agricultural problems. The impact
on production of higher labor costs and the exodus of skilled rural
workers are accounted for by the lure of employment in Cairo and

abroad. Lower crop yields mainly reflect deteriorating soil quality resulting from poor water management.

U.S. aid officials regularly counsel Egypt's policymakers that only by raising official prices closer to world market levels and by dropping production allocations will farmers have the incentive to increase their efforts. In the case of wheat, the assurance of food aid has, as much as anything else, helped to convince the government to lift controls, allowing farmers to move from wheat to crops with a higher degree of profitability. But even if denied foreign assistance, Egypt would still have to deal with the uncompetitiveness of growing wheat on the country's scarce, irrigated land as against producing higher value clover for animals as well as fruits and vegetables. In view of Egypt's consumption requirements, the disappearance of concessional U.S. sales might force a reimposition of government quotas and other restrictive policies in order to ensure higher grain production, thereby reducing farmers' incomes. More probably, rather than stimulating domestic output, a loss of P.L. 480 wheat would lead either to larger external commercial purchases, using scarce foreign exchange, or force a cutback in expenditures in other budgetary areas. In either event, the policy choice would be as much political as economic.

Many Egyptians in and outside of government nonetheless believe that the aid donors, but mainly the pattern of U.S. allocations, divert their country from its desired development priorities. To its critics, AID is seen as enticing Egypt to preempt some of its limited financial resources for programs it either does not need or ones that are only marginal to its interests. The requirement that Egypt provide matching funds for most projects and finance their recurring costs meanwhile adds to the country's large debt burden. Detractors claim that the assistance committed to industrial investment is inadequate and that, in general, too small a direct U.S. contribution goes to building the productive capacity of Egypt's economy. The earmarking of funds for specific U.S. projects often makes it difficult, it is argued, for Egypt to use flexibly the dollars allocated and to capture the large sums promised for projects that may never be completed. The United States is also viewed in some quarters as having monopolized much of the available talent in Egypt through professional and financial inducements. The time and energies of leading economists and scientists are occupied in AID programs that, according to allegations, have been used to gather data detrimental to Egypt's national interests.[12]

According to the government's critics, particularly those on the left, Egypt pays a heavy price in sacrificed economic and political options. Involvement with the United States restricts Egypt's ability to pursue aid arrangements with other countries. The United States is seen as applying its financial leverage at the same time to induce Egyptian policymakers to accept Israeli cooperation in making Egypt's adjustment to world market demand. Using Israel's experiences and marketing channels, Egypt was supposed to gain access to the European community and in the process integrate its economy with that of Israel's.[13]

Few would argue that AID, through its unwillingness to fund every kind of project, influences the contents of the Egyptian development portfolio. Yet U.S. officials counter that they have the right to make their assessments on economic grounds and, in any case, the Egyptian government is always free to use its own resources for more preferred programs. With U.S. assistance, these officials claim, Egypt is usually able to implement its own goals more quickly and efficiently. In fact, the criticisms of foreign aid donors are not so much the result of disagreements about development policy choices as they are expressions of a reemerging economic nationalism. Although not necessarily seeking an end to financial assistance from the West, the skeptical show concern about Egypt's economic dependence on the outside world. Many fear that aid is also being used to purchase Egypt's participation in the machinations of the West's economic managers and political strategists.

The Nature of Dependence

All economic indicators point to Egypt's strong reliance on the outside world for the capital, commodities, and technical services needed to sustain current levels of consumption for its citizens and realize promised economic expansion. Proponents of dependency theory insist that in the context of the world capitalist system, this dependence, as with other less developed countries, means subordination to the more developed, wealthier countries. Because of uneven, exploitative policies, developing countries are kept from adjusting their domestic production and export trading patterns to their own national advantage. In the now familiar arguments, the richer countries are seen as able to force the dependent ones to adopt policies that work essentially to the advantage of the core countries in a world system. There appears, moreover, a symbiosis of interests between key domestic elites and those on the outside who have imposed dependent structures. It is an article of faith among these theorists that the economic circumstances of most poor countries and their failure over time to realize economic growth or extend equity is largely explained by this dominance by the industrial West. The subordinate relationship is perceived for much of the Third World as a successor form to colonial rule because it continues to deny recipient countries opportunities to realize their full economic potential or to exercise their complete political independence.[14]

The investments of multinational corporations are considered a prime instrument of economic penetration and manipulation of the dependent country's economy. Only slightly less pernicious is the perceived role of foreign aid, bilateral and multilateral. It is stressed that outside assistance programs, whether in the form of balance-of-payments support or development loans and grants, help to create long-term financial obligations to Western governments that are given a permanency by the protectionist trade policies of the industrial states. Bilateral aid is seen as creating the most direct opportunities for pressuring recipient countries. It frequently results in high priced imports for a country tied closely to a single major donor. Recipient country policies compliant with donors' interests are likely to preclude chances of a more self-generated process of development. Multilateral aid, through such agencies as the IMF and World Bank (and its IDA affiliate), is a more disguised but still effective way for these same developed countries to shape a recipient country's economy and prepare it for its prescribed role in the world capitalist system. The restrictive monetary and fiscal policies forced on these countries deny domestic policymakers the freedom to manage their own resources and stymie any efforts to redistribute power and wealth more equitably.

Critics of U.S. foreign aid programs are well-armed when it comes to demonstrating how aid works hand in hand with profit-seeking U.S.-based corporations. Worldwide, 75 percent of AID's development assistance funds are reportedly spent in the United States, and in the late 1970s almost one-half of the U.S.-financed procurement contracts were for purchases from just twenty-two U.S. megacorporations.[15] It is frequently pointed out that AID's programs seem tailor-made for big corporations rather than small businesses. Many officials in recipient countries particularly object to financing equipment imports from U.S. firms through the U.S. Export-Import Bank, with its high interest rates and requirements that goods be carried on expensive U.S. flag vessels. Even World Bank projects are said to generate many times the dollar value of the contribution of the U.S. government to the international agency in procurements from U.S. companies.

Some U.S. firms have responded to Egypt's efforts to attract foreign private investment. Petroleum exploration and production companies expanded a presence in Egypt begun in the mid-1960s. Where, in 1974, there had been only six banks in the country, by 1983, seventy-five foreign and Egyptian banks were in operation.[16] Directly or indirectly as a result of the AID program, a number of U.S. management, accounting, and engineering firms were represented in Cairo, along with U.S. construction, telecommunications, and manufacturing companies. Many U.S. exporters gained entry to Egypt during the decade through commodity contracts arranged with AID funding, or they otherwise found opportunities for marketing their products and services enhanced by U.S. development aid. More than four hundred U.S. firms are said to have benefited in some way from commodity aid sales to Egypt.[17] Because contracts going to U.S. firms and procurements from U.S. exporters figure so importantly in the U.S. balance of payments, aid legislation contains explicit provisions to avoid or lessen foreign competition for U.S. industries.

U.S. commercial interests have a high stake in what is presumably the most benevolent form of assistance—food aid. Historically, U.S. wheat surpluses have served as the major motive behind shipments on concessional terms to food-deficit countries. The advantages of food aid have been the indirect price supports for U.S. farmers, the subsidies for the U.S. shipping industry, and the savings to the federal treasury in not having to store wheat lacking commercial markets. U.S. policymakers have made no effort to hide their long-term goal in the Third World of turning a dependence on U.S. aid into a reliance on the United States for commercial grain purchases once a recipient country's economy had sufficiently strengthened.

In the case of Egypt, the United States did not have to wait very long for concessional sales to stimulate commercial ones. Of the $1.8 billion in all exports by United States to Egypt in 1980, including military sales, roughly one-half occurred outside official assistance programs.[18] By 1983, the value of U.S. farm products exported to Egypt had risen to nearly $900 million, up from $123 million in 1973 and $770 million in 1980, and more than one-third was traded on commercial terms.[19] Egypt had joined the top ten world markets for U.S. agricultural exports.[20] Thanks to P.L. 480 agreements, U.S. millers found in Egypt their largest foreign customer. The importance of the Egyptian market was underscored in a budding trade war with the EEC in January 1983; in "retaliation" for the agricultural export pricing policies of the Europeans, Washington directly subsidized 1 million metric tons of wheat flour (worth $120 million) sold commercially to Egypt.

Against the $2.8 billion the United States exported to Egypt in 1983 (about one-third of Egypt's total imports), Egypt's exports to the United States were valued at only $303 million and 85 percent was crude petroleum.[21] There were areas with sales potential for Egypt, notably for cotton yarn, where some Egyptians contend that official U.S. pressure limits sales. They also feel that the United States has not done enough to help Egypt develop new export markets to replace those lost by signing the Camp David accords. Yet the lopsided, two-way trade between Egypt and the United States cannot be explained, in the prevailing structure of trade, simply as an example of industrial nation protectionism.

Egypt's compounding rate of dependence after 1974 was probably unavoidable as a means of financing investment and covering its balance of payments deficits. The choice then, as earlier in the Nasser regime, was not whether to form dependent relationships but with whom and to what degree. Egypt sought credits from both the developed market economies and the centrally planned ones. As discussed in Chapter Two, the cumulative effects of years of deterioriating infrastructure, declining industrial efficiency, and critical shortages of grain had given Sadat a sense of urgency (quite aside from his political motives) to attract capital investment from the West and the affluent Arab states.[22] Egypt thus did not follow the pattern of some countries that discarded nationalist, state-sponsored development under external pressures. An opening was not quietly forced on the country through the penetration of the multinational businesses. Rather, the national laws adopted after 1973 were calculated to entice substantial foreign investment.

The prospect of dependence on the capitalist countries was not, given the Egyptian experience, a matter of giving up a distinctively more equitable aid and trade with the socialist economies. For although barter agreements used extensively by the Soviets and the Eastern bloc countries allowed more flexibility for countries such as Egypt with meager foreign exchange holdings, the goods bartered were not uncommonly dumped by the Soviets and their allies, thereby depressing world prices. Barter deals are likely, as Egypt found out, to allow a developing country's industries that must also continue to sell in wider international markets to become highly uncompetitive over time. For all the praise of the Soviets' willingness to invest in heavy industry and help in augmenting Egypt's productive capacity, the quality of their development contribution is questioned as is their neglect of nonindustrial sectors. The Soviets also stand accused of failing to make the Egyptians fuller participants in their own development process.

A condition of dependence that under *Infitah* left Egypt unable to diversify its production or alter its patterns of trade is not, all the same, necessarily proof of classic dependency.[23] For an exploitative relationship, not merely an advantageous one, the developed country should have used its economic superiority to impel a dependent country to take actions clearly in the interests of the former and to the disadvantage of the latter.[24] Dependency theory posits a deliberate set of strategies designed to transfer or appropriate valued resources from the less developed country and/or to take advantage of a large consumer market and low labor costs—leaving the subordinate country economically weakened and the developed country strengthened. In foreign aid, exploitation describes the case where the interests of the donor are served at the expense or with only minimal benefit to the recipient.

This would undoubtedly be the case if the donor regularly sought to deny the recipient a fair return on its exports or contrived to keep its productive capacity underdeveloped.

Though it is readily acknowledged that U.S. aid programs since 1975, as before 1967, were never devoid of commercial motives, the case is not thereby made for economic exploitation. The relationship has not been so skewed that if the United States and other major donors have profited economically and politically, then Egypt has lost. Although the U.S. programs often provide, in effect, opportunities for U.S. exporters, the advantages are not necessarily one-sided, and the Egyptians may be clearly the gainers when there is at least some international competition to aid or trade. Dependence can be, as the Egyptian case suggests, a needed condition for economic growth, and neglect by the developed countries can be a worse fate.[25] In view of the formidable job of trying to raise the rate of savings and force other means of domestic capital mobilization, the attraction of external resources, private or governmental, may represent the only chance for Egypt to meet both its immediate consumption requirements and have something left over for development. Meanwhile, political dividends aside, the expensive, open-ended aid obligations assumed by the United States may not be either on balance or in the long run economically desirable.

One supposed purpose of bilateral and multilateral foreign aid is to pave the way for private capital by pressing recipient governments to enact protections for foreign investments and by helping to reduce business skepticism about a country's political stability. In Egypt, it is debatable how much external aid has in fact lured direct foreign investment. To be sure, the United States regularly facilitates contacts between private firms and Egyptian government officials and otherwise encourages U.S. private investment. Many businessmen take their cues from AID's investment priorities as well as the results of negotiations between Egypt and other creditors. However, most multinational corporations make their own determinations based on calculations of likely returns on investment and independent analyses of risk. Though foreign investors remain wary of long-term involvement in Egypt, some find it among the more stable countries in the region and are attracted to its potentially large domestic consumer market. Supportive policies by AID and others may be far less determining than the administrative hurdles posed by the Egyptian bureaucracy, the lack of official follow through on specific commitments, and the physical difficulties of doing business in Cairo.[26] Rather than the massive U.S. aid program laying a protective ground for U.S.-based corporations, the reverse is perhaps more valid. Overtures to foreign firms for joint ventures often seem most designed to impress the Western countries with Egypt's commitment to a private sector, liberal approach. Disappointment about the level and kind of direct private investment from the West, especially the United States, forces the Cairo government to rest most of its plans for development financing on foreign, nonprivate sources.

A U.S. aid policy that dismisses the idea that food self-sufficiency is a proper goal for Egypt is often cited as evidence of exploitative designs. The official U.S. view stands in contrast to frequent public assertions by ranking Egyptian officials that self-sufficiency in wheat or at least in carbohydrates is possible by the end of the 1980s. Although lacking a serious economic plan, these policymakers are anxious about the long-run availability to Egypt of grains, whether on concessional or commercial terms. They are also understandably concerned about the annual cost of importing wheat and maize. For many in and outside of government, the answer to food security lies in sharply curtailing food imports together with greatly expanding local production.

The hard sell of U.S. farm products by the Reagan administration and the major contribution of agricultural exports in attempts to offset the worsening U.S. trade balance is confirmation enough for aid critics of an U.S. marketing strategy using P.L. 480 agreements. Predictably, those who interpret concessional U.S. wheat as a device to capture and hold Egyptian markets also conclude that U.S.-funded agricultural programs are intended to ensure that the country does not become more food self-reliant. In all fairness, the United States in its development aid to Egypt appears guided by traditional liberal doctrines. Egyptian planners are advised to forego the goal of food security in favor of producing commodities for which the country has a comparative advantage, a strategy that stresses agricultural exports development over attempts to close the food deficit gap. U.S. aid officials who sometimes question whether U.S. taxpayers should be asked to support the strengthening of Egypt's agricultural sector do so not in fear of a shrinking market but out of frustration with financing a government unwilling to budget sufficient rewards for its own farmers.

U.S. advisors specifically argue that food self-sufficiency, especially in wheat, is unrealistic and economically unsound. At current yields, it is estimated that in order for Egypt to acquire wheat sufficiency it would have to give over to grain production an area equivalent to virtually all its current arable land.[27] To have wheat planted on expanded, reclaimed land is an even more dubious strategy. Even at world prices, the high reclamation costs cannot be covered by the growing of wheat; only higher value crops are economically viable. Any short-term attempt to lessen Egypt's dependence on the United States and others for food grains can come only at the expense of reducing the country's relatively high (74 percent) self-sufficiency in beef production. There is some logic in this choice as the costs of producing meat in Egypt are much greater than the cost of meat imports, and the costs of growing wheat locally are less than those of importing it. But to expect Egyptian farmers to forego livestock production ignores the current profitability of fodder crops, the importance of farm animals as energy and dairy sources, and the contribution of berseem to soil fertility in the crop rotation system.

The question is naturally raised about where in fact Egypt's comparative advantages in international trade may lie. Traditionally it was in agriculture, and specifically in the export of very long staple cotton. But the market for this commodity has contracted with the popularity of synthetic fibers that blend just as well with less expensive, shorter staple cotton. Egypt's shift to this shorter variety has the advantage of reducing the growing seasons and making it easier for farmers to plant horticultural crops and berseem in rotation with cotton. Yet the change leaves Egypt to compete in selling cotton within an already crowded field where prices fluctuate sharply. As is the case for most of the country's agricultural output, there are few large markets abroad waiting to be tapped. Successful export promotion as well as guarantees of free entry are preconditions if the country is to break the present stagnation in agricultural export growth.

Economically efficient, tradeable goods production seems even less promising in the industrial sector. Few believe that Egypt will be able any time soon to count on manufactured exports to maintain a healthy balance-of-payments position. In fact, a competitive industrial export sector seems even more remote than before *Infitah*. Industrial exports in the early 1980s were only 7 percent of total industrial output, lower in real terms than before 1974.[28] Very probably, less than 20 percent of foreign private investment has found its way into the productive sphere, and the Open Door legislation created, by one estimate, no more than 45,000 new jobs.[29] Dominant public sector industry continues to emphasize its role in meeting rising domestic demand and import substitute strategies. For local industries to become competitive in both domestic and foreign markets requires, moreover, that they overcome their traditionally low productivity, poor quality controls, and weak marketing skills. There exists a serious lack of skilled technicians and managers; most of them are abroad earning far higher salaries. (Indeed, the exported labor force, somewhere between 2 and 3 million, has for some time been Egypt's most sought-after commodity, especially by affluent Arab states.) Egypt is also not well-endowed with the non-agricultural raw materials on which industrial development could be based. The country desperately needs retooling and expansion of its industry to cope with high urban unemployment and redundant labor, especially in public industries. Yet most schemes for gaining a larger export market that could help stem imports seem to rest on building modern industry that is unavoidably capital-intensive.

Import substitution industries offer to date little to commend them. The apparent profitability of the country's aluminum and fertilizer factories, together responsible for one-fifth of national electricity consumption, is based on government-subsidized energy prices that hide the true opportunity costs. Policies intended to shield consumers and producers from price increases reduce prospects for either export generation or effective import substitution. Little more than nationalist aspirations prompt the belief that expanded trade can replace aid soon as a way of diminishing Egypt's economic dependence. Similarly, no serious economic blueprint supports the view that local industry can provide substitutes for most imports as a way to reduce consumption and spur domestic investment. Indigenous political elites find it considerably easier to keep aid flows coming rather than to try imposing unpopular, stringent financial reforms. Stated differently, it may be that domestic policies, dictated by internal political imperatives, explain more of Egypt's inability to place its economy on a sound footing than any manipulation by external forces emerging out of dependent economic relations. As Waterbury has observed, in the last analysis the leaders in the Third World states decide the degree of dependence rather than the captains of industry and political elites in developed countries.[30]

Conclusion

Exogenous factors, in particular oil revenues, remittances, and Suez Canal tolls, rather than basic domestic strength account for Egypt's economic growth. The decision reached in the mid-1970s to open Egypt to global economic forces has also increased the country's vulnerability to changes in world oil and grain prices, inflation and interest rates, and the well-being of developed country economies. Although not all recent economic trends have been adverse to Egypt's balance of payments, a lasting effect of combining economic integration with domestic political pressures has been the increasing discrepancy between world and domestic prices.[31] Until the seemingly intractable problems of price controls and subsidies are resolved, Egypt is expected to have little access to the resources or kinds of investment choices that are presupposed in a successful adjustment to a competitive world economy.

In retrospect, foreign aid has not assured Egypt the most effective use of its national resources, induced needed structural changes, or always introduced appropriate technologies. Aid has probably added, even if inadvertently, to the distortions and disincentives in the economy. Still, the proposition that an aid dependence is a drag on overall economic growth is difficult to demonstrate in the Egyptian case. To the contrary, foreign assistance appears to be a necessary condition, albeit hardly a guarantee, of economic development and a rising standard of living for most Egyptians. Were Egypt to refuse aid without compensating export income and other large capital inflows, it would be left with no recourse but to press down strongly on consumption and curtail most of its present development plans. The country's chronic budgetary and current account problems which are expected to become critical in the late 1980s, leave no obvious alternatives to a substantial U.S. assistance program, especially commodity aid. An abrupt break in the U.S. aid connection would also jeopardize other Western bilateral and multilateral aid agreements as well as dim chances of new, direct private investment. Even with the Mubarak regime's efforts to improve ties to other Arab states, the lowered revenues and present disarray of the Organization of Petroleum Exporting Countries (OPEC) give little hope that the regions' states can supply generous, dependable assistance or offer substitutes for the security the West promises against Egypt's perceived enemies.

These observations presume that Egypt has little to gain from trying to pursue highly autarkic policies. It is difficult to conceive Egypt's insulation from the world markets, at a level similar to the 1960s, without a radical change of the country's political alliances and in its aid and trade partners. As already noted, a realignment with the socialist bloc would only substitute other forms of economic dependence and impose new political constraints. Though developing countries do not always find it possible to comparison shop for foreign aid, Egypt has had more opportunity than most to weigh the relative degrees of foreign interference. In any case, Egypt cannot now easily disregard its commitment to international market solutions. Sadat's conviction that prosperity and political objectives are linked to participation in a global economy staked out for Egypt a serious political and economic investment. President Mubarak has sought to avoid both the unpopular elements of Sadat's liberalizing policies and Nasser's command economy. But wherever the middle course is drawn, he remains committed to attracting Western capital. As already noted, even when Mubarak found it necessary to impose deliberalizing measures, the restrictions were not designed to halt economic penetration.

The country's planners had hoped, all the same, to reduce Egypt's dependence on foreign capital by financing development through more internally generated savings and budget surpluses. In the government's 1982/83–86/87 Development Plan, domestic savings were scheduled to increase by at least 20 percent annually, eventually replacing foreign funds as the major source of financing. But even as the plan was implemented most of the optimism behind it had diminished. Economic growth slowed, and slumping or stagnant revenues from Egypt's principal hard currency earners threatened to leave the country unable to pay for its import needs. Petroleum receipts, which account for 65 percent of export earnings, have fallen with global over-production and competitive markets. Workers' remittances are certain to decline as belt-tightening economic policies in the region's major oil-exporting countries force many foreign employees to leave. There seems little likelihood that Egypt will be able to generate new, lucrative sources of foreign exchange. The hard economic facts permit little room, then, for confidence in the economy, certainly in the absence of outside help.

Foreign aid that is bilateral and, as in the U.S. program, essentially politically motivated, offers a form of dependence that carries some advantages to the recipient. The Egyptian experience shows that this aid is likely to be very generous. Egypt receives a far higher level of aid than similar, low-income developing countries whose relationship with the United States is less politically inspired. Political aid is also certain to come on easier terms. By the early 1980s, nearly all U.S. project and commodity financing for Egypt had been shifted to a grant basis, and P.L. 480 loans remain exceedingly soft. This bilateral aid usually sets, for all the advice given, far less stringent domestic economic conditions than those demanded by the IMF. Most important, with Washington committed to authorizing more than $1 billion yearly in economic aid, an important means of leverage over Egyptian economic policy is effectively denied. AID officials cannot with much conviction threaten to withdraw or withhold funds from the government. U.S. influence over Egypt's broad development choices notwithstanding, the U.S. desire to assure Egypt's cooperation in international regional policies limits the demands the United States can impose. Egypt's colonial past and attempts by the Soviets after 1967 to intrude in the country's domestic affairs make the U.S. and Egyptian governments alike sensitive to public criticism. A Cairo government that complains strongly enough and implies that its ability to succeed (and survive) is at stake has during the history of the U.S. aid program received most of what it sought. Ironically, for reasons of Egypt's designated strategic position, the country's leadership can probably count on the United States and other Western donors, perhaps even the IMF, to come forward with whatever financial assistance is required should the economy deteriorate to the point that the regime's stability is threatened.

Notes

1. Morgan Guaranty Trust Co., *World Financial Markets*, June 1983. Debt servicing calculations are based on a survey by Morgan Guaranty in *The Wall*

Street Journal, June 2, 1984 and AID/Washington estimates. Also see World Bank, *World Debt Tables* 1983-84 Edition (Washington, D.C.: Johns Hopkins University Press, 1984), p. 226. The total 1985 external debt is based on an estimate by AID/Washington. A study by the IMF reported in *The New York Times*, September 24, 1985 calculates Egypt's outstanding obligations at $35 billion.

2. U.S. Embassy, Cairo, "Economic Trends Report: Egypt," April 15, 1985, p. 1, from data furnished by the Central Bank of Egypt, the IMF, and other sources.

3. An earlier version of the chapter appears in Marvin G. Weinbaum, "Dependent Aid and U.S. Economic Assistance to Egypt," *International Journal of Middle East Studies*, Vol. 19, no. 1 (Spring 1986).

4. John B. Parker and James R. Coyle, "Urbanization and Agricultural Policy in Egypt," *Foreign Agricultural Report*, no. 169 (September 1981): p. 34.

5. U.S. Department of Agriculture, "Fact File," *Foreign Agriculture* (February 1984): p. 13. In 1984, Egypt imported 1.5 million tons of wheat and wheat flour from the United States at concessional prices. Egypt also turned to foreign sources for much of the sugar, vegetables oils, and meat consumed domestically. Once an important rice exporter, the country is now unable to produce enough for its own market. See also Anne M. Thompson, "Egypt, Food Security and Food Aid," *Food Policy*, Vol. 8, no. 3 (August 1983): 178–186.

6. In all, P.L. 480 sales supply about 20 percent of Egypt's total wheat consumption. Demand for food is rising at an annual rate of 2 to 5 percent ahead of agricultural production, which in recent years has averaged no more than 3 percent. The 48.4 million people Egypt has to feed in 1985 will, if the prevailing rate of nearly 3 percent population growth per annum continues, increase to 70 million by the end of the century.

7. U.S. Embassy, "Economic Trends Reports, 1985," p. 3. However, the book value of direct private U.S. investment in industry and agriculture was only $61 million in 1984. U.S. Embassy, Cairo, "Economic Trends Report: Egypt," April 17, 1984, p. 4.

8. *The New York Times*, February 14, 1985.

9. "Economic Trends Report, 1985," p. 12. Also see World Bank, "Arab Republic of Egypt: Current Economic Situation and Growth Prospects," Report no. 4498-EGT, October 5, 1983, p. 118. A Morgan Guaranty Trust Co. study, cited in Marie-Christine Aulas, "Sadat's Egypt: A Balance Sheet," *MERIP Reports*, no. 107 (July-August 1982): 4., indicates that compared to most less developed countries, little of Egypt's debt is short-term. Of the $5.4 billion in all loans owned by Egypt to private banks at the end of 1982, only $1.5 billion were to U.S. banks.

10. For a lengthy examination of competing theories on aid's role in development see John White, *The Politics of Foreign Aid* (New York: St. Martin's Press, 1974), pp. 122–142.

11. A general treatment of the topic is found in Marvin G. Weinbaum, *Food, Development, and Politics in the Middle East* (Boulder, Colo.: Westview Press, 1982), pp. 147–148.

12. See especially an article by Galal Ahmad Amin in *Al-Ahram Al-Iqtisadi* (Cairo), October 18, 1982.

13. Aulas, "Sadat's Egypt," In fact, Egypt and Israel found very little that was compatible in their two economies. A modest trade, mainly agricultural items from Israel to Egypt, was conducted until the outbreak of the 1982 Lebanon war. Just prior to the conflict an agricultural cooperation agreement between the two countries had been signed that would have allowed Israel to instruct Egyptian farmers on modern irrigation methods and provided for an exchange of agricultural research scientists in plant protection and veterinarian services.

14. For a good summary of the literature see Ronald H. Chilcote, *Theories of Development and Underdevelopment* (Boulder, Colo.: Westview Press, 1984).

15. David Kinley, Arnold Levinson and Frances Moore Lappe, "The Myth of Humanitarian Aid," *The Nation*, July 11–18, 1981, p. 42. Peter McPherson, the AID administrator, contends that 90 percent of U.S. development loans come back in the form of new or increased exports, an argument given credence by the fact that developing countries purchase more than 40 percent of U.S. manufactured exports. "U.S. Aid in Developing Countries: Altruism Pays Dividends," *Enterprise*, November 1981, p. 9. Until the mid-1980s, when overvalued dollars slowed the growth of imports, developing countries' imports were expanding at the rate of 20 percent yearly compared with a growth of 15 percent for their exports to developed countries.

16. U.S. Agency for International Development, Cairo, "Country Development Strategy Statement, FY 1985," Washington, D.C., April 1983, pp. 25–26.

17. James F. Bednar, "Stopgap: U.S. Assistance is Buying Time for Development," *Agenda*, Vol. 5, no. 2 (March 1981): 12.

18. U.S. Embassy, Cairo, "Economic Trends Report, 1984," pp. 4, 15. In 1982, $1.3 billion of the $2.9 billion in total exports were commercial.

19. U.S. Department of Agriculture, *Foreign Agriculture* (August 1981): 5 and *Foreign Agriculture* (February 1984): 12.

20. U.S. Embassy, "Economic Trends Reports, 1984," pp. 15, 23.

21. Ibid.

22. Much of the early investment in Egypt, especially private financing, came from the Arab countries and not the West. Approximately twenty countries in all were involved in aid to Egypt during the period 1974 to 1977. About $7 million of the $12 million total external assistance, including military aid, came from Arab sources. U.S. House of Representatives, Committee on Foreign Affairs, "Economic Support Fund Programs in the Middle East," April 1979, p. 8. The government to government Arab aid was initially used to restructure and ease Egypt's debt burden. Private Arab investment was concentrated in investment companies, luxury housing, and tourist projects. Even after government aid dropped off sharply following Sadat's Jerusalem visit and halted with the Camp David agreements in March 1979, private Arab investment in Egypt continued.

23. The distinction between dependence in terms of need and causal dependence or dependency in the sense of an undesirable relationship from the standpoint of the poorer country is well recognized in the literature. See for example, J. A. Caporaso, "Dependence, Dependency, and Power in the Global System," *International Organization*, Vol. 32, no. 1 (Winter 1978): 13–44. Also see R. D. Duvall, "Dependence and Dependencia Theory: Notes Toward Precision of Concept and Argument," Ibid., pp. 51–78.

24. See White, *The Politics of Foreign Aid*, p. 79.

25. For a discussion of the dependence/growth links see John Waterbury, *The Egypt of Nasser and Sadat* (Princeton: Princeton University Press, 1983), p. 22.

26. Private foreign investment flows from all sources, averaging $650 million yearly by the end of 1982, are rising substantially. U.S. Agency for International Development, "Country Development Strategy Statement, FY 1985," p. 26. The number of new investment projects approved turns largely on the willingness of the government's Investment Authority to ease its own suspicions and streamline procedures.

27. The level of wheat production would no doubt be far lower were it not for the desire of particularly small farmers to assure much of their own food supply and the value of wheatstraw in livestock rearing. Anne M. Thompson, "Egypt, Food Security and Food Aid," *Food Policy*, Vol. 8, no. 3 (August 1983): 180.

28. U.S. Embassy, "Economic Trends Report, 1984," p. 11.

29. *Al-Ahram Al-Iqtisadi* (Cairo), December 6, 1982, quoted in *MERIP Reports*, no. 117 (September 1983): 18. Also see Aulas, "Sadat's Egypt," p. 17. A higher job figure is reported in a government study by the Investment Authority. In an examination that covered 31 percent of the total number of investment projects, it claims that 84,000 jobs had been created through the first ten years of the Open Door. *Middle East News, Economic Weekly*, March 1, 1985, p. 25.

30. Waterbury, *Egypt of Nasser and Sadat*, pp. 32–40.

31. An extended examination of exogenous factors is found in Agency for International Development, "Country Development Strategy Statement, FY 1985," Annex D, February 1983, pp. 26–28.

4

Programs and Projects

Several distinct features and directions are discernible in the still evolving economic assistance to Egypt. Egypt's perceived development needs, the range of U.S. expertise and resources, and the participating U.S. and Egyptian institutions determined at the outset that the aid would be broad and multifaceted. Development projects and transfer programs would not be focused on any single sector or problem but would touch nearly every sphere of the Egyptian economy and society. From the beginning, the aid effort was conspicuously well-funded. The high level of support meant that financial constraints well-known in other U.S. assistance programs had no close parallels in Egypt. The possibilities lay open for new, more creative programs and the fuller testing of development ideas. The shift to a virtual grant basis for development projects and commodities, aside from P.L. 480 food credits, also placed Egypt on a preferred footing as an aid recipient.

Despite some inconsistencies and discontinuities in programs, the U.S. assistance since 1975 has adhered officially to four stated goals. The first is to rebuild Egypt's infrastructure so that it provides adequate services for its citizens and underpins the productive sectors of the economy. The second aims to use projects to improve human resource capabilities and the quality of life for most Egyptians. The third goal seeks directly to expand productive activities, mainly in industry and agriculture, through capital investments, and technology and commodity transfers. The fourth goal is to assist Egypt in managing its balance of payments through programs designed to sustain reasonable levels of food consumption and credits for raw materials and equipment. These programs encompass both short- and long-term objectives. They finance immediate consumption and deal with economic crises but also incorporate projects with long gestation periods and only distant payoffs.

In practice, the package of U.S. aid is a technical approach to development. The various projects and transfer programs are dominated by the view that the provision of adequate and appropriate resources and expertise will best assure economic growth. Ill-conceived domestic

TABLE 4.1
U.S. Economic Assistance to Egypt, Fiscal Years 1974 to 1983

	FY 1974 Thru FY 1983	
	Obligated ($000)	Expended ($000)
Economic Support Fund (ESF)		
Commodity Import Program (CIP)	2,823,852	2,211,341
Projects	3,629,659	1,771,524
Total ESF	6,453,511	3,982,865
P.L. 480		
Title I	1,847,966	1,812,973
Title II	143,362	136,606
Title III	73,511	58,511
Total P.L. 480	2,064,839	2,008,090
Total Dollar Funded Programs	8,518,350	5,990,995

Source: U.S. Agency for International Development, <u>Ten Years of Progress: USAID in Egypt</u> (Cairo: Arab World Printing House, 1984), p. 11.

policies and ineffectual institutions in the recipient country that discount the effect of both received and self-generated resources are considered major obstacles to success. Ethical aspects to aid, namely, the alleviation of poverty and maldistribution of income, are not ignored but remain ancillary and secondary. In these and other respects, the development projects and transfer programs bring to Egypt the values and experiences the United States has gained during years of giving development assistance globally, though they also bear the particular marks of adaptation to the special purposes and conditions in aiding Egypt, as is evidenced by the following descriptions of the AID portfolio of projects and programs.

The AID Portfolio

Table 4.1 presents the obligations and expenditures in the Economic Support Fund (ESF) for Egypt for fiscal years 1974 through 1983 and includes the total for U.S. food aid under P.L. 480. The ESF category encompasses the $750 million to $800 million annually provided Egypt during these years for both development projects, some seventy-seven in place in 1984, and the Commodity Import Program (CIP). The latter, more a fast disbursing balance of payments than development tool, supplied $300 million annually in concessionary loans and grants that enabled the Egyptian government to import U.S.-produced commodities, namely, capital equipment, raw materials, agricultural goods, and consumer products. In all, nonproject aid, CIP and food loans, accounted for 57 percent of U.S. assistance during the decade. Table 4.1 also reveals the slow utilization of funds by the Egyptian government and the AID mission. The pipeline of unexpended AID money, which peaked in 1982, stood at $2.5 billion at the end of the 1983 fiscal year. This funding backlog is probably unavoidable as long as the assistance carries a heavy project portfolio and it remains U.S. policy to commit in advance the anticipated costs of a project rather than to fund in increments so that obligations are more in line with actual disbursements. Although CIP procurements for items ranging from garbage trucks to tallow for soap absorbed about 80 percent of the funds made available during the decade and P.L. 480 obligations were quickly spent, project aid was able to use only 50 percent of allocated funds.

Table 4.2 indicates the funds obligated by sector through the 1984 fiscal year. Plainly, the economic infrastructure (including electric power, water, sewerage, and telecommunications) had prime claims on the U.S. aid dollars, accounting for more than one-half of all project assistance. Industrial, social service (education, health, and population), and decentralization sector (mainly rural public works) projects drew roughly similar shares of AID support, each about 10 percent of the project assistance. Agriculture has captured 7 percent of the funds, with other sectors holding still smaller shares. However, the totals in Table 4.2 can be misleading. Of the more than $3 billion shown for CIP transfers, more than 40 percent were used to support industry, an amount far greater than went directly to industrial-related projects.[1] The infrastructure was the second largest recipient of CIP funding, adding more than $800 million to this sector. Commodities also figured strongly in assistance to agriculture and social development and provided funds well in excess of the $293 million slated for agriculture and irrigation projects.

The several sectors also differed in their ability to absorb the obligated funds.[2] Industrial projects were able to disburse more than 68 percent of the assistance and decentralization projects 60 percent. Agricultural projects managed to use 50 percent of the dollars set aside and social programs about 45 percent. Although overall the infrastructural sector projects also absorbed 45 percent, the subsector of water, sewerage, and housing projects could expend only 28 percent of the allotted funds.

The third largest segment of the U.S. aid program for Egypt after project aid and CIP are P.L. 480 authorized food shipments. Title I of

TABLE 4.2
U.S. Economic Assistance to Egypt by Major Sectors,
Fiscal Years 1974 to 1984

Assistance Sector	Obligated (millions)
Project assistance:	
Infrastructure	$2,189.2
Public industry	431.0
Agriculture and irrigation	293.1
Social services	414.5
Decentralization	432.2
Finance and investment projects	130.6
Science and technology	78.9
Other projects (feasibility studies and small projects)	109.9
Nonproject assistance:	
CIP	$3,119.8
Cash transfers	101.9
Total	$7,301.1

Source: U.S. General Accounting Office, *The U.S. Economic Assistance Program*
for Egypt Poses a Management Challenge for AID, Report to the
Administrator of the Agency for International Development, July 31,
1985, p. 4.

the food program offers highly concessional loans—at 2 percent during
a ten year grace period and 3 percent during the remaining thirty years
of repayment. (Since 1981 the shipments have included only wheat and
wheat flour. Once-furnished corn, tobacco, and beans are now financed
through the CIP.) Through FY 1983, almost $1.85 billion has been
obligated under Title I. By contrast to the rest of the aid program, the
aproximately $250 million committed annually in recent years has, as
Table 4.1 indicates, nearly always been spent. Loan obligations incurred
under Title I sales are forgiven in a separate Title III program for
development activities. A 1980 agreement set aside $75 million for five
years for rural infrastructural construction in twenty-one governates.
This support became absorbed the following year, however, in a larger,

$145 million AID grant for a Basic Village Service Program. Another program, Title II, is normally for emergency relief. Because Egypt faces no food crises as such, the $143 million obligated through FY 1983 and $11.2 million committed in FY 1984 were targeted for specific groups in need. Food commodities are channelled to two U.S. voluntary agencies, CARE and Catholic Relief Services, which, working with the Ministries of Health and Education, support a number of programs. The largest is for maternal child health centers in a nationwide nutritional education program. Another provides food assistance to a small number of orphanages and other institutions serving children. A substantial lunch program for rural primary schools has been funded, although U.S. participation was scheduled to end in 1985. Title II also furnishes food commodities to the United Nations World Food Program as part of the U.S. annual pledge.

Infrastructure and Industry

In the drive for industrial development and broader strengthening of the economy, Egypt's run-down physical infrastructure has stood out as a serious obstacle and therefore obvious target for aid investment. AID's initial project in 1975, worth nearly $30 million, was to supply electrical distribution equipment to the war-ravaged canal cities. It was soon followed by a series of agreements for power plants, telecommunication systems, and urban water and sewerage improvements and expansions (see Table 4.3). In the case of a $190 million grant in 1979 for a thermal plan in Shoubra El Kheima in Cairo and the loans and grants awarded for telecommunications projects, the AID financing was supplemented by several international concessionary loans. A $91.4 million loan and grant was made available for the rehabilitation and expansion of Cairo's Rod El Farag Water Plant, built in 1903; after modernization, the plant was expected to provide almost one-third of the water for central Cairo.[3] Agreement in 1982 to rehabilitate and modernize twelve hydroturbine generators at the Soviet-built Aswan High Dam carried special symbolic importance for the United States. AID provided funds for a housing project designed eventually to benefit thousands of low-income people in Helwan, south of Cairo. Additional electric power, water, and sewerage obligations were approved and new infrastructural projects were discussed through 1984, but most major infrastructural agreements were initially funded in the 1970s. Aside from the very first in the canal cities, every one of these projects was still under construction in the mid-1980s and, for some, equipment and design contracts remained unsigned. The largest of these projects, the $250 million power steam plant at Ismailia, approved in 1976, was not expected to be completed until 1986 or later. This slow progress in Egypt's highly visible, AID-funded infrastructural sector prevented the United States from being able to deliver an important part of the "peace dividend" that Sadat had so badly needed.[4] It remained a source of embarrassment for his successor and continued to stand for much of what was wrong with U.S. aid.

From the outset, AID planners designated industry, together with related trade and service fields, as the major loci of future employment gains. U.S. misgivings about assisting government-owned industry are strong and, in fact, no new funds have been committed to capital projects in the public sector by the United States since 1978. Notwithstanding this, the dominance of the public sector in Egypt's economy has made it inevitable that U.S. assistance aimed at enhancing the efficiency and productivity of industry would go in large part to public companies. During the history of the program, as much as 90 perent of CIP allocations for industry were programmed for public sector enterprises.[5] In all, the public sector has received in grants and loans three-quarters of the aid committed to rehabilitate and expand industry.

Financial assistance to the public sector was supposed to address not only the need for capital facilities and equipment but also management and technical problems. This assistance has included programs intended to train middle-level management, finance vocational education programs, and better link researchers, planners, and industrial users.[6] In AID's Industrial Production Project, $130 million has been specifically earmarked to renovate public sector companies, train Ministry of Industry personnel and plant managers, and introduce pollution controls.[7] Experiences with the Industrial Production Project have, however, been largely disappointing. AID claims some success in helping to increase management autonomy and in enabling these public enterprises to introduce new product lines. The project takes credit for some indirect effects in circumventing price distortions. But in most of its subprojects, AID faces difficulty negotiating with the Egyptian bureaucracy, and plans have been only slowly implemented.[8]

The single most notable public sector projects, listed in Table 4.3, are the $93 million spent to rehabilitate the Misr Company for Weaving and Spinning at Mehalla Al-Kobra and the $195 million in U.S. support for construction of two (mainly publicly owned) cement plants at Suez and Quattamia. Many of the credits made available under CIP for the transportation infrastructure have particular relevance for industry and related trade. These include purchase of cargo handling equipment at the Alexandria port, more than 700 heavy trucks, 1,000 AID-financed freight cars, and 250 marine diesel engines for Nile River barges. Grain silos and edible oil and tallow storage facilities under construction are

TABLE 4.3
Major Aid-Funded Activities, Fiscal Years 1974 to 1983

General Economic Support	$ Millions
A. Balance of Payments	
Commodity Import Program (CIP)	2,825.0
Food for Peace -- Title I	1,848.0
Food for Peace -- Title II	143.4
Food for Peace -- Title III	73.5
B. Development Planning	
Technical and Feasibility Studies	77.1
Technology Transfer and Workforce Planning	37.3
Applied Science Technology Research	24.4
Development Planning Studies	15.8
Sinai Planning Studies	2.7
INFRASTRUCTURE	
A. Electricity	
Electric Power Distribution Equipment	29.8
Ismailia Steam Power Plant	250.0
National Energy Control Center	43.5
Gas Turbine Generators (Talkha and Helwan)	67.3
Urban Electric Power Distribution Equipment	56.0
Shoubra El Kheima Thermal Power Plant	190.0
Aswan High Dam Turbine Rehabilitation	85.0
B. Water and Sewerage	
Cairo Water System	91.4
Alexandria Sewerage System	15.0
Canal Cities Water and Sewerage Systems	169.0
Alexandria Wastewater System Expansion	198.7
Cairo Sewerage	129.0
C. Telecommunications	
Telecommunications Systems	242.0
D. Housing	
Low Income Housing and Community Upgrading	80.0
DECENTRALIZATION	
Development Decentralization	26.2
Basic Village Services	145.0
Provincial Cities Development	30.0
Decentralization Support Fund	100.0
Neighborhood Urban Services	54.5

(continued)

TABLE 4.3 (Continued)

TRANSPORTATION, INDUSTRY, COMMERCE, AND FINANCE

A. Transportation
    Suez Canal Clearance   44.0
    Hydrographic Survey for the Suez Canal   7.1
    Road Building Equipment   13.9
    Cargo Handling Equipment (Port of Alexandria)   30.2
    Grain Storage Facilities   57.7
    Grain, Tallow, Oil, and Fats Facility   37.0
    Suez Port Development   11.3
    Vehicle Maintenance Training   4.5
    Safaga Grain Silos   80.0

B. Industry
    Suez Cement Plant   100.0
    Quattamia Cement Plant   95.0
    Industrial Production   130.0
    Industrial Productivity Improvement   69.5
    Port Said Salines   13.0
    Mehalla Textile Plant Rehabilitation   93.0
    Mineral, Petroleum, and Groundwater Assessment   20.7
    Energy Policy and Renewables   7.8

C. Business and Finance
    Development Industrial Bank I & II   34.0
    Private Investment Encouragement Fund   10.8
    Private Sector Feasibility Studies   5.0
    Tax Administration   3.7
    Private Sector Production Credit   68.0
    Business Support and Investment   9.1

FOOD AND AGRICULTURE DEVELOPMENT

    Water Use and Management   13.0
    Irrigation Water Management Systems   38.0
    Agricultural Development Systems   14.9
    Poultry Development Systems   5.5
    Aquaculture Development   27.5
    Major Cereals   47.0
    Small Farmer Production   25.0
    Agriculture Cooperative Development   5.0
    Small-scale Agricultural Activities   1.7
    Agricultural Mechanization   40.0
    Rice Research Center and Training   21.7
    Agricultural Management Development   5.0
    Agricultural Data Collection and Analysis   5.0
    Irrigation Pumping   19.0
    Canal Dredging Equipment   30.2
    PVC Pipe Drainage   20.0

(continued)

TABLE 4.3 (Continued)

SOCIAL SERVICES

Rural Health Delivery System	12.3
Urban Health Delivery System	37.2
Integrated Social Work Training Centers	2.5
Family Planning	87.4
Peace Fellowships	54.0
University Linkages	17.5
Suez Community Health Personnel Training	8.1
Control of Diarrheal Diseases	26.0
Basic Education	85.0

Source: U.S. Agency for International Development, Ten Years of Progress: USAID in Egypt (Cairo: Arab World Printing House, 1984), p. 13.

also significant U.S.-funded additions to an intended productive infrastructure.

Despite this attention to the public sector, the showcase for U.S. assistance to Egyptian industry was designed to be in the private sector. The United States planned to demonstrate, by joining adequate financial stimulus to an appropriate investment climate, how a largely socialist economy could be transformed into a mixed one. Funding for the private sector necessarily stressed expansion, mainly by providing grants to the Egyptian banking system for private sector borrowers. Investors could draw on short term credit for raw materials, simple machinery, and spare parts, and longer term credit to start up large industrial enterprises and agro-industry. A reported 325 businessmen received more than $100 million in U.S. credits offered to the private sector through mid-1982.[9] U.S. advisors had hoped to distribute at least $50 million annually to be used by private entrepreneurs.[10]

Yet AID has largely failed in its goal to expand substantially private sector industry. At best its financing has succeeded in modernizing certain industries in both the private and public sectors. In general, progress has been minimal in key programs that aimed to increase industrial productivity and improve the quality of management. As conceived by AID planners, new private sector enterprise was to have set an example for a government-run sector burdened by redundant labor and overcentralization, among other problems. Despite the enabling legislation of *Infitah*, the United States found that its efforts to promote free enterprise in industry were repeatedly stymied by official and unofficial government policies as well as by the practices and values of the Egyptian business community. AID is critical of Egypt's reluctance to adopt the policy instruments believed necessary to create incentives for private initiative. Public industry is also favored over private enterprise through electricity and other hidden input subsidies. The once-promised equality between the two sectors has not occurred.

The Egyptian bureaucracy remains suspicious of the private sector and foreign investors. The Private Investment Encouragement Fund financed by AID to provide loan money to private Egyptians through the banking system waited nine months for the government to set up and another nine months to designate an executive director. Meanwhile, $30 million in possible loans were held up. Feasibility studies to attract private U.S. investment capital to Egypt, underwritten by $5 million from AID, were taking up to a year to complete because of delays in the ministries and poor working relationships with contracted AID advisors.

Frustrated by attempts to get projects going with private U.S. participation, AID has sometimes bowed to pressures from the Egyptian government to agree to finance publicly owned business ventures. A factory designed with $300,000 in seed money from the United States to extract chemicals from an oasis lake and a projected glass manufacturing plant costing the United States $1 million were flops that have soured AID officials on similar undertakings in the future. Not atypically, $132,000 in financing for nine Allis Chalmers forklifts to be used in an AID project were found by U.S. auditors to have been virtually unused because the Egyptians could not afford the gasoline to run them.[11] Few projects have proven more publicly embarrassing for AID than the $16 million it allocated through CIP funding beginning in 1979 for the construction of automated bakeries, not one of which is now expected to be completed.

By locating the responsibility for distributing credits to individual private investors in Egypt's Development Industrial Bank and the wider banking system, the United States sought to avoid close identification with loan decisions. But because financing became so often associated with personal favoritism, marginal enterprise, and get-rich-quick schemes, often using CIP imports, AID was unable to avoid accountability entirely. The Development Industrial Bank was particularly unpopular within the government because three-quarters of the allocated funds had gone back to the United States in the form of commodities, advisors, and training programs. The U.S. loan required, moreover, a local financial contribution that the Egyptian bureaucracy saw as tying up scarce funds it could apply to other purposes. AID officials were no more pleased with the Development Bank's transfer of resources to private sector industry. Credits for U.S. imports moved through the Egyptian institution much more slowly than World Bank funds also available to entrepreneurs.[12]

Popular criticism of U.S. efforts to assist industry tends to focus on the time it takes to complete projects. The Suez Cement Plant first went into production six years after its approval by both governments, and it took seven years to finish the Misr Mehalla project. Egyptian businessmen specifically complain that AID's project approval process is too slow. Government officials are more concerned that the terms of several U.S. grants for new industries amount to dictation—that the product be sold at international prices, that Egypt submit its marketing plans to AID for approval, and that a certain portion of the enterprise be sold to private sector ownership.[13] Officials further resent that grants to be used for subsequent Egyptian loans to industry frequently require the purchase of expensive U.S. goods and services, and that these funds cannot be used to finance other projects receiving foreign assistance. Overall, U.S. aid to industry is found too inflexible and, by some, seen as contradicting the Egyptian government's general economic and political policies.[14]

A contradiction of sorts, familiar in Third World aid, runs through AID's program of assistance to Egyptian industry. On the one hand, aid is aimed at helping the country to build its export industry. On the other, U.S. officials concede that any new industry must be reasonably labor-intensive to absorb the large surplus urban workforce. However, most Western experience in industrial development demonstrates that to be competitive, even traditionally labor-intensive industries must modernize in a way that involves the introduction of labor-saving equipment. U.S. aid that assumes a comparative advantage for Egypt in lower labor costs may dictate inappropriate strategies for industry and assure that, exclusive of oil, agriculture remains Egypt's major export income source.

Agriculture

During the decade of assistance, agriculture has been subject to more studies than any other development area. Most are aimed at identifying the means to overcome constraints to further growth and productivity. By itself, agriculture has not been highly competitive for funding with other sectors. As shown in Tables 4.2 and 4.3, just under $300 million was obligated specifically for agricultural research, training, and technology transfers through FY 1984, leaving agriculture with a relatively small portion of the development funds committed for Egypt. However, if related sectoral expenditures are counted, e.g., the construction of grain storage facilities, canal dredging equipment, and irrigation pipes, the amount is appreciably higher. In recent years, AID has pushed a rural development and decentralization strategy promoted by AID meant to complement agricultural gains. The U.S. program is designed, then, to make farmers more productive and enhance their contribution to the national economy and also to increase the well-being of rural dwellers in general, giving them a greater opportunity to influence those development decisions affecting their lives. As such, the objectives for agriculture and rural development conform, more than in any other sector, to both the aid priorities of the 1980s and the basic needs mandate of the 1970s.

The prominence of agriculture in the national economy is readily documented. More than one-third of Egypt's domestic labor force is employed in agriculture full or part time, and the sector accounts for one-fifth of the Gross Domestic Product.[15] Yields for most crops in Egypt are the highest in the Middle East and rank well above those for most of the Third World. Despite this, the country's agricultural system is in sharp decline. Its contribution to foreign exchange earnings, as much as 90 percent of total merchandised export in 1950, stood at less than 15 percent by the early 1980s. Average yields for most major crops have shown little improvement since the early 1970s. Problems from rising water tables resulting from poor water management are serious in Egypt where less than 4 percent of the land, or roughly 6 million acres, is cultivated. The expansion of mechanized approaches to increasing production has clear limits in a country whose average farm is less than three acres. Egypt's difficulties in increasing productivity also stem from weakened institutional support for agriculture in the breakdown of its cooperative system and from inadequate research and extension services. Price incentives are such that farmers have shifted away from those crops critical to export earnings, principally cotton, that the government tightly regulates, to higher value products, namely, horticulture and clover for animals, that can be sold under free market conditions. The increase of only 2 percent in food production during the last decade has not kept pace with the population growth rate, not to mention the rising per capita consumption of wheat, meat, and dairy products. In recent years, as noted earlier, the government has been obliged to import nearly 50 percent of all its food requirements and as much as three-quarters of the wheat consumed.

AID's announced strategy is to help Egypt realize its potential for diversified high-value export crops. Because national food self-sufficiency is conceived as an unrealistic goal for Egypt, progress toward greater food security is expected to come through producing those crops for which Egypt is presumed to hold a comparative advantage based on the country's relatively low labor costs, its good soils, and, most importantly, its continuously available sources of water.[16] Although such traditional export crops as cotton would expand with technical assistance,

output of other crops, including fruits, vegetables, and rice, is expected
to increase more sharply as new markets for Egyptian crops are found
in the Middle East and Western Europe. Meanwhile, much of Egypt's
needs for food grain cereals, pulses, and meat would be met by imports
paid for by the revenues generated from agricultural exports. U.S. funding
for the sector is based on the long held conviction that higher productivity
must come from rehabilitation of traditionally cultivated land in private
hands and through low-investment projects. Capital-intensive undertakings (however desirable elsewhere in the economy) on new lands
are considered unprofitable, involving too costly development and maintenance. U.S. experts insist that the past performance of reclaimed lands
supports their case; they discount the relevance of non-economic criteria
or secondary benefits from new lands development.

The U.S. programs for assisting agriculture and rural dwellers have
three dimensions. The first and most significant is technological—to
introduce the most modern farming methods, which despite the already
high yields could probably raise wheat output by 50 percent, corn by
70 percent, and rice by 30 percent nationwide on the same total acreage.
Aside from more intensive farming with modern inputs, AID plans seek
to rehabilitate irrigation systems, improve drainage, and expand research
and development. Rising labor costs in the countryside have also made
AID officials strongly supportive of the Egyptian government's determination to accelerate agricultural mechanization. The second funding
dimension is institutional development, aimed at strengthening government agencies that deal with agricultural resource and extension services
and provide credit for farmers. Although the U.S. agencies prefer that
credits be made available from private sources, they also realize the
pivotal role of government in view of the lack of interest by private
sector creditors in small farmers. The third aspect involves policy reform.
The aim is to alter domestic agricultural policies believed responsible
for disincentives to production, distortions in the agricultural economy,
and inequities for the rural sector. The Egyptian government is encouraged
to free up agricultural prices, reduce or remove acreage controls, and
liberalize controls of agricultural exports and the domestic marketing
of major crops. By the same token, a large role is encouraged for the
private sector in marketing such farm inputs as seeds, animal feed, and
fertilizer, with less recourse to public subsidies. Overall, policy reforms
are expected to improve the presently unfavorable terms of trade for
the rural areas.

Sixteen AID-funded programs officially classified as agriculture and
food related were in place in Egypt during 1984. All were on a grant
basis. They ranged in size from a $47 million major cereals project
(AID's largest technical assistance project in the country), designed to

increase grain and legume production by improving research and extension, to a $1.7 million project intended to provide assistance to Egypt's Ministry of Agriculture to support the adoption and modification of appropriate intermediate technology. Principal activities also included $40 million in aid for agricultural mechanization that involved the research and planning, training, and servicing of equipment and a grant to assist a government agricultural development bank to expand credit to smaller farmers. Other projects included water use and management, poultry development, and aquacultural cooperative development. The installation of pumping stations along the Nile in upper Egypt, equipment for dredging and maintaining irrigation canals, and facilities to produce plastic drainage pipes were among the capital projects. All but three of the sixteen projects were funded initially by the late 1970s and, with the notable exception of the major cereals project, were scheduled to carry into FY 1986 and beyond. Looking at the second half of the decade, aid planners promised to expand small farmer credit programs and a new project for the further development of high-value crops. A consolidation of research projects and reorganization of data collection and analyses were projected. The ongoing aid projects were also expected to require less construction activity and fewer procurements of U.S. commodities than in the past.[17]

The Egyptian government and AID together share responsibility for the lack of progress in many development projects in the agricultural sector. The bottlenecks often involve contracting delays, deficiencies in project design, and problems involving staffing, especially those associated with the hiring of advisory agricultural teams from U.S. universities.[18] Problems extend as well to poor inter-ministry coordination and difficulties in understanding U.S. procedures and regulations. The unavailability of counterpart funds can be a factor in project delays, even though AID has usually tried to minimize local currency constraints. It is not uncommon to have AID-supplied equipment that cannot be installed, as in the case of irrigation pumps waiting for the building of structures to house them, or a grain storage facility that cannot be completed without the government's construction of a related railway line.[19]

The only modest gains to date in Egyptian agricultural development raise a number of other issues about the role of U.S. aid. Probably the most serious is the charge that the United States, by asserting its own priorities, has obliged the Egyptian government to sink its scarce investment resources into areas of development where U.S. funds are expected to be available. Even if unintentionally, the United States has established at least some economic goals and strategies that limit the freedom of Egypt's planners to determine how they wish to allocate their resources, both those received through external aid and those generated domestically. An obvious and frequently cited case in point, merit aside, is the diversion of local resources away from investment in new lands development. AID's alleged contribution to the widening income gap in rural Egypt is another area of criticism. Together with the possible effects of food aid on lowering domestic production, U.S. aid activities are widely believed to be helping perpetuate government policies that do little to relieve the credit problems of the smallest farmers, and U.S. policies show insufficient interest in appropriate, low-cost technology. AID's support for the mechanization of agriculture may seem justified in the face of recurrent labor shortages in the countryside. Yet it remains unclear what long-term rural employment will look like if over-capitalization is allowed to occur. U.S. assistance may accelerate those forces likely to condemn the economy to a future burdened by large labor surpluses.

At least initially, many of AID's programs in the agricultural sector were formulated without adequate information and experience with Egypt. Their stress on technological solutions frequently underestimated, for example, problems in the agricultural supply system. In retrospect, few would disagree today that AID should have channeled more assistance to revamping and strengthening the structure of extension, research, and training, especially the linkages between research and extension. It is debatable how much the building of a modern agricultural system requires the existence of a modern developed economy to be successful. Certainly, Egypt has managed to maintain a relatively productive system even with many traditional modes of farming. As is often the case in low-income, developing countries, the problem of agriculture cannot be treated in isolation from the broader economy and society. Too frequently the development assistance in agriculture is implemented with highly fragmented projects, without full consideration of domestic policy constraints, intersectoral impacts, or the need to improve human capital.

The extent to which Egypt can effectively absorb large sums of assistance to agriculture from the United States and other donors has long been at issue. The technical and management capacity of Egypt's institutions are doubted, as are the government's ability to meet matching funds requirements and provide the recurring costs associated with agricultural and other projects. Ideally, the challenge of aid is to take Egypt's limited absorptive capacity not merely as an obstacle to be accommodated, but as a set of constraints that can be addressed and overcome. In the final analysis, progress may hinge on how prepared the Egyptian leadership is to mobilize the country's resources for agricultural development and make the difficult domestic policy choices necessary to expand its capacity to utilize foreign aid and investment.

To encourage this, aid donors, but principally the United States, will probably have to permit in all sectors more flexibility in Egypt's use of aid resources and fewer restrictions on the purchase externally of goods and services.

Rural Development and Decentralization

Rural development activities have naturally loomed large for U.S. aid planners as the most direct strategy to reach impoverished majorities. Even so, these programs have not been preeminent throughout the decade of U.S. assistance examined here. The financing of commodity transfers and infrastructural urban bias in aid initially left few resources and personnel for a large-scale attack on the economic and social problems of the rural poor. Most other programs for Egypt were, in any case, more quickly and easily designed and involved less need for intra-bureaucratic coordination. As a single package meant to deliver the benefits of development to the countryside, Egypt thus for some time lagged behind changes in orientation that characterized U.S. and other donor efforts elsewhere in the Third World during the 1970s. When the most important of these programs finally reached their implementation stage in Egypt, they had to be molded to the development values and approaches of the 1980s.

The rural development aided activities launched in Egypt are in several other respects somewhat distinctive from those found elsewhere. In the multiplicity of programs approved for Egypt, the U.S. effort has been a comprehensive one. It encompasses sectoral and special programs, including education, health, and family planning. Still, the approach in Egypt deviates from the prescriptions for successful integrated rural development suggested by an extensive literature.[20] Aside perhaps from the decentralization sector (described below), there are few unifying themes. The various rural programs, instituted in a serial fashion, do not fit together as a coherent approach to Egypt's problems. Food assistance, social programs, public works, and credit facilities for farmers have not, for example, been conceived as aspects of a single blueprint. Attempts to influence crop export strategies are treated separately from local consumption requirements. Educational expenditures have not been directly related to preparing students for rural life and employment. Assistance for local community-run enterprises too often fails to take into account rural market constraints, and agriculturally related technologies are seldom calculated for their likely managerial requirements, social costs, and implications for labor displacement. All the same, the U.S. assistance effort usually avoids overly complex rural projects and has tried to deal with many of the simpler problems first.

Assistance to Egypt largely discards the idea that characterizes so many development programs that peasants are backward and deeply resistant to change. U.S. advisors have come to view the Egyptian farmer, who is less physically and psychologically isolated than most in the Middle East, as highly skilled, innovative, willing to take risks, and usually rational in response to economic signals. Program designs have been unusually sensitive in trying to understand the mentality and attitudes of Egypt's rural poor. With much of the administration of rural programs left to indigenous country personnel, the cultural barriers affecting aid are also probably fewer. By the same token, AID advisors in Egypt are spared the experience of having development activities caught up in regional, caste, race, or ethnic conflicts. The rural population is comparatively homogeneous, although differences between farmers and agricultural systems in the Nile Delta and Upper Egypt can be instructive for planners.

The commitment through rural development to the social and economic betterment of Egypt's small farmers, tenants, and landless also has not, as in many other countries, obliged the United States to address the issue of agrarian reform. Current ideological inhibitions in Washington aside, land redistribution as a means to agricultural growth and development is absent from the U.S. aid agenda. Coming on the scene after Egypt's far-reaching reforms were completed, AID personnel have concentrated on the need for adequate resources and sufficient incentives for farmers. Although significant land and income disparities separate small and middle farmers, this is no more an issue for U.S. officials than it is for today's Egyptian policymakers. Indeed, the more generously assisted middle farmers are conceived by both as being indispensable as food producers and consumers in the internal market. U.S. aid personnel have worked within the Egyptian cooperative system and accept it as a solution to Egypt's problems of land fragmentation and economies of scale, but AID disparages the central government's use of cooperatives as coercive instruments for crop output and pricing controls.

In stressing that the lot of the rural poor can be improved and a community spirit created by allowing rural people to participate in solving their own problems, the United States has been orthodox in its approach to rural development. However, although AID has sought in several programs to invigorate local popular institutions that can reflect the priorities and aspirations of the poor, it has carefully refrained from using its assistance as a lever to alter existing rural power relations. AID accepts the need to work with provincial and local authority figures and to provide material incentives for them to cooperate, and it assumes no direct role in identifying or encouraging new leaders or in assuring that they are representative. At most, AID officials applaud when, as sometimes happens, those in positions of influence and authority agree to involve the powerless in decisionmaking.

Several AID programs in the social service sector directly impact on the lives of farmers and other rural people. One such grant by the United States, first approved in 1976, was for a $12.3 million project to assist the Ministry of Health in maintaining a basic health services program in the rural areas. The grant has provided funds for reducing population growth, although a separate, far larger U.S.-sponsored program for family planning has also been in existence since 1977. Another project, begun in 1981, was intended to increase the access of Egyptian rural children, especially girls, to the upper levels of primary education. The $85 million allocated for the life of the project provides for the construction of facilities, instructional materials and equipment, and technical assistance to introduce a basic educational system.[21] The best financed program for meeting the basic needs of rural dwellers in Egypt has been Title II of P.L. 480. Funded for a total of $143.3 million between 1975 and 1984, it is carried out by U.S. voluntary agencies working with Egyptian ministries and provides food commodities as well as support through commodity sales for maternal/child health centers and a nutritional educational program.

The most ambitious and, many believe, potentially most effective form of U.S. aid for rural areas comes as a wide-ranging set of development activities known collectively as the Decentralization Sector Support Program. The funding is rationalized as a cooperative effort to enable the Egyptian government to realize its commitment to decentralization, expressed in a series of laws enacted since 1975. By the early 1980s, decentralization was the fastest growing part of the AID portfolio in Egypt. It encompassed five closely related aid activities brought together in 1981. One program provided government-administered AID grants to village councils as revenue for revolving loans financing income-producing public projects. Poultry raising, food processing, beekeeping, and bus services have, for example, qualified for support.[22] Early in 1984, 560 relatively small loans worth $14 million had been made in 450 of Egypt's 870 village units from a total of $26.2 million obligated by the United States.[23] A second decentralization program, called Basic Village Services, provided funds to 21 rural governates for infrastructural improvements at the village level. These included such undertakings as market roads, water and sanitation systems, the lining of canals, and drainage programs. More than $200 million in grants and forgiven food loans repayments (P.L. 480 Title III) were set aside with about one-half spent by the beginning of 1984, and more than 3,500 small projects had been completed or were being implemented.[24] Another program obligated $100 million, of which 40 percent had been disbursed, for the supply of U.S. equipment to rural governates and had funded such purchases as road maintenance equipment and water filtration plants. Still another decentralization grant earmarked $30 million for enhancing local government institutional capacity in three provincial cities.

The decentralization concept was also carried to the major cities. Four grants since 1981, totaling almost $110 million, were given to improve the quality of life in Cairo, Alexandria and other urban governates in a Neighborhood Urban Services Project. The parallel urban decentralization fund (including a Cairo government $13 million contribution) made local currency available to low-income districts for such rehabilitation projects as paving streets, building a pedestrian overpass, and refurbishing a local school. The many small grants were meant to impress urban dwellers with the relevance of American aid to them personally. In some neighborhoods, however, rather than income-generating, productive projects were reportedly used to buy furniture and cars.[25]

Underlying decentralization policies is the principle, already suggested, that greater authority and responsibility should be passed to local government and institutions. The identification and execution of urban projects are left to local officials working with elected neighborhood councils and, in their frequent absence, the community's "natural leaders" in private voluntary organizations and neighborhood associations. Village aid, administered by the specially created government unit, the Organization for Reconstruction and Development of the Egyptian Village (ORDEV), is conceived as using U.S. resources to give elected village councils an active role in selecting, designing, and maintaining projects. More broadly, the program is expected to help develop the technical capabilities and improve administrative networks within local, district, and governate levels of rural government.

Decentralization sector support by the United States carries a number of distinct advantages for the recipient. Unlike so many of AID's larger programs, the aid is disbursed with relative speed. Except for the financing of U.S. equipment for the governates, there is a very limited need for imported commodities and thus little of the recycling of aid dollars to U.S. firms common to AID's programs. Minimal requirements exist for outside contractors and the services of foreign advisors, and U.S. officials are not directly involved in the administration of loans to local jurisdictions. Control over disbursements is left to Egypt, and the rules governing decentralization assistance permit more flexibility by the Egyptian authorities in shifting funds sectorally than in most U.S. aid programs.

Attitudes among AID's higher echelons in Washington toward decentralization efforts are actually somewhat ambivalent. On the one hand, officials are impressed with the progress and impact of the programs to date. Decentralization has probably benefited directly tens of thousands of rural Egyptians and has involved the participation of as many as 14,000 village council members around the country.[26] New equipment clearly identified as U.S.-donated is believed good advertisement and suits the increased demands from the Reagan administration for greater visibility in U.S. aid programs. Exposure through local expenditures complements a portfolio otherwise heavy with large, more remote U.S. projects. The growing number of completed projects across the countryside also helped to reverse the image of U.S. aid programs as designed to help only a wealthy few line their pockets. Moreover, decentralization is in accord with the aid philosophy of the administration so far as it entails the transfer of decisions away from a central bureaucracy and allows resources to be used in better conformity with local priorities. To some, the institution-building and more participatory democratic processes are viewed as contributing to a more stable Egypt.

The decentralization grants have, on the other hand, gone exclusively to public sector projects. Although the income-producing loans are limited to likely profitable enterprises, the aid is not primarily designed to stimulate local private sector activity. An erroneous view among those higher U.S. officials unacquainted with the details of the program is that decentralization is necessarily administratively intensive, leading to the proliferation of more government agencies. Doubts are also raised about the large number of decentralization loans contributing to the rural social infrastructure and equity objectives rather than going to Egypt's more economically productive sectors—where aid for the 1980s is supposedly targeted. Detractors believe that, for the price, greater visibility for the United States can be generated with urban, infrastructural undertakings. Despite AID's distancing itself from the actual disbursements of loans, some U.S. officials fear that the United States will be unable to avoid charges of interference in Egyptian affairs in the many local discretionary decisions.

Aware of the vulnerability of decentralization to criticism in Washington on ideological grounds, AID personnel supervising the sector's programs have argued that government-to-government aid is largely unavoidable because private construction firms are usually uninterested in small municipal-level projects. They insist that decentralization projects are not inimical and can be supportive of indigenous private enterprise. Replications of local public projects by private individuals in a "demonstration effect" have been observed. An AID report to the U.S. Congress claims that decentralization has in fact promoted a "modest boom" in rural private sector construction and service activities.[27] Physical infrastructural improvements, such as road maintenance, obviously enhance the marketing opportunities of small farmers. Egyptian-owned equipment firms, representing U.S. manufacturers, can benefit by helping to service and supply spare parts for equipment.[28] There are cases, moreover, where individual villagers have risked equity capital in joint productive investments with village councils receiving AID's revolving loans.[29]

The principal obstacles to implementing and extending decentralization assistance lie with the Egyptian government itself. Although the legal structure for decentralization is in place, many of the implementing laws remain inadequate. More critically, there are individuals in the central government ministries, including officials at the highest levels of development planning, who are set against any program that keeps funds and investment decisions out of their hands. Several ministries, moreover, covet the resources of ORDEV, not one of the more powerful units in the bureaucracy. Provincial governors are among the few influential friends of decentralization. Generous credits for heavy duty equipment furnished the governates function as incentives that have helped to overcome doubts or objections among the governors to the decentralization idea.

Specifically at issue in the mid-1980s was approval of a second phase of a somewhat refocused U.S. decentralization support program. The aid was expected to mobilize local resources through block and matching grants to local governments for the operation and maintenance of basic infrastructures and for policies aimed at promoting the autonomy of local popular institutions. The aid policy also was more explicit in trying to create a climate conducive to private enterprise development.[30] Anticipating bureaucratic opposition in Cairo, AID officials tried to involve Egyptian counterparts in setting priorities for the new proposal. But to survive, decentralization aid was expected by the same officials to require the direct intercession of the U.S. ambassador at the highest official levels in Cairo. The government, it was hoped, would find it difficult to refuse this U.S. program and still maintain its claim to support the principle of decentralization.

Social and Technological Development

Funds supplied by AID for human development have a potentially deep impact on the quality of life in Egypt. Nearly all agreements with Egypt were signed in the late 1970s and were clearly meant to implement the basic needs approach of the period. Although the sum total for programs in the social services sector pales by comparison to physical infrastructural expenditures, the more than $400 million obligated through FY 1984 (see Table 4.2) are substantial by Third World aid standards. The heaviest support has gone to family planning, which the United

States in fact began supporting through international organizations as early as 1971. AID grants have funded since 1977 two projects coordinated by the Egyptian Ministry of Health and several other government and private organizations. The financial aid has gone mainly to institutionalize family planning through the use of contraceptives in thirteen rural governates, toward the training of physicians in four governates, to urban clinics, and for a marketing program to promote and distribute contraceptives through pharmacies and private physicians in several urban areas.[31] Separate grants are intended to improve rural and urban health delivery systems (see Table 4.3). The rural projects involve the training of Egyptian physicians, nurses, and sanitary personnel, outreach activities, and the strengthening of various health services. An additional $2.6 million was committed to the project in 1984 beyond the $12.3 million funded earlier. A larger urban health delivery system project with $37.2 million obligated in several grants had, by 1983, trained in-country more than 2,500 health personnel. The program was aimed particularly at maternal/child health, family planning, and nutrition and emphasized community involvement. It was designed to benefit approximately 6 million mothers and children in Cairo and Alexandria.

One of the most heralded of AID's projects is an effort to reduce infant and child mortality due to diarrhea-caused dehydration. Pilot studies and community distribution of oral rehydration salts have been supported along with publicity campaigns. The $26 million grant also funded a consultancy signed in 1982 between the Ministry of Health and a private U.S. firm to explore private sector possibilities for the production and marketing of salt packets that are presently produced by a public sector company financed by UNICEF. Another $8.1 million has gone for medical education to bring basic community health services to the governates bordering the Suez Canal. A project assisted by a small AID grant to the Ministry of Social Affairs to train social workers was completed in 1983.

Three nonhealth related educational programs were ongoing in 1984. The largest, an $85 million basic education grant, was designed to improve access of rural children, especially girls at the upper grade school levels, to a primary education. The project also funds instructional materials and equipment and supplements Egyptian funds allocated toward the construction of 6,600 new classrooms by 1986. At the university level, the Peace Fellowships, a legacy of the Camp David agreements, were designed to expand the pool of qualified younger personnel able to contribute to Egypt's development through scholarships abroad in certain disciplines for up to two years. The program, administered by AMIDEAST, is scheduled to provide up to 1,900 scholarships, mostly in the United States. It has managed to draw people, after needed revisions in program design, not only from Egyptian universities but from government ministries, research centers, and private and public sector enterprises. English language training is also included in the program. A third AID agreement involves Egyptian and U.S. universities in a cooperative program called University Linkages. The funding is designed to improve Egyptian faculties in critical skill areas as well as strengthen the universities' research capacity through joint projects to solve specific development problems. The linkages project also contains a CIP procurement component for equipment. Administrative under-staffing and caution in the unit of the Egyptian Supreme Council of Universities that acts as reviewer, disbursing agent, and program manager for activities gave the linkages program a slow start since its initial funding in FY 1980; but by early 1984, 129 projects covered by the agreement had been approved.

Social infrastructural improvements also include a grant worth $80 million for housing and community upgrading. The project in Helwan, mentioned above, takes a unique approach in helping to finance both public and private sector housing. One aspect assists the Government of Egypt in the design and construction of a new model community for 7,200 low-income families. The second offers credits to 4,000 families in six of the poorest neighborhoods in Helwan and Cairo to expand and improve the quality of existing housing through home improvements, especially additions and vertical expansion. The latter approach was expected to allow a substantial recovery of loans advanced to families. The grant's mixed character also reflects the conviction of AID officials that government-built housing is too expensive and that the informal housing market is more dynamic and more cost-effective. Detractors could point to the severe delays during the first few years in the planning and construction of the model community in Helwan, a result of a number of factors, including local project management. Ever since the initial obligations for the housing sector, made in 1978, the United States has repeatedly balked at Egyptian requests for new commitments for public housing.

Roughly $79 million in AID funds were obligated through FY 1984 for science and technology. But depending on how the category is defined, as much as $100 million can be identified in authorizations for this sector. The expenditures have been for a set of projects designed to upgrade the skills of Egyptian scientists and technical personnel. The grants, begun in 1975, have financed the training in the United States of almost 2,000 Egyptian experts and administrators in such disparate fields as agriculture, civil aviation, and public administration and also includes assistance from U.S. sources in various technical areas and provision of critically needed research equipment. Also noteworthy is a $24.4 million grant agreement, initially funded in 1977, that has provided for a contract with the U.S. National Academy of Science, among others, for assistance in policy planning, management, and research and development. A stated aim of this applied science and technology research grant has been to strengthen the links between Egypt's scientific community and industry.

Because of the nature of many of these programs aimed at improving human resources and technology transfers, their origins in U.S. assistance are not popularly known. In most cases, the target populations for educational programs are middle-class Egyptians and others who are already highly Westernized. Typically, those programs with a broader base have not lent themselves to advertising the U.S. financial connection. As described more fully later, the United States has always had some ambivalence about how much credit it should take for basic programs. Also, it becomes awkward to try stressing its role as benefactor when the project financing is not provided by the United States alone.

International Cooperation

The effective use of AID resources in Egypt's development projects frequently depends on coordination with other aid donors. Although the United States is the largest single international contributor of economic assistance, it is only one of twenty Western bilateral and seven multilateral development aid programs.[32] Excluding the United States, gross disbursements of official development assistance from the Western industrial countries, including Japan, totaled $1.9 billion during the period 1978 to 1983.[33] Loan and grants to Egypt constitute for France, West Germany, Britain, and others a sizable share of their foreign aid programs for the Middle East and North Africa. In some economic sectors, moreover, these donors are regularly more supportive than the United States. In specific years, France and the Netherlands, for example, have committed more for food and agricultural projects than has the United States. As compared to the approximately $250 million obligated by the United States through 1983 for active agricultural projects, the World Bank, Egypt's second largest aid source, had earmarked $465 million.[34]

To some extent, assistance tends to follow presumed donor advantages. France's program includes food aid and food related projects and financing and technical expertise for the building of a metro system for Cairo. The Germans have supported telecommunications and the Egyptian railways, among other projects. (Additionally, private German capital had participated in more than fifty joint ventures through 1981, including such areas as banking, tourism, construction, and agroindustry.)[35] The nearly $200 million obligated annually in loans and grants by Japan have gone for commodity and technical transfers, including the purchase of iron reinforcement bars, land reclamation projects, and expansions of the Suez Canal. Easy loans from the Dutch have focused on agricultural projects and social and health programs. Although not on the scale of the U.S. aid, these bilateral donors have, by and large, also used their aid to develop long-term markets for their commodity exports and to secure contracts for private national firms.

Attempts to coordinate international assistance to Egypt have occurred on two levels. One involves dividing up the burden of meeting Egypt's budgetary and development needs. To some extent, a rough division of labor has been created among Western countries and international organizations since a spring 1977 Paris meeting of a Consultative Group sponsored by the World Bank and the International Monetary Fund. An Aid Donors Group has continued to monitor Egypt's current accounts and provides an overview of aid strategies and policies. At a second level, partnerships and responsibility for different stages or segments of development projects require closer coordination among the aid donors. The World Bank frequently co-finances projects with the United States and others, especially in the area of agricultural development. A Helwan waste water scheme involves the EEC, the Netherlands, and Italy, with contractors from France, Italy, Britain, and West Germany as well as Egypt. British and U.S. consultants have worked together with Egyptian officials on the rehabilitation and development of Cairo's sewer system. Japan contributed loans for projects in which the United States was also involved, including improving the Alexandria port and the Shoubra El Kheima power station. Swiss financing for the Misr Spinning and Weaving Company supplemented a U.S. loan.

Although a common sense of purpose often prevails among the various donors, differences in development approaches and operating styles can strain cooperation. Communication among the donors and the synchronization of efforts are often poor. At least in the earlier days of the West's current aid programs to Egypt, a shortage of projects also led to keen competition among the donors for projects involving highly advanced technology. In several instances, the United States pulled out of proposed financing when Egypt awarded critical parts of a project to other Western donors.[36] Probably more than any other factor, stresses in cooperation between donors reflect donor difficulties in dealing with the Egyptian bureaucracy and the related uncertainties in the implementation phase of projects.

Lengthy delays are by no means peculiar to the U.S. aid program. Of the eight projects identified in protocol between the EEC and Egypt to cover the period from 1978 to 1984, most of the grants were unused, and no project had been implemented by 1982.[37] In the same year, the

World Bank had forty active agreements with Egypt worth $1.43 billion, but $904 million were still unspent.[38] Poor international coordination and the costs of delays are well documented in the case of a U.S.-funded $31 million project to build three plants to manufacture plastic pipes for irrigation drainage in Upper Egypt. The pipe could not be installed, however, until cement collector pipes were also in place. Production of the collector pipes were financed under a separate World Bank loan. AID was unaware how far the World Bank project was behind schedule, and the plastic pipe plants were allowed to produce at full capacity without facilities to store the pipe.[39]

Absent from the official aid consortium were the Arab states and their development funds that had helped in restructuring and easing Egypt's debt between 1973 and 1977. As already noted, President Sadat nevertheless considered the level of assistance inadequate and made no effort to disguise his disappointment with the generosity of his Arab brothers. The economic boycott of Egypt did not prevent private Arab investment, sometimes in partnership with Western businessmen, to continue quietly after 1977. By the early 1980s, although official Arab aid had not resumed, private Arab banks, particularly those in the Gulf, had begun to participate openly in international consortia to provide loans to the Egyptian government.

Soviet and East European commodity and technical aid did not cease entirely with the eviction of the Soviet military in 1972 and Sadat's entente with the United States after 1973. Communist bloc economic assistance that had run $2.5 billion, concentrated mainly between 1960 and 1970, continued at very modest amounts through the 1970s. Except for a brief period, Soviet technical personnel have been a fixture in the country as advisors for Egypt's Soviet-built industrial plants. Development loans were signed in the early 1980s with Hungary and Romania. But the generally low levels and limited kinds of aid from the Soviet Union and East bloc countries eased Egypt's task of keeping this assistance apart from U.S. and other Western programs.

Alternative Modes

A continuing debate goes on within the U.S. aid community in Cairo and Washington about whether there are better programming approaches for assisting Egypt. These discussions involving delivery modes underscore differences of opinion on the desirable size and visibility of the programs as well as the degree of control the United States should exercise. The arguments intersect with the dialogue in progress with Egyptian officials on the best ways to achieve mutually agreed development goals and plans for domestic policy changes. The discussions reflect dissatisfactions on both sides with the prevailing approaches and pressures for some modifications, if not more radical changes. Much of the debate questions whether AID in Egypt should move away from its primary project orientation in favor of more cash transfers, sector grants, and commodity transfers, and what combination of modes is both optimal for development and politically feasible.

Cash transfers refer to the simple transfer from the United States to Egypt of dollars with which the Cairo government would presumably be free to spend as it wished.[40] Examples of cash transfers are not uncommon in the U.S. global aid program, usually for specific reasons and short periods. Israel is of course the most conspicuous recipient, on a seemingly permanent basis; but Turkey in 1980 and El Salvador more recently have received cash transfers, in the first case to reward Ankara for signing an agreement with the International Monetary Fund, and in the latter for balance-of-payments support. In FY 1984, Egypt received for the first time a cash transfer of $102 million, which was repeated in FY 1985 at $100 million, and later supplemented with an emergency economic grant.

High Egyptian officials leave no doubt that they favor this mode and would like to see more project support converted to cash transfers. Some U.S. planners also find advantages in this approach. Cash transfers would no doubt reduce the administrative burden in aiding Egypt. With decisions on how to employ more of the funds left to the Egyptians, very little AID staff would be required in the country. Advocates also insist that with the Cairo government freed of most U.S. aid restrictions, the United States would become less a target of the regime's opponents and avoid being held accountable for popularly perceived development failures. In the improved political climate, AID might be better able to capture the attention of government leaders for macroeconomic reforms and to sustain Egypt's political/military cooperation with the United States. The critics of increased cash transfers stress the near impossibility of monitoring how aid dollars are used. It would be difficult, if not impossible, to ensure that the aid went to priority areas or, in fact, was devoted to development purposes. These critics are convinced that without AID and other foreign donors, most notably the World Bank, the Egyptians would be under no pressure to think systematically about their development program.

Sector grants represent something of a compromise between the familiar project approach and cash transfers. These general grants to the recipient designate that projects be located or funds otherwise used in particular sectors or subsectors of the economy. After that, however, the Egyptians could have considerable leeway to reobligate the funds within a sector without U.S. approval. AID's involvement would be greatly reduced or eliminated entirely in the identification and monitoring of projects. The proponents of the grant approach insist that the Egyptians would become more directly responsible for the design and implementation of projects, thereby strengthening their own development-related institutions. They point with some pride to the flexibility and overall success of the quasi-sector grant approach when five ongoing projects in the decentralization program were combined. The aid money in a sector grant approach can also be disbursed more quickly, cutting the backlog of unexpended funds. Like cash transfers, sector grants could reduce stresses on U.S.-Egyptian aid relations. The Mubarak government has left no doubt that it sees sector grants as more responsive to Egypt's own development ideas. Those who criticize this mode as a major alternative to AID projects often point out that it is not well suited to address specific development bottlenecks identified by AID. Most of all, they question the feasibility of sector grants in view of institutional weaknesses, governmental and private, in most sectors of the Egyptian economy. They contend that the sectors better able to manage the funds may not be the ones that should have the highest priority.

Another alternative is to expand commodity imports. This mode of aid delivery, as described earlier, disburses more quickly, is less staff-intensive, and has during the history of U.S. economic assistance been viewed positively by the Egyptian government as balance-of-payments and budget support. The approach furnishes Egypt with dollar credits to import commodities largely of its choice from the United States and allows the government to earn local currency from their sale. Few doubt the contribution of the Commodity Import Program to particular economic sectors and its critical early role in the rehabilitation of the infrastructure and industry. Its supporters argue that in addition to meeting consumption needs commodity aid can assume a supporting role in development efforts. For some, such aid has special advantages in avoiding most of the normal oversight that projects must endure. However, development professionals have never been enamored of AID's commodity program. The CIP transfers are in practice seldom related to development goals, and the program does little to upgrade those Egyptian institutions engaged in development activities. There is also some resentment, particularly in recent years, because most commodities end up in the public sector. Misgivings among AID officials with CIP funding, which had held constant at about $300 million annually, contributed to its reduction to $200 million in fiscal year 1985.

AID officials, notably those in Washington, remain committed to projects as the dominant delivery mode for Egypt. Their reasons are both professional and political. They argue that the present approach has achieved significant development benefits and that lacking the present control and accountability inherent in the project mode, the United States will yield up what little leverage it has over the Egypt government. AID also believes that without close scrutiny over how Egypt spends its aid dollars, justifying continued high levels of support before the U.S. Congress would be difficult. Instead of greatly changing the mix of delivery modes, AID expects to improve its programs in Egypt by concentrating on a smaller number of discrete projects, giving the assistance a more consistent focus, and making it easier for the AID mission in Cairo to manage.[41] At least of late, Washington also shows a willingness to allow AID officials in Egypt more latitude in approving projects and disbursing funds—constant sore points in relations between the mission and home office as Chapter Five describes. Evidence of AID's continued faith in a project-oriented approach is demonstrated by the increase in funds obligated for development projects in FY 1985.

Through the years, U.S. Embassy officials in Cairo have led a quiet campaign for a strong commodity program and, later, for cash transfers. The diplomatic community also has been more sympathetic to sectoral grants. In general, they have been partial to any means that promised a more rapid expending of aid funds. Foreign policy officials believe that the diffuseness of AID's project portfolio impairs the desired political effect of aid. They are especially leery of AID's often not too subtle attempts to link desired revisions of its assistance to the Egyptian government to movement on domestic policy changes.

Quite predictably, offers by AID to exchange possible sector grants or cash transfers for economic reforms are deeply resented in Egyptian government circles. Even the appearance of a deal creates apprehension, lest it seem that basic policies are being dictated by the United States. The Ministry of Agriculture broke off negotiations with AID for a sector grant proposal to compensate the government for costs of raising prices paid to farmers for major crops when it became clear that AID had injected itself into a too politically sensitive area.[42] The Egyptian bureaucracy is, however, not always united on the type of aid it prefers. Top policymakers seek anything that promises greater flexibility and control, even when they may have no clear alternative plans. But the technical ministries are understandably suspicious of sector grants and especially cash transfers. For without U.S. aid clearly earmarked and committed during the life of a project, these ministries are concerned that the funds may be diverted by the regime from projects in which they have a stake. Intrabureaucratic differences and rigidities within Egyptian and U.S. aid-related communities as well as divergent perspectives and goals separating the two are explored more fully in the next chapter.

Notes

1. U.S. Agency for International Development, Cairo, *Ten Years of Progress, USAID in Egypt* (Cairo: Arab World Printing House, 1984), p. 6. U.S. Agency for International Development, Cairo, "Status Report of United States Economic Assistance to Egypt as of January 1, 1984," p. 1.

2. "Status Report," p. 1.

3. U.S. Agency for International Development, "Status Report of United States Economic Assistance," p. 9.

4. See discussion in William J. Burns, *Economic Aid and American Policy Toward Egypt, 1955–1981* (Albany, N.Y.: State University of New York Press, 1985), pp. 196–198.

5. Interview with Michael Stone in *Rose El Youssef* (Cairo), October 3, 1983, pp. 29–31. Even in fiscal year 1984, most of the $300 million in CIP continued to go to the public sector.

6. U.S. Agency for International Development, "Status Report of United States Economic Assistance," pp. 20–23.

7. Ibid., p. 21.

8. U.S. Agency for International Development, "Country Development Strategy Statement, FY 1986, Annex D: Industry Strategy Statement," April 1984, p. 9.

9. U.S. Agency for International Development, Cairo, *Change* (Cairo: Arab World Printing House, 1983), p. 8.

10. Donald S. Brown, *Economic Development in Egypt—An American's Perspective* (Cairo: U.S. International Communications Agency, March 1982), p. 12.

11. Rick Atkinson, "Political Goals Dictate Form of Aid to Egypt," *Kansas City Times,* September 28, 1983, circulated by the USIS to the U.S. Embassy, Cairo.

12. U.S. Agency for International Development, "Country Development Strategy Statement, FY 1986, Annex D," p. 9.

13. Remarks by Dr. Fawzi Riyad Fahmi at a seminar on "Assessment of USAID Program in Egypt," Institute of National Planning, Cairo, June 1, 1983.

14. Ibid.

15. U.S. Agency for International Development, "Country Development Strategy Statement, FY 1986, Annex C: Egypt: Agricultural Sector Strategy," April 1984, p. 1.

16. Ibid., p. 5.

17. Ibid., p. 27.

18. U.S. General Accounting Office, "Report to the Congress: U.S. Assistance to Egyptian Agriculture: Slow Progess After Five Years," March 16, 1981, p. 37.

19. U.S. Agency for International Development, Cairo, "Decentralization Sector Review Analysis, Sector II PID," May 1984, p. 10.

20. For a useful overview see A. Dawson, "Suggestions for an Approach to Rural Development by Foreign Aid Programs," *International Labour Review,* Vol. 117, no. 4 (July-August 1978): 391–404.

21. U.S. Agency for International Development, "Status Report of U.S. Economic Assistance," p. 47.

22. Brown, *Economic Development in Egypt*, p. 19.

23. U.S. Agency for International Development, Cairo, "The Government of Egypt's and USAID's Decentralization Sector Support: Its Accomplishments and Expenditures," Offices of Local Administration and Development and Urban Administration and Development, April 1984, p. 1.

24. Ibid., pp. 1, 5.

25. Essam Raffat, "Egypt and American Aid," *Al-Ahram Al-Iqtisaadi* (Cairo), November 15, 1982, pp. 4–6.

26. U.S. Agency for International Development, Cairo, "Rural and Urban Development: The Decentralization Program," Office of Local Adminstration and Development, February 1984, pp. 1, 2.

27. U.S. Agency for International Development, "Country Development Strategy Statement, FY 1985: Egypt," Washington, D.C., April 1983, p. 33.

28. U.S. Agency for International Development, Cairo, "Mid-Term Evaluation of the Decentralization Support Fund," Office of Local Administration and Development, February 1983, p. 19.

29. Robert J. LaTowsky, "Egyptian Labor Abroad," *MERIP Reports*, no. 123 (May 1984): 16.

30. U.S. Agency for International Development, "Rural and Urban Development," pp. 1–4.

31. U.S. Agency for International Development, "Status Report of U.S. Economic Assistance," p. 44. Information for much of this section is based on this document. Also, U.S. Agency for International Development, "Country Development Strategy Statement, FY 86, Annex E: Population and Health Strategies," April 1984.

32. Aswan Aid Donors, *Egypt: Economic Update 1981* (Cairo: Fiani and Partners, 1981), p. 7/4.

33. U. S. Agency for International Development, "Congressional Presentation, FY 1986," April 1985, p. 25.

34. U.S. Embassy, Cairo, "Egypt: Annual Agricultural Sector Report—1983," February 28, 1984, p. 9. Total assistance from the World Bank from FY 1946 through 1984 came to $2.5 billion. In FY 1984 the bank's commitment to Egyptian programs was $458 million. The next highest international contributor was the EEC with $25 million committed in FY 1984. U.S. Agency for International Development, "Congressional Presentation, FY 1986," p. 25.

35. *Middle East News, Economic Weekly* (Cairo), March 26, 1982, p. 4.

36. U.S. General Accounting Office, "Egypt's Capacity to Absorb and Use Economic Assistance Effectively," report to the U.S. Congress, September 15, 1977, p. 15.

37. *Egyptian Gazette* (Cairo), January 26, 1982.

38. Ibid., February 9, 1982.

39. U.S. General Accounting Office, "U.S. Assistance to Egyptian Agriculture: Slow Progress After Five Years," report to the U.S. Congress, March 16, 1981, p. 41.

40. See U.S. General Accounting Office, "The U.S. Economic Assistance Program for Egypt Poses a Management Challenge for AID," report to the administrator of the Agency for International Development, July 31, 1985, pp. 31–42 for a fuller examination of the alternative modes.

41. Ibid., pp. ii, 13, 46, 53.

42. Ibid., p. 39.

5

Bureaucratic Constraints

Conditions of AID

The U.S. AID mission to Egypt occupies what is to some a curious position in economic assistance and development activities. Despite its popular image in Egypt and, for that matter, in the United States, the AID mission does not function as an operating, "hands-on" agency. Officials in the field at times may be conspicuous and deemed influential, but their influence derives from their work as facilitators or middlemen. For AID in Egypt as elsewhere in the Third World is essentially a bureaucracy of planners and financial managers. Its role is, moreover, one of gaining approval and monitoring project spending rather than supervising projects, furnishing technical expertise, or acting as a procurement agency. Strategies of implementation often get the least attention. Prior to the 1970s, AID personnel did indeed play a more direct part in implementing development programs. Although the basic mode of channeling aid through public bureaucracies has not changed, a revised conception of field missions as composed of generalists rather than development technicians, and an overall reduction of personnel (down one-quarter of the agency's size worldwide in the late 1960s) required a more detached role.[1] By contracting out projects, funding the hiring of mostly private U.S.-based consultants and experts who would not appear on the books as government employees, AID was able to convey the impression to Washington lawmakers that it was cutting back on staff. For some country programs, including Egypt, AID also transfered to recipient government banks or ministries the task of distributing funds for specially earmarked purposes. On a day-to-day basis, the AID mission is Cairo is left to identify projects, write strategy papers and lengthy project justifications, process and pay vouchers and, most importantly, smooth the relations between the contractors and their employer, the Egyptian government.

AID finds itself after three decades the beneficiary of experiences gained in giving assistance worldwide and the inheritor of a legacy of rules and regulations that have frequently served to rigidify the aid process. The lessons that successive AID employees in the field and officials in Washington have learned about the ineffectiveness of various approaches and the dangers of mismanagement and corruption have left attitudes and procedural safeguards that handcuff field missions and reduce their ability to act appropriately, responsively, and promptly in disbursing aid funds. Observers have enumerated more than one-hundred restrictions, frequently labeled as "barnacles," in the foreign aid program.[2] These occur in the form of provisions in the Foreign Assistance Act of 1961 and its amendments that govern the disbursement of foreign aid. Many of them were added in the period just prior to the beginning of massive aid to Egypt, placed there as one of the ways that Congress reasserted itself in foreign policy after the Vietnam and Watergate experiences. Some see AID as one of many scapegoats, not just through congressional action reducing funds and personnel, but also in the introduction of complicated procedures covering virtually every area of its operation from project identification to financial reporting.[3] At least some constraints are self-imposed, the result of AID's trying to anticipate the criticisms of congressional subcommittees. The striving to protect prerogatives and resources is perhaps understandable for an agency without independent statutory recognition surviving on annual congressional authorizations and appropriations. Whatever the reasons, AID's rigidities have forced clients, in this instance the Egyptians, to endure a labyrinth of details and delays.

The procedures for project development and implementation are prescribed in internal AID regulations. The documentation required for assistance is designed, ideally, to assure a sense of fairness, to prevent abuses, and to provide for the efficient and effective use of AID's resources. With this in mind, enormous effort goes into writing (in consultation with the Egyptians) specifications for projects and into preparing feasibility studies and evaluation procedures to justify approval and secure funding. The elaborate procedures are supposed to avert such problems as biased selection of contractors, misuse of funds, and implementation bottlenecks. Along with increasing chances of project success, the various rules and criteria are also expected to furnish a model for the Egyptian bureaucracy, thereby influencing its attitude and behavior in project administration. The cost of these safeguards and guidelines comes high, however, in terms of time and money. Indeed, nearly everyone associated with U.S. assistance, including the mission officials themselves, finds the red tape frustrating and often inexplicable.

Earlier in the aid relationship, many difficulties could be explained as arising from Egyptian ministries' unfamiliarity with AID procurement and contracting practices and AID's inability to articulate its requirements adequately. Less confusing and better appreciated requirements have in recent years helped to expedite the flow of assistance. But beyond the communications problems, the rules, regulations, and procedures under which AID operates are themselves inhibitors of project progress. An approach to development aid that is essentially project-oriented involves procedures and paper work that local officials find not only unnecessary but at times perverse, even deliberately demeaning. Competitive bidding procedures and expensive feasibility studies have been among the most time-consuming and criticized features of the usually cumbersome U.S. aid process. The accumulated body of regulations and procedures, together with the prevailing ideas in Washington about development aid, condition what the mission can hope to accomplish in Egypt and what the Egyptian government can expect to gain from its aid relationship.

The desirability of U.S. aid makes it prudent for Egyptian officials to accede to the rules and regulations laid down by U.S. law and AID practices. Just the same, Egyptian ministry officials do not hesitate to complain, and their criticisms are occasionally amplified in Egypt's semi-official press. U.S. programs in particular come in for attack for making it more attractive or requiring the government to engage foreign expertise rather than employ their own nationals. There is much that to the Egyptians seems patronizing and unnecessary, especially in the area of technical assistance. Because of specifications and regulations, for example, U.S. engineering firms are almost always engaged, and at least 10 percent of capital project costs go for engineering services. At the same time, AID refuses to allow its funds to be used for the salaries of Egyptians where monetary incentives, it is argued, could attract and hold the best people in sectors critical to Egypt's economy and basic services. U.S. consultants are said to cost too much because of their high compensation packages, and their salaries together with procurement requirements make it appear that aid dollars, supposedly designated for Egypt, are being recycled back to the United States. Although the AID mission claims that the amount spent on salaries for U.S. contractors and consultants amounts to less than 5 percent of the annual program for Egypt, even this figure strikes many as extravagant.[4] Egyptians also dispute the need for feasibility studies and prolonged contracting processes. They call them costly and repetitive, of little value to the country or, ultimately, to the donor. Ministry officials will point to other aid programs where, once a general authorization is made, an embassy officer of the donor country will alone decide whether to fund a request. By comparison, AID's feasibility studies and reviews are likely to take eighteen months (from six months to a year can pass before a contractor is selected). Behind much of the resentment lies a comparison between the supervision of U.S.-sponsored projects in Egypt and U.S. economic assistance to Israel that is delivered without an AID mission.

The AID Mission

The AID mission in Cairo occupies several floors in one of the city's most modern office buildings, on one of its busiest streets. The large glass-dominated structure (the Bank of America's location on the ground floor adds to the symbolism) corresponds with AID's apparent image, that of an imposing, influential bureaucracy, alienated from most of Egyptian society. The U.S. presence is certainly formidable in another sense: There are about 1,000 U.S. citizens associated with an official community that includes embassy officials one block away, a project contractor population numbering another 1,000, and hundreds more U.S. citizens in Egypt in a military advisory capacity. The AID mission by itself has 132 authorized direct U.S.-hire positions in addition to 175 contract personnel and about 90 foreign national professional employees. In 1984, the mission was organized into 22 offices and divisions, most of them reporting to 6 assistant directors, all of whom were directly responsible to the country AID director (see Figure 5.1).

Comparisons are naturally made with other economic assistance programs operating in Egypt, bilateral and multilateral, but most are either far smaller efforts or have an approach to aid delivery that obviates the need for many resident professionals. Parallels are of course also drawn with the more than 20,000 Soviet military advisors as well as economic and technical personnel who were so prominent before 1972. Against this presence the body of U.S. consultants and specialists does not seem too striking. A full accounting of U.S. citizens must, however, also include many businessmen, a category obviously absent from Soviet representation. The U.S. resident community of about 15,000 people is still far fewer than the community in Iran before 1979 or in Saudi Arabia today.[5] Yet affluent aid-related U.S. personnel in Cairo are a source of growing uneasiness, particularly among U.S. foreign service officers familiar with the high U.S. profile in Iran during the 1970s.

A project mode country program as expensive and extensive as that in Egypt logically requires the large professional and support staff. By 1984, with almost eighty major projects underway, the agency had succeeded in increasing the staff needed for program control by 50 percent over 1977. Congressionally mandated regulations as much as any factor necessitate sufficient personnel to assure that auditing and oversight requirements are met. Many on the staff are therefore management, administrative, and technical support personnel rather than staff involved with project management. (AID has long been accused of being a top-heavy agency with about 65 percent of its total professional staff based in Washington.) It is often asserted that the mission in Cairo has not become more efficient as it has grown but instead has become

Figure 5.1
Mission Organization Chart AID/Cairo, June 1984

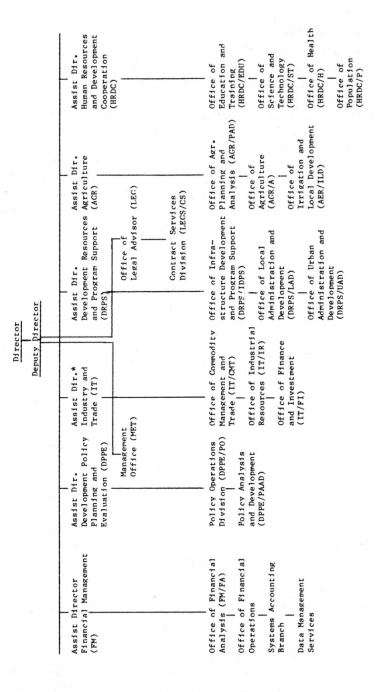

*Being reorganized

subject to many of the organizational problems that typically beset large bureaucracies.

Because the Cairo mission directs so vast and expensive a program, with its high political stakes, U.S. personnel assigned to Egypt are among AID's most senior, experienced people. Still, although the level of professional competence among many in the administration of the aid program is unusually high, the preparation and commitment of those in the mission vary considerably. Only a notable few project managers, for example, arrive with or acquire a good familiarity with Egyptian culture or the economic and political system. It is a rare AID official who has good facility in Arabic. In fact, there is for most little opportunity or incentive to become country experts. Most personnel are rotated in country assignments every two or four years. They may never again in their careers find occasion to use specialized information about Egypt. Moreover, because projects normally take five to eight years from conception to completion, officials know that they will not see a project through and have their individual initiatives rewarded or penalized.

Even the more dedicated officials have little knowledge of what is going on outside their offices and certainly outside of Cairo. They have very limited contact or acquaintance with the kind of people who ultimately benefit from U.S.-funded programs. Many of AID's local-hire Egyptian professionals do maintain regular contacts with their Egyptian government counterparts, and in some departments of the mission, members of the U.S. staff take the initiative in meeting U.S. contractors and local officials. For the most part, however, AID's U.S. personnel acquire little field experience and come to know very few Egyptian officials during the course of their stay in Cairo.

As previously pointed out, the AID mission is involved in the routine of transferring funds, defining appropriate monitoring procedures, and finding ways to coordinate project participants. Consultants, often from U.S. universities or specialized firms and institutions, provide most of the extensive studies. Because of the legal constraints under which the mission operates, its small group of lawyers are key figures in the aid process. But rather than using their skills to find more innovative ways to disburse aid, the mission's lawyers see their job as protecting the mission and its officials. With the lawyers so cautious, their eyes constantly focused on the legal requirements of the Foreign Assistance Act and appropriation bills, it is left to project managers, if anyone, to find ways to bypass some of the numerous legal requirements.[6] A good portion of the staff is tied down in writing policy papers mainly to satisfy AID headquarters in Washington. The important planning office does not coordinate its activities closely with functional departments. Although many officials are qualified as economists and development practitioners, they are far removed from the day-to-day problems associated with projects or the efforts to influence Egyptian government policy. The expertise of many on the staff makes them qualified to oversee infra-structural projects where engineering design and work loom largest. Less certain, however, is the competence of AID officials, working within the structure and processes of the mission, to promote the now more numerous private sector-oriented projects. For these, the staff's lack of entrepreneurial experiences and innovative, flexible thinking is often obvious.

At the AID mission's helm during most of the recent history of U.S. aid to Egypt had been one man, Donald Brown. As director, Brown came to lead the development assistance efforts just as they were beginning to take off in 1977, after a period when the program was limited to commodity transfers and budgetary support. Brown remained director in Cairo until the summer of 1982, by which time he had left his own personal stamp on the mission. The noncommodity program expanded during these years from one focused largely on a few major infrastructural projects to a highly diversified development portfolio motivated by the need to spend annually the nearly $500 million authorized for project support alone. The two ambassadors whom Brown served gave him a free hand. Both seemed to be satisfied so long as the aid monies flowed smoothly; they were, in any case, largely preoc-cupied by their facilitating role in an Egyptian-Israeli peace. The entire tone and direction of the mission reflected Brown's own style and impressive talents. He kept informed about every program in progress and participated in most decisions. Although Brown was, of necessity, too removed at the top to understand how to operationalize some of the mission goals, in other respects he tried to act as a ubiquitous project manager. Many of the programs undertaken were ones that he personally championed and defended to Washington. Subordinates admired Brown for his professionalism and knowledge of detail. He was less appreciated, however, for what some perceived to be his inability to delegate authority easily and for a managerial style that was viewed at the same time as overbearing and loose. For Egyptian officials, Brown almost alone could speak authoritatively about the U.S. aid program.

Brown's relations with the Egyptian bureaucracy were cooperative and cordial even though, as a reserved person, he often seemed to find it difficult to interact in the effusive, informal manner expected of him. Contacts between the mission director and the Egyptians were strongly influenced by the personalities in the government and the structure of decision-making in the Egyptian bureaucracy. For the most critical years of the Brown tenure (the later Sadat years), Abdel Razzak Abdel-Meguid tried to consolidate ministerial authority. His direct access to President

Sadat assured Meguid both power and wide-ranging responsibilities. The AID director had regularly to compete, then, with many others for Dr. Meguid's time and could anticipate long intervals before ascertaining an Egyptian position. The official most directly responsible for dealing with Brown, Fuad Iskandar, was easier to reach and quicker to respond but, taking his cues from Meguid, was aggressive in trying to demonstrate the bureaucracy's desire for increasing its self-determination in development planning.

The Reagan administration's efforts to revise the AID mandate and put its stamp on foreign assistance were ultimately incompatible with Brown's style of operation and his diffuse programs. Brown was a carryover from the Carter administration, and his instincts about development aid were considered by the AID leadership in Washington to be out of step with the new themes. An early decision to replace Brown would, however, have possibly suggested displeasure in Washington with the course of the aid program to Egypt or, more specifically, given support to criticisms about U.S. financial backing for Sadat's economic liberalization. Sadat's assassination placed an added premium on continuity in Egyptian-U.S. aid relations. Brown meanwhile cooperated with Washington's ordered reassessments of the program and modifications in sectoral emphases. Perhaps despite personal doubts, he participated in discussions promising more flexibility to the Egyptian government in the use of assistance funds. When Brown finally stepped down, it came as no surprise that his slated successor was a Republican whose professional background included neither development administration nor extensive international experience.

Michael P. Stone had been running a large, successful California wine firm. He was presumed to be the kind of person to transfer private sector skills to the large AID operation which, given its size and financial responsibilities, in many respects resembles a major corporation. Stone was expected to be a more efficient business manager, able to delegate authority to his subordinates, including freedom to deal directly with the ministries. Though Stone was not a personal friend of anyone in the Reagan administration, nor a known ideologue, it was felt that he held the personal confidence of the AID administrator, Peter McPherson, and could reduce tensions between the mission and Washington. With direct access to McPherson, Stone was also believed to be in a stronger position to impress on the Egyptian government Washington's desire to have it undertake unpopular economic reforms, particularly the lowering of subsidies for food and energy considered essential for Egypt to effectively absorb U.S. aid.

To the surprise of most, Stone's talents lay not in management but in promotion. From the outset he showed little interest in the mission's administrative operations, patience for detail, or creativity in program development. Microeconomic studies, a priority activity under Brown, were largely ignored. Stone was accustomed to being the corporate "outside man." Using his strong public relations skills, the director appeared to feel most comfortable trying to explain the aid program to Egypt's decisionmakers and a public that had become increasingly suspicious of U.S. intentions. Stone's desire to better focus the mission's far-flung efforts in fewer, larger projects offered a way to more easily justify and sell programs as well as to spend the massive aid funding for Egypt. In the mission, he proposed to consolidate responsibilities in a functional reorganization of his top subordinates with the aim of creating a more controllable operation with less dependence on outside expertise. But when the proposal met with resistance internally and Stone failed to win the backing expected in Washington, he allowed his ideas for reorganization to die. Stone succeeded only in abolishing for a time the position of deputy director, a post held by a Brown-era holdover whose liberal, activist views were less a problem than his incompatibility with a director whose self-starting style permitted no alter ego. Although the mission's six assistant directors and nearly two dozen office directors were given greater freedom in day-to-day operations than they had exercised earlier, Stone failed to accomplish a flattening of the mission's hierarchical structure that could have facilitated a better flow of information. Previously, some observers felt that Brown had been unable as mission director to communicate adequately with his subordinates, possibly reflecting his perception that he knew more than anyone else. For Stone, a loner role naturally suited what appeared to be his disdain for administrative, bureaucratic systems.

Relations with Washington, which had been expected to improve under Stone, in fact grew more confrontational. Program oversight and procedural requirements by the home office tightened (see below), making any new program initiatives nearly impossible. Stone's ability to go over the heads of the Washington AID bureaucracy, directly to the administrator, was sorely resented by many veteran bureaucrats and the top AID political appointees who also complained about a lack of professional orientation. The Cairo director also could not escape the attacks of those officials who objected to so large a share of AID's resources going to Egypt. Criticisms of Stone's performance as an administrator were compounded by doubts about whether his essentially pragmatic, goal-oriented views would allow him to push energetically enough Washington's more doctrinal demands on Egypt for increased private sector involvement in programs and meaningful economic policy reforms. Because of Stone's apparent desire to please the Egyptian client, top AID officials viewed him as having too much sympathy for Egyptian complaints about the diffuse character of U.S. aid, expensive outside consultants, and lack of control over project funds.

If Stone seemed best suited to defining and publicizing AID programs for the Egyptian media and building a good personal rapport with Egyptian leaders, by 1984, he was experiencing setbacks even in these areas. A post-Meguid reassignment of bureaucratic responsibilities and accompanying personnel shifts helped to reduce somewhat the adversarial tone in contacts with some Egyptian officials. Stone had easier access than Brown did to ministerial levels and even to President Mubarak. The director was perceived by the Egyptian leadership as a political figure, less well informed than his predecessor but more directly a spokesman for the AID administrator and, through him, the White House. But the mission director's blunt style did not go over well with all Egyptian officials at the top, especially the Minister of Investment and International Cooperation, Wigih Shindi, who was now involved in all the key decisions on the Egyptian side. Stone's often candid remarks also drew much criticism from the Cairo newspapers to which he gave a series of interviews in fall 1983.

Stone, all the same, seemed to gradually learn to appreciate the constraints of operating in Egypt, particularly that in the local bureaucratic culture it is far easier to reach agreements than to have them implemented. Perhaps he came to understand better that he could not set a few businesslike targets for the mission and expect them to be implemented quickly. Stone's sensitivity to the difficulties faced by his subordinates improved. In turn, morale in the mission also rose, despite continued objections by some to his priorities and style. Stone drew some sympathy, moreover, in trying to defend the mission in its ideological and procedural battles with the Washington AID establishment. The restoration of a deputy director post, a decision imposed on Stone by Washington late in 1983, also improved the running of the mission. The new deputy, Art Handly, a former mission director in Tanzania, quietly succeeded in gaining the confidence of the staff and although given by Stone only limited formal responsibilities, was able to provide informally the needed management direction and an understanding of development issues. The deputy accomplished this, moreover, without upstaging the mission director or otherwise threatening his authority. Stone's detractors in AID/Washington finally prevailed, however. In November 1984, Frank Kimball, a seasoned AID official with extensive managerial and overseas experience, then serving as counselor to the agency in Washington, was sworn in to replace Stone.

That Kimball might be less impeded by Washington than was his predecessor seemed likely after a September 1984 internal study of AID concluded that the home office should confine itself to general policy questions.[7] Apparently as a condition of accepting the post of director in Cairo, Kimball was promised greater autonomy for the mission. The redelegation of authority in 1984 and 1985 permitted him to amend project and nonproject activities and added to his powers over project implementation. AID in Washington retains the right, however, to approve initial proposals in excess of $20 million, or most of the mission's proposals, and the AID administrator is allowed to exercise concurrent authority over the same functions as the mission director in Egypt.[8] But assuming that this latter provision is not abused, Kimball acquired important new tools of program management.

Intrabureaucratic Differences

Conflicting professional orientations and intrabureaucratic conflicts for control and personal advancement account for most of the competing perspectives and priorities among U.S. aid officials. The differences show up clearly in the dynamic core shaping American aid policy that includes, along with AID's mission in Cairo, its Washington bureaucracy, the U.S. Department of State, the U.S. Embassy in Cairo, and the U.S. Congress with its relevant subcommittees. The executive branch's Office of Management and Budget and the U.S. Department of Agriculture are interested if more occasional actors.[9] U.S. business works hard at times to influence the AID portfolio in Egypt, with the communications industry being especially persistent. Even U.S. public opinion and its perceived level of tolerance for foreign aid and assistance to Egypt in particular set a notable parameter for policy.

Lack of agreement about development strategies among the mission staff in Cairo is an expected consequence of varying programming responsibilities and competition for recognition in funding. These divisions typically come to the surface during preparation by the mission of a Country Development Strategy Statement, required until recently on a yearly basis by AID in Washington. More serious, however, are differences that have emerged in recent years with the home office. These tensions with Washington at times overshadow even the difficulties that AID officials in Cairo have with their Egyptian counterparts. The disagreements are in part an expected outgrowth of a divergence in views between field and center policymakers, each having its own constraints and pressures, even where they may share similar professional orientations. AID in Cairo is preoccupied with problems involving the disbursement of funds and the mission's relations with the Egyptian government. In Washington, officials focus on trying to rationalize programs in accordance with the agency's perceived mandate and, in so doing, to satisfy the current administration and legitimize its efforts before the Congress. But the conflict in the early 1980s also represented a significant change between Cairo and Washington as the latter tried to exercise tighter controls over the management of overseas programs. The very size and salience of the program in Egypt ensured that Washington's quest for greater supervision of programs would be strongly felt in Cairo.

Through 1984 at least, the mission expended considerable energy trying to retain some of its earlier flexibility in determining projects and setting the terms of aid. Administrative rules that required Washington's approval for the simplest decisions involving expenditures have always limited the field's freedom of action. Cairo-based AID officials have constantly had to face delays, for example, caused by awkward and often unnecessarily drawn out bidding procedures and U.S.-dictated specifications for construction. But in the past the mission in Cairo could usually count on approval of program and money requests, even if much delayed. Washington increasingly began, however, to shower the mission with demands for additional information and justifications before projects were considered, and many were rejected. This close supervision seemed at some variance with a managerial approach enunciated by the AID administrator—to draw more clearly the lines between the Washington office and field missions.[10]

Aid officials in Washington deny that the agency has turned its back on the 1970s mandate so much as it has decided on different means to accomplish the job. But the tighter executive direction and management that emerged in the early 1980s was inspired if not dictated by an economic philosophy injected into foreign aid by the Reagan administration. The narrowing of the AID mission's discretion was in large part an attempt to adjust to doctrinal and political signals from Washington. Closer scrutiny of the Egyptian policy environment and reduced funding for some problem areas and projects mark some of the differences. Not a few proposals were questioned and turned back by the home office through the mid-1980s because they were perceived as violating free-market precepts. Mission officials found it difficult to identify new development projects in any sector that could pass muster in Washington, particularly when there was a public sector component. As a result, AID was unresponsive to a number of major funding proposals made by the Mubarak government. The large aid sums that had to be obligated yearly forced the mission to seek approval in Washington for costly, expanded infrastructural projects and, at least in the view of some AID staff, obligated the mission to settle for increased support for several peripheral programs. Many of the mission's development professionals, nurtured on the more idealistic beliefs and strategies of the 1970s, believed that the AID ideologues in Washington supported unsound notions of development and were indifferent to the lowered esprit de corps among mission personnel.

The crucible in which U.S. aid policy in Egypt is formed also includes those managing U.S. foreign policy in Cairo and Washington. Embassy officials in Cairo for a long time have stressed the political significance of economic assistance, particularly at the time when it strengthened President Sadat at home so that he could pursue risky policies abroad. From the (Department of) "State" perspective, the aid effort should be in the first instance consistent with overall U.S. policy toward Egypt and U.S. regional aspirations.[11] Officials are regularly concerned about Egypt's short-term economic difficulties and their possible effects on the regime's political viability and willingness to retain cooperative relations with the United States. Specifically, as described in Chapter Four, they have called for the transfer of quickly consumed food and supplies intended to overcome immediate shortages and relieve foreign exchange problems. In general, the Department of State view favors less fettered use of aid dollars. It also offers muted criticism of AID's attempts to pressure the Egyptians to introduce belt-tightening economic reforms that it fears could be ineffective and adversely affect larger U.S. political objectives.

The counterperspective, shared by most AID officials (and key members of the U.S. Congress), disparages relatively short-term, high-impact programs, preferring investment in carefully designed development projects. Proponents of this view have usually defended grants for major capital projects which, though slow to show returns, are expected to rehabilitate and modernize the economy. At least for the first five years of the aid program in Egypt, these development professionals also tended to favor a diversified portfolio of smaller projects planned to raise productivity in industry, agriculture, and other sectors in association with an appropriate domestic policy climate. They have normally measured their efforts against a broad set of development criteria and hold attitudes that grow out of professional training and experiences often very different from those of embassy foreign service officers. Chapter Four has already described how these different perspectives during the mid-1980s influenced attitudes toward proposed changes in the mode of aid delivery to Egypt. More regularly, discussions concern the selection of projects that provide early evidence of U.S. political support or those that promise relatively longer term economic benefits.

Still, it is easy to overstate the gap between the political and development orientations. The choice of aid approaches rarely comes down to an either/or one but rather a proper mix of the two. The legitimacy of both goals is generally appreciated. Much as policies seeking short-term political benefits need not necessarily sacrifice long-term solutions to problems, political goals can also serve developmental ends. AID's professional staff is not politically naive or insensitive to the geostrategic purposes of the U.S. presence in Egypt. They pride themselves on having created a credible development program for Egypt despite the dominant political motives in aid, and they concede that without political stability there can be no long-term assistance role for the United States. The AID mission cooperated with the embassy in pushing specific, politically symbolic policies, including many initial CIP proposals, the quick repackaging of funds to increase commodity and food aid in the wake of Egypt's January 1977 food riots, the Peace Fellowship program, and the emergency aid grant for the 1985 and 1986 fiscal years.

For their part, those politically oriented officials admit that successful development and sound reforms can be important political assets. These U.S. officials realize that although interim risks are reduced through reliable commodity and financial support, political aims can also be served by helping Egypt to improve its economic self-reliance. The need for "quick fixes" through commodity financing and other budgetary supports in fact diminished with improvements in the Egyptian economy in the late 1970s, making possible increased emphasis on capital projects as well as more modest efforts to assist agriculture, small business, and science and technology. Moreover, the supposed political dividends from equipment grants and intermediate goods often fail to take full account of the time-consuming requirements for competitive bidding and Egyptian-side appropriations, not to mention the possibility that, as in the case of the noisy, defective Cairo buses, U.S. equipment may be ridiculed rather than praised (see discussion in Chapter Seven).

The Other Bureaucracy

Much as the Egyptians have had to become accustomed to U.S. procedures and conscious of AID's priorities, so too, U.S. officials have been forced to adjust to the organization of Egypt's economy and its bureaucratic values and practices. U.S. aid personnel view the economy's management as cumbersome, fragmented in its decisionmaking, and pulled in several directions by vested interests in the ministries. The Egyptian bureaucracy is faced with many of the same problems of administrative inefficiency and corruption frequently identified elsewhere in the Middle East and Third World. The public ministries display the familiar patrimonial qualities of defensiveness and informal decision processes. The bureaucracy is marked by telltale signs of rivalries and jealousies and failure to share and assume responsibility.[12]

Yet Egypt is also in many ways unique among less developed countries. As Ayubi points out, there exists alongside the personalistic or oligarchical strand in Egypt's political culture a bureaucratic one that is highly centralized and authoritarian. Bureaucratic attitudes are often traced to a mentality that dates to the centralized administrations of the pharaohs and their basis for legitimacy.[13] For four thousand years Egyptians have accepted that a single bureaucracy would dominate their lives. A modern, powerful bureaucracy, one that intrudes into every area of the economy, is certainly evident by the mid-nineteenth century, well before bureaucratic experiences in most Third World countries. Egypt's 1952 revolution and the nationalization laws of 1961 brought its government bureaucracy the primary responsibility for the productive sector of the expanded public-dominated economy and administrators the task of implementing Egypt's new social programs. Whatever the policy changes since Nasser, the country's economic and social development continues to be tied closely to the performance of this bureaucracy. Although the U.S. aid program encourages revised administrative practices and supports efforts to decentralize and limit the public bureaucracy, its assistance by no means offers a direct challenge to the bureaucratic structures. By and large, the United States has accepted Egyptian institutions as it has found them. It is also clear that the character and pace, and ultimately the success, of foreign assistance are fundamentally influenced by the prevailing bureaucratic norms and behavior. Egypt's large and ineffective bureaucracy is considered by many in the AID mission to pose as formidable an obstacle to economic growth (and especially private enterprise development) as is found anywhere in the Third World.

The bureaucratic practices and values in the Egyptian bureaucracy often appear highly irrational or nonrational to Egypt's Western aid donors. They find that administrators tend to oversimplify problems and delay dealing with them. The duplication and inflexibility of rules are maddening to outsiders who also disparage the personal influence that it takes to cut through the endless decision processes. Wishful thinking and public pronouncements often substitute for action. Resistance to change and the absence of initiative are conceived as partly the result of older attitudes toward risk-taking. That many higher administrators were trained during the socialist era of the 1950s and 1960s and influenced by the Eastern bloc is seen as contributing to the overly centralized, secretive, and poorly informed government ministries and agencies. The slow, inefficient services and weak coordination of the bureaucracy is laid to self-serving, competitive personnel. Government ministers resist delegating authority to their deputies who they perceive more in staff than line relationships and who, in most instances, are none too anxious to assume responsibility. Inadequately trained lower ranking officials are usually fearful of making mistakes and embarrassing supervisors and thus try to pass on or ignore problems. These officials are assigned tasks without either ample material support or expectations of reward for their accomplishments; they understand that benefits are normally awarded for loyalty, regardless of one's competence or efficiency.

Critics admit, however, to another kind of rationality at work. Criteria of status and individual security in the Egyptian bureaucracy often count as much as efficiency measured in temporal and monetary terms. Attitudes and behavior may be highly appropriate (if not laudable) in the pursuit of economic and social benefits and may contribute to reducing tensions.[14] What is to the outsider an unconscionable disregard for the national interest is sometimes as much a matter of policy priority. AID officials, unable to explain attitudes toward rural and agricultural needs in the bureaucracy, for example, sometimes fail to appreciate the long held orientation of administrators toward a philosophy of urban/industrial development.[15]

Ayubi writes that solving Egypt's complex development problems is "not due to technical ignorance of *how* to do something but to social and political considerations related to *why* one should do them."[16] Low motivation and morale are in part an economic consideration. Government salaries that were modest in the Nasser era became even less adequate during the 1970s as the regime did not have the means to reward good administration and, in any case, preferred to create financial incentives elsewhere in the economy. Poorly paid administrators depend on favors and gratuities for economic survival. They remain in their positions because it affords personal security and opportunities to promote other interests, including personal profit from aid contracts and advantages for friends and relatives.[17] Ironically, the same ministry employees who sit idly most of the day in an office they share with a dozen others are examples of individual industriousness in hustling to make extra cash once off the job.

Ayubi's conclusions about Egypt's rich pool of talent may have been more accurate in the 1960s. Some of the country's most qualified citizens (e.g., its engineers, doctors, teachers, accountants, plumbers, and electricians) are attracted by far higher wages elsewhere in the Arab world or in the West. Experienced employees also leave public service when they can for jobs in the domestic private sector. Meanwhile, the bureaucracy is bloated as the employer of last resort for Egypt's recent university graduates who wait several years for an actual appointment. Swamped with employees, the Ministries of Electricity, Health, Industry, and Communications allocate most of their budgets for salaries, with the aid donors, in effect, picking up the ministries' operating expenditures.

Problems of direction, coordination, and control by the Egyptian bureaucracy are obvious obstacles for the successful absorption of external aid. The list of complaints compiled by AID officials and others in Cairo is long and pointed. Administrative vagueness and procrastination in the formative stages and inattention and inefficiency in the implementation of projects are familiar criticisms. In the mid-1970s, difficulties in getting development programs going was blamed on the limited experience of Egyptian planners with international and Western donor organizations and countries. It was quickly realized, however, that many of these problems were more endemic. From the U.S. perspective, decisions are never made quickly and are all too often highly personalistic. High turnover, especially at top ministerial levels, means that officials appear to have no personal commitment to programs or familiarity with their objectives. The Egyptians, it is contended, have difficulty in articulating what they want because it would force them to be more specific in assigning costs and indicating their priorities. Wherever development proposals originate, from AID, foreign consultants, U.S. private investors, or within the ministries, a definitive "yes" or "no" from the bureaucracy may take months, years, or never be announced. Proposals are frequently shelved, and technologies may be unemployed rather than directly refused. Firms awaiting approval for joint ventures under *Infitah* laws are often discouraged and give up. Commodities financed by AID, including such project-related equipment as roadgraders and bulldozers, sit in warehouses because no official will take the responsibility for clearing them. If decisions are finally made, or initiatives taken, they occur typically only after intervention by officials at the highest ministerial levels.

The nationally centralized bureaucratic structure is, nevertheless, hardly monolithic in its decisionmaking process. To the contrary, like the political system itself, the bureaucracy is fragmented and uncoodinated in planning, approving, financing, and executing development projects. The dialogue between the U.S. donors and the Egyptians is often indecisive simply because bureaucratic policy-setting is so broad and diffuse.[18] In their own sphere, the ministries and other agencies exercise considerable independence of action, subject only to the government's annual budget process.[19] At times, they aggressively promote their own projects. Even under the tighter control of planning, investment, and finance instituted by Abdel Rassak Abdel-Meguid, ministries frequently could overrule or ignore him. The priorities of the ministries are quite often in conflict, and the relationship among these entities can be more critical to the progress of development then the discussions with aid sources. Egyptian officials usually lack a centralized data base or the means to synthesize and gather additional data. Very little of the information used by ministries to determine agricultural policy, for example, is accessible to any foreign aid agency. Some of the most pertinent information is guarded as having political and security value, and AID tries to avoid the appearance of competing with the ministries through a separate collection and analysis of agricultural data.[20]

In the absence of bureaucratic agreement, the United States and other donors cannot avoid getting mixed signals. Programs designed with these external sources frequently underscore the ministries' inability to work in a coordinated fashion and point up their vested interests. Government officials do not welcome projects that would, for example, require them to share responsibilities with other units in the bureaucracy. Ministry-sponsored studies by foreign consultants are expected to endorse existing policies and assist efforts against encroachment by others. AID consciously tries to avoid entanglement in these bureaucratic in-fights but cannot be unaffected by the unproductive competition and its outcomes. As a way out of the bureaucratic imbroglio, AID officials have considered the chief administrative officers of the twenty-seven governates, with their considerable autonomy and status, capable of furnishing effective coordination within their areas of jurisdiction.[21] In a few cases, at least, the governors have not disappointed them.

Some sectors of the bureaucracy, in effect, continue to balk at working with foreign donors, especially the United States. The institutional history of each bureaucratic unit and the age and training of its administrators influence the degree of cooperation with AID officials and the speed with which U.S. funds are absorbed. More than a few Egyptian administrators view AID's attempts at institution building and technology transfers as likely to reduce their own influence over the economy, and they particularly resent U.S. encouragement and support for liberalized, private-sector-oriented policies.[22] Working with the U.S. planners can also add to an official's work load, with no increment in salary.[23] But often what appears to be a ministry's uncooperativeness or indecision is simply its weakness in the policy setting councils of the Egyptian government. Cases in point are the long-term inability of the Ministry of Agriculture to win bureaucratic battles on such important issues as farmers' incentives and procurement prices, or the undependability of the Ministry of Rural Development in a bureaucracy where it lacks clout.

A lack of clear definition of responsibilities within and among ministries can preclude effective preparation of projects and increase the pitfalls in large, complex development undertakings. AID cannot avoid dealing in its agricultural development planning, for example, with a bureaucracy where the Ministries of Agriculture, Land Reclamation, and Irrigation often represent different interest constituencies, champion disparate development philosophies, and engage in bitter institutional rivalries. The administration of small rural projects, such as providing safe water to villages, requires the reconciliation of interests and coordination of procedural practices of diverse ministries including Construction, Local Government, Health, and Finance. AID's aims have perhaps been most directly thwarted by the lack of coordination in the activities of the Ministry of Planning, which develops Egypt's Five Year Plans; the Ministry of Finance, which prepares the country's annual budget; and the Ministry of Investment and International Cooperation, which, together with the implementing ministries, had until 1984 the most direct contacts with AID officials.[24] The frequent changes in Egyptian cabinet positions and higher level ministry posts in themselves assure frequent redirections in policy and neglect for adequate long-range development plans.

The shortage of managerial skills in the Egyptian bureaucracy is generally agreed to be the major constraint to the early and successful completion of AID-sponsored projects. Even when qualified personnel in the public bureaucracy are available, they may not be the ones assigned to a project. AID is reluctant, however, to challenge the Egyptians' selection of counterparts on projects, though it privately disagrees with the selection criteria.[25] Staff assigned to projects are very often chosen on the basis of position and tenure in the bureaucracy and an ability to speak English rather than for their technical competence. Those designated as co-project directors are, moreover, frequently expected to retain previous responsibilities, which naturally limits the amount of time they have for the project and retards its implementation.[26] The Egyptians have also been slow in providing promised salary incentives to their staffs. Even though Egyptian law limits the salaries U.S. contractors can offer to Egyptians they hire directly, foreign firms can easily drain off well-qualified personnel from national institutions. Also, as already observed, many of the best trained and most experienced people are working outside the country. Contractors have difficulty in many instances, moreover, in establishing a rapport and adjusting to the style of their Egyptian counterparts whose professional environment of centralized management contrasts with the normally decentralized U.S. experience.

Egypt's bureaucratic pathologies are also matters of concern to its highest policymakers. As Ayubi observes, the bureaucracy's performance satisfies neither its clientele nor its masters.[27] The low quality of information passed from administrators to top decisionmakers plainly impedes the country's capacity to plan. With administrators frequently oblivious and sometimes contemptuous of the broad public, the government is in a poor position to institutionalize feedback and assess the progress and failures of these programs.[28] Meanwhile, development setbacks, delays, and scandals during the last decade have contributed substantially to a growing popular cynicism. With promises still largely unfulfilled, Egypt's political leaders have cause for worry.

The Interface Between Bureaucracies

Normal interface between the U.S. and Egyptian bureaucracies takes place on several levels. Basic decisions, especially in the initial phases, occur at the highest levels and bring together the AID mission director and his top associates with Egyptian ministers and undersecretaries in the functional ministries and the ministries of economy, planning, and international cooperation. Parallel technical discussions are likely to be going on simultaneously between people from AID offices and their peers in the Egyptian bureaucracy. Once a project is underway, however, the project officer maintains the primary contacts with the government and the third party, the U.S. contractor. These AID officials have a corresponding Egyptian ministry project officer with whom they are in contact, usually about problems with the contractor, the application of AID regulations, and contract renewal. The degree of cooperation varies, not surprisingly, with how well the two project officers get along personally. Often the relationships are cordial; in other instances, Egyptians in the ministries object to interference from an AID officer whose role they see as merely to "sign off" where required.

Despite the frequent agreement between the two bureaucracies on long-term economic goals for Egypt, U.S. and Egyptian planners do not always see eye to eye on programmatic priorities. Nor have their development strategies always coincided. It has already been observed in Chapter Four that Egypt's planners have normally preferred commodity rather than project aid. Transfers of durable and consumer goods are quickly absorbed into the economy, making a direct impact on the balance of payments and requiring little administrative effort. AID officials, by contrast, have regularly stressed that commodity aid, although defensible as a temporary policy, makes little positive contribution to the process of economic development. Even in project aid, Egyptians have not always received financial assistance in the sectors identified by them as critical. U.S. funds have been unavailable, for example, except on a token basis, for projects involving public housing, hospital construction, youth activities, and postuniversity vocational training as well as land reclamation and new cities. Although the grounds for disagreement are frequently technical and analytical, or reflect bureaucratic misunderstandings and contrasting social and cultural values, the basis for differing priorities is often also doctrinal. Most seriously, failure to accommodate the preferences of the Cairo government raises the issue

of Egypt's economic independence and control over its development
that has implications for wider bilateral relations.

AID officials insist that they are in the country to fulfill Egypt's own
wishes and to abide by its priorities. They claim a right and obligation
to express their opinions but deny any intention or even the ability to
dictate decisions. The Egyptians may be unable to gain financing for
all they seek, but they can nevertheless bar those projects and programs
to which they object. The Egyptian bureaucracy in the first instance
identifies specific projects and, if the United States refuses to support
them, the Cairo government is not prevented from finding other donors
or investing on its own. Indeed, the U.S.-financed basic commodities
are supposedly a way of freeing up additional resources for development.
But U.S. influence remains indirect and subtle. Because the Cairo government seeks concessional external financing for all major projects, the
policy agendas of Egyptian ministries are unavoidably influenced by
AID's decisions.[29] The ministries feel encouraged to list projects in those
sectors and with those approaches that are believed likely to win AID's
consent. Moreover, project portfolios shaped by U.S. aid policy marshal
a sizable portion of government investment resources through local cost
contributions and drain off many of Egypt's qualified, available personnel.
Many ministry officials and an increasingly large public perceive the
United States, through its aid program, as steering development in a
highly self-interested way, making decisions that should be legitimately
left to Egyptian authorities.

Cooperation between AID officials and Egyptian ministries and agencies varies considerably. With some Egyptian officials, especially those
who are Western-trained, there may be little need to explain or justify
the use of classic liberal economic theory. These officials agree in principle
with the free-market policies advocated by the United States, most other
Western donors, and the IMF, although they also may feel irritated at
times by advice based on studies of cost-effectiveness that they believe
fails to give adequate weight to social costs, political risks, and national
aspirations. Egyptian policymakers often express confusion as to why
United States, in a aid program that is admittedly so political, insists
on employing predominantly economic criteria to decide what to finance.
It is unclear why when political motives are supposed to loom largest,
U.S. officials allow project aid to become so weighted down by feasibility
studies, protracted contracting provisions, and other procedural requirements. Relations have become confrontational where practical differences
exist about what the U.S. programs should accomplish. The Egyptians
differ in the emphasis they give to public sector industry and desert
reclamation, as already noted, but they also would prefer that the United
States cut back its investment in health and education and other social

sector projects in favor of the economic infrastructure. The sources of friction between AID and officials in the development-related ministries have also been of a more fundamental kind. AID officials frequently encounter preeminent Islamic, socialist, and nationalist ideas in development plans, approaches that to the U.S. policymakers usually seem heretical to the building of a modern state integrated into a global market economy.[30] Obstacles are most regularly thrown up in the Egyptian bureaucracy to the promotion of private sector investment.[31] Therefore, any policy dialogue with "Nasserist" officials is inevitably slow and is likely to become antagonistic.

AID officials more often express their inability to detect among the Egyptians a coherent economic vision or systematic plan, whether ideological or practical. Officials in the ministries are perceived as having little conception of development aside from what seems to be a "resource view." Where U.S. advisors tend to see problems of implementing projects in terms of administrative determination and skills, their Egyptian counterparts seem to feel that most objectives can be realized by getting the United States or other donors to furnish more resources. This notion of development has during much of the history of the program expressed itself in "build us this."

The consequences of an absence of agreement about objectives in aid projects are often serious. When goals are left too broad or vague, the project implementor, usually a contractor, lacks direction and authority. Attempts to incorporate the separate agendas of Egypt and the United States in the same project normally lead to a design that is unable to integrate or prioritize aims adequately. At other times, designs left vague offer no clear basis for implementation in their wide interpretations.[32] The resulting slow progress on many projects breeds further disappointment and distrust. Although some of the differences, substantive, conceptual, and procedural, cannot be easily resolved, failures of communication between the two bureaucracies and their parallel operating components very often exaggerate disagreements.

As the primary deliverers of technical services and providers of managerial supervision for development projects, private U.S. contractors are a common source of friction in the aid relationship. Most U.S. advisors and firms, though AID funded, are directly employed by an Egyptian ministry or agency in a "host-country contract."[33] Although AID reserves for itself the right to advise ministries on selecting and negotiating with U.S. experts and firms, and specifies what can and cannot be done under the aid agreement, most contractors have no direct contact with AID officials in Cairo. In fact, often neither AID, the contractors, nor the Egyptian government are certain about the extent of the mission's responsibility for assisting or monitoring AID-funded projects.[34]

The mission assigns a project committee and project manager who are only expected to backstop and monitor the contractor's relations with the government. This arrangement is designed to give Egyptian authorities ultimate responsibility for implementing projects and to improve opportunities for the transfer of technical, institutional, and administrative skills. The mission's monitoring of the progress of projects is, however, not as a rule systematic, and much is left to the project officer's individual initiative. A lack of staff may explain insufficient monitoring. A 1984 report found that the existing staff was overburdened. Only 15 AID mission direct-hire personnel were said to be responsible for overseeing the activities of about 140 contractors involved with direct and host-country contracts/projects.[35]

The AID bureaucracies in Cairo and Washington are frequently critical of their own contractors. Audits have found that aid funds have not always been efficiently or effectively used. Washington investigators have turned up inept project administration and budget accounting problems. Some of the most serious accusations are leveled against university contractors whose recruitment difficulties are alleged to have failed to provide the expertise necessary to implement projects.[36] Other studies have concluded that despite the limited size of the Cairo mission, its staff could probably assume greater responsibility for some programs, as, for example, when contractors are assigned to explain AID's own rules and regulations to Egyptian administrators. Yet U.S. domestic pressures preclude letting the Egyptians use aid dollars for non-U.S. exports and suppliers.[37] AID remains reluctant to contract with Egyptian engineering or architectural firms whose reliability and capacity the mission still questions.

Washington has throughout the aid program rejected the idea of a largely turnkey approach to aid where local bureaucratic and political constraints are presumably avoided by handing over completed projects, managed and built entirely by U.S. personnel, to the Egyptian government. It has always been a stated purpose of U.S. development aid that it transfer managerial skills and share responsibility with the recipient country's development bureaucracy. Yet AID in Egypt has showed little interest in going the next step by gaining authorization under the Federal Procurement Regulations for a system used in several other aided countries that transfers broader responsibility—reimbursing recipients (with dollars buying local currency) for projects completed by them within a specified time period. The reimbursable or voucher schemes can reduce or eliminate competitive bidding and most U.S. procurement requirements and construction specifications. Whatever the legal and political reasons for hesitating to go forward with these approaches in Egypt, there is most of all a continuing lack of confidence by U.S. officials that local contractors and the Egyptian ministries have the skills and motivation to go it alone. Indeed, in the mission's frustration about multiple contractor coordination and manpower problems, officials had in the early 1980s opted in several projects, including the rehabilitation of Aswan Dam turbines and Cairo water activities, for turnkey contracts with U.S. firms.

There is much in Cairo that is reminiscent of the heady days of economic expansion in the Shah's Iran. (Not that anything can compare with the free spending of the oil boom years after 1973 and, of course, AID's program had ended in Iran years earlier.) The sheer number of U.S. and other foreign firms, most of them involved in large capital projects, makes for obvious comparison. So, too, do the motives of the expatriot advisors and technicians. For every conscientious firm under contract there appeared to be many more with no apparent interest in the country or its problems—aside from making a quick profit. Indeed, the incentives of high salaries and opportunities to promote their company's programs were sufficient in themselves to guarantee participation—successful results from the project often seemed only incidental.

The relations between Egyptian officials and the personnel of many of the U.S.-contracted firms are often acrimonious. Each side blames the other for project delays. U.S. contractors are quick to point out the poor work values and the corruption they find among their Egyptian counterparts and credit official inertia with most of the responsibility for project delays. The low morale found among Egyptians working on projects is frequently a result of the Cairo government's personnel policies and failure to deliver on promised salary incentives. Egyptians, aside from resenting the higher salaries and generous allowances given U.S. consultants, complain about the lack of relevance of the foreigners' experiences to conditions in Egypt. Sometimes, as in the major cereals project, they directly question the contractor's expertise.[38]

At times, the Egyptians have had difficulty in attracting and retaining qualified private U.S. contractors. Whether a result of the well-known frustrations of living in Cairo, reports of haggling with Egyptian counterparts, profit margins, or the competitive bidding system itself, the United States has not always offered first-rate professionals or technical advisors to Egypt. People who could be passed off as experts elsewhere in the Third World may not win the respect of their more technologically sophisticated Egyptian colleagues. No doubt the objections raised to U.S. advisors is at times simply bureaucratic jealousy and national pride. But at least for some projects where AID provides the funding and prescribes the source of contract personnel, U.S. companies may not compare well with other countries in providing the kinds of models, training, or experienced personnel that Egypt requires.

Egyptians express considerable irritation about being forced to engage U.S. firms when they believe they could stretch their AID dollars further by having the option to contract with other foreign experts and suppliers or use their own. Some critics contend that U.S. firms frequently raise the price of services and goods when AID is the source of funding. The very process of selecting contractors is considered too time consuming and is seen as a major cause of funds being held up in the aid pipeline. To many Egyptian officials, AID appears as an agency whose function is to steer contracts to U.S. firms. Indeed, there are examples of AID loans and grants materializing only when Egyptians, using their own budgetary resources, were about to close a deal with a European firm. Egyptian officials complain that the advice given by outsiders too often runs at cross purposes with the bureaucracy's own plans and priorities.

Conclusion

Students of foreign aid often note how the missionary zeal is gone from U.S. aid programs worldwide. They observe that idealistic, enthusiastic program administrators have increasingly given way to lackluster aid bureaucrats who seem most adept at minimizing risks and following regulations.[39] Economic assistance to Egypt, commencing when it has and in the proportions it has, understandably draws such criticisms, and this study lends support to many of these conclusions. However, the fault probably lies less in the quality of U.S. personnel, many of whom are individually dedicated and hard working, than in an aid process that constrains their actions and stifles initiative, and with an Egyptian system whose bureaucratic inertia leaves them frustrated and cynical.

U.S. advisors and their Egyptian counterparts have come to expect that underlying cultural and bureaucratic differences will create interpersonal stresses. In some respects, mutual trust has improved since the first years of the program, and close working relationships between individuals have formed during the years. But even as the two have come to better understand one another, the dialogue has also grown tougher. Through most of the 1970s the Egyptians looked upon AID as a gift-giver and nodded approval to almost everything offered. Officials often took the attitude that donors should decide how they want to spend their own money. During recent years, the government has insisted on being a more active partner in the process. Increased centralization of contacts with aid donors in a strengthened economic management structure in the early 1980s encouraged ministries to become more attentive to project details and to exercize more scrutiny about how funds were being used. Ministries have shown concern for the effectiveness and impact of programs and the possibility of foreign aid altering their priorities and restricting their development choices.

More independent attitudes among higher level Egyptian officials negotiating for U.S. aid are perhaps best revealed by the increasing tendency to offer competing proposals to those initiated by AID. During 1984, Egypt, which must concur in the use of U.S. funds slated for project development and used to pay consultants, refused to release these funds and deliberately courted delay in authorizing projects. These same officials have waited, moreover, often until the eleventh hour, before agreeing to accept U.S. funds when the terms have been other than those preferred. These more forceful attitudes cannot be divorced from Egypt's sense of having new political options and its need to demonstrate its freedom of choice during a time when popular and elite disapproval of U.S. foreign policy in the region is on the upswing.

A common refrain is that Egypt, as a Middle East country, must follow its own development course. There exists considerable nationalist appeal in this notion and some factual basis for the view that Egypt's historical and ecological context calls for solutions that are somewhat distinctive. Nonetheless, the models of development that Egypt's governments adopted after 1973 and that continued into the 1980s rest on Western concepts of the primacy of economic growth, even while retaining a commitment to social responsibility. The only limited success in absorbing these liberal economic ideals and giving them application has been defined in this chapter as, in part, the result of shortcomings in the Egyptian bureaucracy and its U.S. aid benefactors. In some respects, borrowed concepts and technologies have proven inappropriate. Yet Egypt is for the time being likely to continue basing its development plans on strategies prescribed by the West and to use imported indices to gauge progress. Ironically, the success Egypt achieves may depend on the emergence of patterns uncharacteristic of Egypt—greater local and sectoral decentralization and greater citizen participation. For although the historic concentration of authority at the center has no doubt been critical to an Egyptian civilization and inspired political leadership at the top remains indispensable, administrative inflexibility and overcentralization are probably the most serious obstacles today to the initiation and management of change. Experimentation in local governance and increased popular involvement in decisionmaking should lead to development programs more sensitive to people's needs and more efficient use of the country's domestic resources and foreign aid.

Notes

1. AID employed approximately 5,400 people in the early 1980s, with operations in 60 countries.

2. William Sommers, "Rescuing AID," *Foreign Service Journal*, Vol. 59, no. 5 (May 1982): 16.

3. Martin Tolchin, "The Role of 'Barnacles' in Foreign Aid," *The New York Times*, July 5, 1983.

4. U.S. Agency for International Development, Cairo, "Questions and Answers on AID Program," a paper distributed by the mission in Cairo, November 1981, p. 7.

5. Jennifer Seymour Whitaker, "Cairo: They Don't Miss Sadat," *Atlantic Monthly* (January 1982): 17.

6. There are, to be sure, ingenious ways to avoid requirements. In one case, after an Egyptian request to build a laboratory to produce an urgently needed vaccine that would take years to construct according to U.S. specifications, an arrangement was worked out where AID furnished (in a nonproject designation) the necessary "commodities" for the laboratory, channeling them through a private voluntary organization.

7. U.S. Agency for International Development, "Near East Reviews, Staff Utilization Report for Egypt," September 12, 1984, cited in U.S. General Accounting Office, "The U.S. Economic Assistance Program for Egypt Poses a Management Challenge for AID," Report to the Administrator of the Agency for International Development, July 31, 1985, p. 8.

8. Ibid., p. 9.

9. Even the Department of Health and Human Services and the National Science Foundation can apply pressure, as in early 1984 when they pressed the mission to provide funds in order to replace the now depleted P.L. 480 Special Fund that had supported science and technology research in Egypt since 1961.

10. U.S. Agency for International Development, "Administrator's Message to Employees on the State of the Agency," Office of the Administrator, March 2, 1984, p. 24. The administrator argued that the Washington office should be involved in developing policy and strategies, assuring project consistency with these objectives, and evaluating the portfolio performance by the mission. The field mission was expected to work with the host country in designing the implementing projects, ensuring their technical feasibility, and making adjustments in projects with the changing conditions.

11. By law, the Department of State is charged with providing the political and security justification for Egypt's qualification for the ESF category of foreign aid and for helping to establish the amount needed to meet this objective.

The U.S. Agency for International Development is, of course, a component unit of the Department of State. However, the AID administrator in Washington reports directly to the secretary of state. The formal bureaucratic structure also obscures the extent to which AID, with its traditionally separate identity, is able to set its own agenda and have its personnel assume a different professional perspective from others in the foreign service community.

12. For a discussion see Marvin G. Weinbaum, *Food, Development, and Politics in the Middle East* (Boulder, Colo.: Westview Press, 1982), pp. 96–101.

13. Nazih N. M. Ayubi, *Bureaucracy and Politics in Contemporary Egypt* (London: Ithaca Press, 1980), pp. 479–499.

14. Elia H. Tuma, "IBM: A Non-Development Model of the Egyptian Economy," an unpublished paper, p. 11.

15. Middle East Center, University of Pennsylvania, "Conference on Policies and Strategies of USAID in Egypt," January 18–20, 1978, p. 16.

16. Ayubi, *Bureaucracy and Politics*, p. 507.

17. Tuma, "IBM," p. 28. The starting salary for a government employee with a college degree runs less than $750 a year. A minister may earn no more than $2,500 yearly.

18. U.S. Agency for International Development, "Country Development Strategy Statement, FY 1984, Annex: Agricultural Prices," February 1982, p. 54.

19. Timothy Curtin, "An Appraisal of the USAID/USDA Report on Agricultural Development in Egypt," unpublished report, Cairo, Egypt, 1983, p. 8.

20. U.S. Agency for International Development, "Country Development Strategy Statement, FY 1984, Annex: Agricultural Prices," p. 52.

21. U.S. Department of Agriculture, "Egyptian Agriculture and the U.S. Assistance Program," Office of International Cooperation and Development, Technical Assistance Report, no. 2, June 1979, p. 25.

22. Ibid.

23. Objections raised to U.S. programs are frequently highly personal. The perceived obstructionism of one Egyptian minister was alleged by AID officials to have resulted from his failure to win a AID-funded contract. Key Egyptian officials have in recent years often seemed to obstruct the agreement process in an effort to demonstrate their personal authority as well as to remind the United States that Egyptians can still be masters in their own house.

24. The ministry was abolished in July 1984 at the time of the appointment of a new prime minister. International cooperation became a responsibility of the Ministry of Planning, which was renamed the Ministry of Planning and International Cooperation. Investment authority was shifted to the Ministry of Economy and Foreign Trade.

25. U.S. General Accounting Office, *U.S. Assistance to Egyptian Agriculture: Slow Progress After Five Years* (Washington, D.C., March 1981), p. 51.

26. Ibid., p. 40.

27. Ayubi, *Bureaucracy and Politics*, p. 500.

28. Monte Palmer and Ali Laila, "Innovation and Development: The Case of the Egyptian Bureaucracy," a paper delivered at the 17th Annual Meeting of the Middle East Studies Association, Chicago, Illinois, November 3–6, 1983, p. 5.

29. See the discussion by Stanley F. Reed, "Dateline Cairo: Shaken Pillar," *Foreign Policy*, no. 45 (Winter 1981-82): 177.

30. U.S. Agency for International Development, "Country Development Strategy Statement, FY 1985, Annex C: Development Administration Constraints to AID's Work in Egypt," February 1983, p. C4.

31. A case in point is the attempt to get the Egyptians to encourage fertilizer imports through the private sector. Citing the goal of increased agricultural production under the "self-help" provision of P.L. 480 legislation, AID officials have prodded the Cairo government to break its monopoly on imports and rein in those pro-public sector officials in the bureaucracy intent on undermining the government's stated commitment to expanding private sector activity.

32. U.S. Agency for International Development, "Country Development Strategy Statement, FY 1985, Annex C," pp. C2–C3.

33. There are two types of host-country contracts. One is a contract for the delivery of commodities under AID's Commodity Import Program. Eligible commodities are listed by AID, and Egypt identifies those it wishes to purchase. Foreign exchange is made available by AID. The second type, and the kind mainly of interest here, is a host-country contract for goods and services intended for AID-financed projects. For purchases by Egypt, AID contract officers in Cairo and Washington draw up project tenders for U.S. bidders. These tenders are then advertised in the Commerce Department's *Business Daily*.

34. U.S. General Accounting Office, *U.S. Assistance to Egyptian Agriculture*, p. 40.

35. U.S. General Accounting Office, "The U.S. Economic Assistance Program Poses a Management Challenge for AID," a report to the administrator, Agency for International Development, July 31, 1985, p. 24.

36. U.S. General Accounting Office, *U.S. Assistance to Egyptian Agriculture*, pp. 45–49.

37. When no U.S. producer or only a single firm exists, as in the manufacture of motorcycles, one AID agricultural development proposal illustrates a familiar way to circumvent the requirement. Extension workers in need of transport were to get an allowance that would enable them to buy any brand on credit arranged themselves.

38. U.S. General Accounting Office, *U.S. Assistance to Egyptian Agriculture*, p. 19.

39. Elliott R. Morss and Victoria A. Morss, *U.S. Foreign Aid: An Assessment of New and Traditional Development Strategies* (Boulder, Colo.: Westview Press, 1982), p. 105.

6

Aid and Policy Reform

Egypt has undergone considerable economic change during the period since 1974. As Chapter Two describes, Anwar Sadat's *Infitah* sought a decisive reorientation in political-economic strategy, even if it fell far short of its goal to restructure the economy and assure its growth. The liberalizing tendencies in Egypt were established despite an economic management that remains highly centralized and reluctant to abdicate to market forces. Nowhere is this contradiction more apparent than in the commitment of Egyptian governments to the underpricing of consumption. In keeping faith with still popular socialist legacies of the Nasser era, Egyptian authorities steadily increased subsidies on basic commodities and services and maintained price stabilizing policies. These consumer-shielding measures helped in the early 1980s to revive a balance-of-payments and budgetary problem. In the absence of new sources of national income, the heavy public expenditures to cover subsidies cut deeply into resources for investment. Direct and indirect food and energy subsidies were also held responsible for the improper signaling of investment choices in both industry and agriculture.

The real growth projected at 8.1 percent in Egypt's Five Year Plan (1982/83–1986/87) was predicated on fundamental economic reforms that would, above all, spawn a more competitive export sector and new sources of foreign exchange. Yet prospects seem dim for corrections in budgetary and fiscal policies in general and for major adjustments in the structure of pricing and subsidies in particular. Slowness to reform is not unexpected where so many have benefited from income transfers, and the probable political costs of change are more immediate and incalculable than the anticipated economic benefits. A weak, unreformed economy may eventually, however, undermine Egypt's commitment to minimal consumption levels for its citizens and make aid inflows even more crucial to the country's economic stability. Meanwhile, foreign aid can play a role in helping to promote new policies as well as in sustaining older ones.

The Dimensions and Magnitude of Subsidies

Pricing and subsidy policies are critical and sensitive issues in the Egyptian economy.[1] Consumer prices for a wide range of basic commodities and services are held down by the government through a system of direct and indirect subsidies and controlled marketing channels. The subsidies for food cover to some degree all the items considered basic to the Egyptian diet, including bread, beans, lentils, refined sugar, rice, tea, cooking oil, red meats, chicken, and fish. Even some foodstuffs not designated as basic, such as margarine and sesame, and such nonfood items as soap and cotton fabric, are sold at artificially low prices. Aside from bread, restrictions apply to consumer access to all subsidized food. Sugar, tea, cooking oil, rice, and other items are rationed and available at their low, fixed prices only at consumer cooperatives and government-owned shops.[2] Consumers are also subsidized through the considerable underpricing of public transportation and utilities, especially electricity. Gasoline and other petroleum-based products are marketed substantially below market value as well. In addition to subsidies, the government has tried to control overall consumer costs through low procurement prices for certain agricultural crops and through rent and credit controls.

Allocations for all direct or explicit consumer subsidies for 1984-85 were at the equivalent of about $2.5 billion in a central government budget approaching $22 billion.[3] But with indirect and unbudgeted food and energy costs included, the actual magnitude of subsidies is far greater. Direct food subsidies are the difference between what the government pays, for example, for the purchase and handling of wheat and flour internationally, or the amount it pays Egyptian farmers (usually much lower than the import price), and the price at which these commodities are sold to bakers who, in turn, sell bread for regulated prices in shops. Indirect food subsidies include such expenditures as those for farm inputs. Together, direct and indirect food subsidies ran to just under $3 billion in 1984. Indirect energy subsidies for fuel and electricity are found in the reduced input prices that result in lowering production costs of goods and services. The costs to the government represent the differences between the price of energy for local consumption and the opportunity costs to the Egyptian economy based on their export sales value. Added to explicit subsidies for electricity, gasoline, kerosene, and butagas, the full underwriting of energy is figured at $4 billion or more.[4] Not only were these along with food subsidies a $7 billion burden on the national budget but, in the case of food, every 10 percent rise in government expenditures for subsidies, other things being equal, was estimated to bring a 5 percent increase in the inflation rate and a 2 percent decline in the country's balance of payments.[5]

To understand why the current subsidy system has become so extensive and expensive requires an historical perspective that reveals changing domestic priorities and international conditions. Government intervention to keep domestic prices of wheat in short supply from rising sharply first occurred in the aftermath of the World War I. Consumer rationing and subsidies, designed to assist lower income people in purchasing basic commodities, began with wartime scarcities in 1945. But the amount allocated at the time for subsidies was modest, less than L.E. 1 million.[6]

The Free Officers who seized power in 1952 were said to be politically innocent, without a clear ideology and any notion of what to do or how to do it. They were, of course, first and foremost a closely knit band of military professionals who were only marginally, if at all, connected with any political party. Michael Hudson observes that, in fact, "they proved to be consummate politicians."[7] Soon after coming to power they destroyed both the right and left wing opposition in the country and "were able to fashion, in bits and pieces, a set of positions [that] preempted their rivals and touched a responsive chord in the Egyptian people."[8]

Although transnational symbols became important later on, the initial thrust of the Free Officers' appeal was domestic. The corruption of the monarchy and the failure of the previous governments to reduce socio-economic disparities were conditions that lent themselves to political exploitation. Domestic reform was uppermost among the priorities of the new government. Its first major act was land reform. These and later interventions in the economy were designed, on one hand, to further the new regime's strongly felt but undeveloped sense of social justice, and, on the other, to undercut the influence of members of the old political and economic elite. The trend toward increasing government intervention culminating in the socialist decrees of 1961 has been seen by many observers as pragmatic, incremental responses to circumstances as they unfolded.

Throughout the 1950s, the costs of subsidies in the government budget did not rise steeply and by 1960 totaled only about L.E. 9 million, going mainly for wheat and rationed kerosene and sugar. The nationalization and centralization of Egypt's economy that began in earnest in 1960-61 under Nasser's first Five Year Plan sought to contain consumption as a principal means to provide resources needed for development. Although also committed to income redistribution, this strategy was pursued through raising taxes and establishing social insurance schemes rather than through commodity subsidies. The government efforts to help insulate Egypt from sharp swings in international grain prices rationalized the small subsidies for wheat and served as much as a subsidy to Egyptian producers as to urban consumers.[9] The country was assured, in any case, adequate, affordable food supplies during the first half of the 1960s and spared heavy outlays of foreign exchange, a savings in large part due to the U.S. P.L. 480 program that provided agricultural products through highly concessional financing.

Ample grain supplies were less certain after a politically peeved United States reduced and then finally cut off its food program to Egypt in late 1966. Rising domestic prices and a weakening economy forced the Nasser government during this period to restructure its rationing system, which now covered many basic but mostly unsubsidized commodities. Because welfare policies such as rent controls and minimum wage levels had improved the real income of most Egyptians of modest economic means, there had been no need for a major expansion in the scope of subsidies. But the defeat in the 1967 War, which Nasser survived largely through his own charisma and effective internal security, exposed grave cracks in the legitimacy of this regime. In the face of a subsequent failure to do anything to reestablish national self-respect, Nasser had to tread carefully. One of the decisions taken was to prevent rising prices from becoming a source of resentment. The infrastructure for price control was already in place, and it was in the aftermath of the war that subsidies were firmly if, by later standards, still modestly established. By 1969-70, the budget appropriations for subsidies on commodities had grown to L.E. 11.6 million, of which nearly all went to support consumption of edible oils and bread.[10] To the end of the Nasser years, then, the regime had succeeded without great cost in stabilizing food prices, even if supplies were short at times. In doing so, it also instilled the idea that Egyptian governments would be committed to cheaply priced food, a popular expectation that could threaten domestic stability should it go unmet.

Sadat was unable to exert the same personal magnetism as Nassar had, and in the initial period of his rule, when he had still not won the power struggle within the Arab Socialist Union, Sadat tried to avoid making decisions or letting inflation become rampant. Also, in the aftermath of the 1967 War, the old issues, mainly ideological in nature, around which political factions used to gather, were replaced increasingly by concerns about the standard of living as the economy deteriorated. The 1973 War brought Sadat the kind of power and popularity that Nasser had, but only for a short while. Real increases in prices of subsidized goods occurred immediately after the war, and Sadat chose to let the state take over the burden.

Subsidies became a problem of crisis proportions beginning in 1973. Poor wheat harvests worldwide had already pushed up sharply the costs of grain imports before the 1973 War, and rounds of OPEC price hikes in the months following the conflict found their way into everything imported, including food. Subsidies for food had stood at about L.E. 11 million in 1972. Within a year, the figure jumped to L.E. 89 million and then leaped to L.E. 329 million in 1974.[11] Per capita expenditures on food subsidies rose from L.E. 1.8 (in constant Egyptian pounds) during 1967–1969 to L.E. 11.2 per capita by 1973–1975.[12] Subsidy costs for wheat and flour alone were up 174 percent. Even without substantial increases in the volume of imports, the cost of trying to insulate the Egyptian consumer from the impact of global inflation had become a heavy burden on Egyptian government finances. In the space of a single year, from 1973 to 1974, food subsidies as a share of total current expenditures rose from 7.6 percent to 23.3 percent.[13]

Policies pursued during the rest of the decade must be viewed in the context of Sadat's economic liberalization and its goal to attract Western and Arab capital, both private and government. If successful, *Infitah*, along with the economic dividends promised from peace with Israel, could create a new climate for private investment, increase employment, and, with higher productivity, generally raise the society's standard of living. Meanwhile, subsidies to protect the consumer were seen by the regime as a necessary price for keeping the urban population in particular patient and peaceful. Any doubts about the wisdom of this approach were dispelled by the urban food riots of January 1977 when, at the insistence of the IMF, the government tried to reduce some food and energy subsidies (see below). After the Camp David accord, the increase in domestic political opposition ruled out a serious effort to reform the subsidy system.

In spite of rising world wheat prices during the late 1970s, the government was spared from having to dig deeply into its meager hard currency holdings by generous U.S. P.L. 480 sales, resumed in 1975. Even so, the costs of direct food subsidies alone rose from L.E. 450 million in 1978 to L.E. 880 million in 1979 according to official sources and just over L.E. 1 billion according to unofficial ones (see Table 6.1).[14] Per capita expenditures rose to an average of L.E. 20 during the years 1979–1981.[15] Much of this substantial change reflected the gradual devaluation of the Egyptian pound, by 56 percent, that increased import costs. Since 1979, the fiscal losses due to subsidies for food and energy have continued an upward spiral. Aside from more costly imports and a further devaluation in 1981, this largely uncontrolled growth arises from decreased domestic production of some subsidized items coupled with an expanded demand for imported products, labeled the "new consumerism," that has come with higher real incomes in some segments of the Egyptian population.

TABLE 6.1
Summary of Egypt's Food and Energy Subsidy in 1979 (L.E. Million)[a]

		Urban	Rural	Total
I. Food (All Direct)		1,019	0	1,019
	A. Wheat	590	0	590
	B. Oil	200	0	200
	C. Sugar	44	0	44
	D. Meat	44	0	44
	E. Other	141	0	141
II. Energy		1,171	725	1,896
1. Direct		569	243	812
	A. Kerosene	163	176	340
	B. Butagas	82	7	89
	C. Electricity	199	24	222
	D. Gasoline	125	36	160
2. Indirect		602	483	1,085
	A. Fuel	472	378	850
	B. Electricity	130	105	235[b]
III. Total[c]		2,190	725	2,915

[a]The exchange value of the Egyptian pound was 1 L.E. = $.69 in 1980.

[b]Does not include L.E. 54 million estimated indirect electricity subsidy provided in the production of exported aluminum.

[c]Totals may not add due to rounding.

Source: U.S. Agency for International Development, "Egypt's Food and Energy Subsidies in 1979" (Cairo, 1981), p. 13.

Distributive Inequities

During the 1970s, Egypt's food and energy subsidies and accompanying price controls came to serve as a means of supporting and stimulating consumption among *all* Egypt's economic groups. Whatever the initial social welfare objectives, the system went well beyond putting more buying power into the hands of the lowest income groups. To be sure, the increasingly expensive subsidies, even if not primarily aimed at improving nutrition in the society, did ensure that no part of the population would suffer malnutrition or hunger through a lack of access to food. Though health problems in Egypt abound, most result from poor sanitation and impure water. Low, stable prices for bread, sugar, and rice, among other commodities, has meant a sufficient caloric intake for even the poorest Egyptians, a portion of the society that spends more than one-half of its meager income for the purchase of food. Indeed, Egypt's average of 3,500 calories per day ranks it with countries having per capita incomes up to twice as high.[16]

The actual distributional effects leave no doubt, all the same, that the subsidies were not designed as a system of income transfers for the most needy. Ration cards required to buy most subsidized items are available to urban households regardless of income. That these subsidies had become significant increments to the buying power of every income category is evident in a 1981 study by AID economists.[17] In examining the distribution of the 1979 subsidies, it found that food and energy subsidies were critical, as expected, for urban households at the lower end, those expending less than L.E. 778 and L.E. 1,114 yearly (see Table 6.2). For these categories, which make up more than 50 percent of the urban population, the subsidies represent, on average, roughly one-half of all their household outlays. Food and energy subsidies for the next 28.5 percent, the middle class in terms of expenditures, accounted for nearly 42 percent of their household spending; and for the top group, with expenditures of more that L.E. 1,783, subsidies constituted one-third, most of it going toward energy costs. Even if, as a more recent estimate finds, most Egyptians now receive closer to 30 percent of their real incomes in subsidies, any reduction in subsidies without compensating wage increases or offsetting income transfers would still be devastating to the lower income groups.[18] Cuts would also bring a substantial deterioration in the living standards of much of the rest of the urban population. Controlled prices on key commodities are especially important to government employees and other middle-income groups that during the 1970s suffered most in the inflation that accompanied Egypt's economic liberalization.

An examination of the 1979 data also indicates that the poor receive disproportionately less from the subsidy system than Egypt's economically better-off citizens. The bottom half of the urban population, those with yearly household expenditures under L.E. 1,114 in Table 6.2, receive only about 43.8 percent of the value of the food subsidies going into wheat, wheat flour, and other items. The lowest category, with expenditures less than L.E. 779, moreover, share in 21.7 percent of the subsidies with 26.6 percent of the population. At the same time, the two highest expenditure groups together take more than 56 percent of the subsidies, and the 21.2 percent of Egyptians in the category with more than L.E. 1,783, most of the urban middle class, did proportionately best with 27.1 percent of the subsidies. This group's share of subsidies in oils, fats, and meat was especially large. No doubt the easier access of the higher expenditure group to subsidized food is a major reason for the

TABLE 6.2
Distribution in the Urban Sector by Household Expenditure Class of Egypt's 1979 Food and Energy Subsidy (in percentages)

Household Expenditure Class (L.E./yr)[a]	Urban Population Distribution	Subsidies as a Percent of Expenditures			Distribution as a Percent of Subsidy		
		Food	Energy	Total	Food	Energy	Total
0-778	26.6	28.5	23.4	51.9	21.7	15.5	18.4
779-1113	23.7	25.5	24.0	49.5	22.1	18.1	19.9
1114-1782	28.5	20.1	21.6	41.7	29.2	27.1	28.1
1783+	21.2	12.5	20.8	33.3	27.1	39.3	33.6

[a]The exchange rate was 1 L.E. = $.69 in 1980.

Source: U.S. Agency for International Development, "Egypt's Food and Energy Subsidies in 1979" (Cairo, 1981), p. 3A.

disparity. For example, these households may be able to send servants to the market to wait on the long lines for government sold items. Wealthier individuals often offer *baksheesh* (small bribes) for preferential treatment by shop clerks and, with their ready cash, can take advantage of gluts in normally scarce, rationed commodities.[19]

A skewed distribution among urban households is more pronounced for energy subsidies. Whereas the lowest 50 percent, those expending less than L.E. 1,114 (see Table 6.2) received together just 33.6 percent of the value of the subsidy for electricity, kerosene, gasoline, and butagas, and the next 28.5 percent of the population accounted for 27.1 percent, the highest 21.2 percent captured more than 39.3 percent of the total energy subsidy. With food and energy taken together, the top 21.2 percent took away almost 33.6 percent of the total value of subsidies, and 18.4 percent went to the bottom 26.6 percent of urban households. The differences are of course particularly curious for what is intended to be a progressive policy of income transfers.

Striking disparities have also prevailed in the distribution of food and energy subsidies between Egypt's urban and rural populations. About 75 percent of the subsidy is estimated to have gone in 1979 to residents of Cairo and Alexandria.[20] In the AID study's findings, none of the direct food subsidy, then L.E. 1 billion, went outside the urban areas, and only 37 percent of the energy subsidies were absorbed in the countryside—which contains more than 50 percent of Egypt's total population (see Table 6.1). Often those in the rural areas pay half again as much for subsidized items as city residents. Thus, if subsidies represented in all a 41 percent addition to household expenditures of urban families in 1979, the effective income transfers were far less for Egypt's rural population.[21]

The benefits available to urban consumers through government pricing and subsidies policies are believed to be a major factor in the migration of rural populations to Egypt's cities. Food subsidies expressed in the form of low prices are attractive to those initially seeking jobs in the cities or trying to get by until more satisfactory employment is found. The subsidies thus bear some of the responsibility for agricultural labor shortages, stagnant production, and increased food imports. It is to these kinds of impact on the domestic economy that the discussion now turns. The high economic stakes in the subsidies for certain economic groups in the cities also figure, as we will see, in the forms of political action they are prepared to engage in to protect their interests.

Distortions in the Economy

The long-term trends in Egypt's economy are not especially bright. As already noted, the country's deficits on current accounts are again rising along with government budget deficits, and there are disquieting signs in the growth of the money supply and external debt. If subsidies appear a logical target for reductions, it is probably because so much else in the government's outlays, including defense, are even less touchable. As it stands, Egypt must not only find ways to finance present subsidies for consumption and the operation of public enterprises but must find the means to cover the increases in costs inevitable in continuing these policies. Funds for the subsidies on food and energy can only come from transfers from other sectors of the economy, in earned foreign exchange, or through external assistance. The diversion of scarce resources in order to hold down prices obviously comes at the expense of investment opportunities in industry and agriculture. The consumption-oriented policies act, then, as an open-ended drain on funds needed for the kind of cost-effective investment that Egypt requires to expand production and promote sufficient and efficient employment for an expanding urban labor force.

Food and energy subsidies compound the country's financial problems in other ways. The subsidizing of commodities that helps to ease the burden of higher prices to consumers also results in a stimulation of demand that, in turn, brings the need for still more subsidy financing and the use of scarce foreign exchange for costly imports. Annual per capita wheat consumption rose by more than 110 percent between 1960 and 1980, making Egyptians one of the world's largest wheat consumers. The consumption of sugar was growing in the early 1980s by 11 percent annually as the general rates of food consumption in the country were rising by as much as 8 percent a year.[22] The subsidization of meat in the cities is credited with the sharp jump in recent years in poultry consumption, costing the government more than $100 million annually. Low energy prices are linked to the overconsumption of oil and the consequent losses incurred to Egypt's most valuable export commodity. Internal consumption of petroleum grew by an average of 11 percent annually between 1974 and 1983, and more than 35 percent of oil production was being diverted during the early 1980s to domestic use.[23] Overall domestic energy consumption rose by 15 percent in 1984. Rather than encouraging conservation of electricity, artificially low prices that are one-fifth of what a free-market price would be, no doubt stimulate inefficient consumption. Subsidies of basic commodities serve, moreover, as implicit transfers of income, in raising demand for other, nonrationed items. Upward market pressures result in price increases in these noncontrolled goods and demands among the middle-income groups for more luxury goods than Egyptian production may be able to meet quantitatively or qualitatively. Subsidies that were intended to insulate consumers from inflation force the government to engage in deficit financing that, together with other factors, in fact also fuels inflation.[24]

Efforts to minimize the public costs of urban consumer subsidies result in the kind of discrimination against agriculture so familiar in the Third World.[25] This bias in Egypt takes the form of an indirect tax on the sector: The farmer is effectively prevented from receiving the border price for his production of several key crops, of which cotton is the most important and conspicious. By one estimate, low farm prices amount to a tax equivalent of 40 to 50 percent on agriculture which, when reduced by the input subsidies going to farmers, leaves as much as a net 30 percent loss to the sector.[26] The low, fixed prices offered farmers, enforced by annual cropping plans and mandatory procurements, make it inevitable that producers shift where they can to other crops in high demand but outside the price controls and quotas.[27] Much of the shift has been to fodder crops at the expense of Egypt's highly remunerative, hard currency earning cotton production. As a result of price distortions, for example, farmers have during the years sometimes used fertilizer allocated for cotton instead for vegetables and delayed cotton planting, settling for reduced yields in order to permit two or three cuttings of clover. In the 1983 cotton harvest, cotton was left standing in the fields because the official procurement price was so low that many farmers in the Nile Delta were unable to pay for the labor required for more than one of the three pickings.[28] Most Egyptian farmers find themselves, moreover, in no position or feel little incentive to take advantage of high yield producing techniques. With agricultural products thus denied the protection extended to many domestically manufactured goods, the terms of trade were turned solidly against agriculture, and the sector had great difficulty competing for investment and halting its labor outflow.

Another serious indictment against Egypt's cost/price structure is its effect in distorting industrial development. Prices set by government fiat, out of line with international prices, are believed to misdirect Egypt's resources. The wrong signals are sent for investment in industry (and agriculture), and chances are lost to build competitive production for either domestic or export markets. The subsidized energy prices that figure in production inputs and outputs lead to investments that are probably not cost-effective, thereby starving other areas for funds. Actual costs of production, including the low wages facilitated by food subsidies, are disguised, and the real profitability of industry is confused with its paper profitability. One study found that if Egypt exported the oil it used to produce electricity at its government-owned Nag Hamadi aluminum plant in upper Egypt, it could earn enough foreign exchange to import all the aluminum produced at the plant and pay the wages of all its workers.[29]

Inappropriate investment decisions based on low-cost energy often result in the favoring of capital-intensive strategies over labor-intensive ones, where the country's comparative advantage probably lies, and further aggravating Egypt's unemployment. On these grounds, increased mechanization in some industries may not always be economically or socially defensible. Moreover, because the growth of certain industries is predicated on consumption of cheaply priced petroleum products, Egypt's only limited proven resources cannot be ignored in long-term development planning. At the present rate of extraction, Egypt's oil is expected to last at most another fifteen years. If domestic consumption increases at the present rate, it is estimated that Egypt's exportable production will disappear by the early 1990s, and the country will be importing oil not long after.[30]

External Pressures on Economic Policies

The remarkable international transfers of capital and commodities to Egypt since 1974 can take much of the credit for the survival of pricing and subsidy policies. Put simply, without programs such as those offered by the United States, the Cairo government would have lacked the resources to sustain its consumption-oriented policies. U.S. P.L. 480 grain sales and the Commodity Import Program have, in particular, propped up the country's urban pricing system and allowed Egypt's economic planners to avoid facing the worsening problems in the food and agricultural sectors. No doubt, commodity aid postpones indefinitely the kinds of crises that might impel difficult economic reforms. The readiness of the United States and others to assist in financing Egypt's import food bill permitted authorities to meet the rapidly expanding costs of the subsidies program, especially when other external revenue sources were also flourishing in the late 1970s. Indeed, it is frequently charged that foreign aid exacerbated the very problems it was supposed to alleviate. Although a national bias against agriculture did not begin in 1974, increased deliveries on highly concessional terms of food sold at subsidized prices resulted in unfair competition for domestic producers.[31] The availability of reliable foreign supplies took the pressure off the government to raise prices paid to Egyptian farmers. The higher imports needed to compensate for subsequently discouraged domestic production brought additional foreign exchange burdens and a deepening food dependence.

The irony here is that so much international advice and pressure have been directed at Egypt to improve the efficiency of the subsidy system by limiting open-ended subsidies, trying to target needy groups, and instituting a means of regular price adjustments to reflect rising costs.[32] Ultimately, the aim has been to have authorities eliminate fixed prices and subsidies—moving domestic prices toward world ones. U.S. aid experts have long argued that badly flawed policies constrain economic growth and lower productivity, despite the stimuli of external aid. Moreover, inappropriate policies are said to undermine AID's development assistance. These assessments based on classic economic analyses have, as already discussed, coincided with the more general outlook in the Reagan administration that a linkage ought to exist between offers of capital assistance, commodity aid, and other programs, and a recipient country's readiness to undertake policy and/or institutional reforms. Officially at least, P.L. 480 sales are supposed to be predicated on a country's willingness through procurement pricing to create stronger agricultural incentives and its demonstration of favorable attitudes toward the private sector (e.g., as in fertilizer distribution).[33] As a condition for financing development, Washington argues that projects should also be designed for full cost-recovery through removal of government subsidies.

The contradiction both in calling for reform and underwriting prevailing economic policies has, of course, a political explanation. For all the contention that progress requires an economy geared to market forces, the United States refuses to withhold resources or to otherwise "get tough" with an Egyptian government whose importance as a recipient is measured primarily in strategic and geopolitical terms. After all, a friendly regime forced to implement radical changes might not survive; or Egyptian leaders, pushed too hard, could, however reluctantly, become alienated from the West. To deny P.L. 480 wheat would, besides damaging political ties, succeed in worsening Egypt's economy because the government would in all probability find it necessary to divert foreign exchange in order to buy additional wheat on commercial terms.[34] There is also sensitivity, in the official U.S. community in Cairo, that Egyptian policymakers who may agree with them on liberal economic principles must acknowledge and pursue goals of a noneconomic kind. Economists from the two sides appreciate the other's arguments and problems better than their public dialogue often suggests, even if they do not always feel free to advocate policies that fully satisfy one another. Where U.S. officials in Cairo and Washington have so far drawn the line is in their refusal to accede to Egyptian pleas for, in effect, a complete "blank check" form of aid in payment for political cooperation. They doubt that the government would be able to resist using funds normally earmarked for development activities for anything other than financing the pressing subsidies bill.

Plainly, the United States is unable to dictate policy changes. The symbolic importance of consumer subsidies as a token of official concern for economic justice necessarily limits the influence of foreign advisors. On those occasions when AID has used its leverage more aggressively, it has often looked foolish. The Reagan administration has, all the same, tried to move away from the cautious, nonconditional approach; the United States pushed Egypt hard, for example, to raise electricity tariffs to industry sufficient to recover recurring costs. When AID threatened to withhold funding for electrical generating projects and specifically the Abu Sultan hydroelectric plant, the Egyptians agreed to raise utility charges. Yet AID failed to specify how much of an electricity increase it would consider adequate. After U.S. officials complained about its size and demanded a further increase, the Egyptians reportedly felt misled.[35] In 1983, the United States, under its own pressure to obligate large dollar amounts to Egypt, in fact granted $100 million for the Abu Sultan project, and AID justified its decision by observing that the Egyptian leadership had at least tried to keep energy prices even with inflation. Similarly, the United States eventually gave in with a $100 million grant for water and wastewater projects after having admitted that reforms by the government were inadequate.[36]

As a practical matter, the United States finds itself in the position of continuing to encourage economic policy adjustments by supporting those inclinations to reform that already exist. Using more a carrot than a stick, American advisors are ready to support any changes, however incomplete, if they appear in the preferred direction. Most AID officials concede that they can provide at best the analytic capacity on which sound choices can be based and assist with financial and technical resources in implementing government decisions on reform. These advisors have been disappointed frequently enough by Egyptian government statements that reform is imminent. They are now unlikely to underestimate the obstacles posed by the public sector bureaucracy and other interests or the importance of adequate managerial expertise and policy-related data in developing and instituting reform.[37] It is now felt that even if full agreement with the Egyptian government on the desirable policy climate for aid were possible, the implementation of changes would be, at best, slow and uneven.[38]

It was under strong outside pressure that the most far-reaching single attempt to cut subsidies was made. Promoting his Open Door policies, President Sadat appointed Dr. Abdel Aziz Hegazi as prime minister in 1974; but in March 1975, he replaced him with Mamdouh Salem, a former policeman from Alexandria, with instructions to speed up the changes that Sadat wanted in the economy. Hegazi was removed following serious riots on New Year's Day 1975 during protests against the high cost of living and shortages of basic commodities. Security forces reacted swiftly to the riots, arresting hundreds of suspected dissidents. Several other violent strikes, similarily motivated, occurred in 1975 and the following year.

These outbreaks were minor compared to the riots that took place on January 18–19, 1977, when a clumsy effort by the government to restructure part of the economic apparatus put the Sadat regime in serious danger for thirty-six hours. The government had agreed to an IMF-sponsored economic reform package in which subsidies on many items were to be cut. Economic planners hoped to save L.E. 227 million, approximately 35 percent of the 1977 subsidy budget.[39] Both the United States and Saudi Arabia, Sadat's two main monetary backers, made it clear that meeting IMF conditions was a must if financial support were to continue at the required expanding level. On January 17, 1977, the government cut subsidies by more than L.E. 200 million. The following day prices of one type of bread as well as of tea, sugar, bottled gas, and many other items went up by from 10 to 60 percent. Overnight the cost of small luxuries increased dramatically. As news spread through Cairo and other cities, huge mobs took over the streets. Shopkeepers closed their shops while roaming gangs chanting anti-Sadat slogans smashed, burned, and looted. Passersby cheered them and, during the first day, Cairo's ill-paid policemen did not seem to know which side they were on. Of Egypt's major towns only Ismailia and Tanta were calm. In Alexandria, guns were soon out on the street. For one day, perhaps hoping that the political fuse would burn itself out, the government did nothing. On January 19, however, after rioting continued into the night, the government rescinded the subsidy cut and the higher prices. Only then was the army sent into the streets, a sequence of events that led many to suppose that Sadat was worried about the army's own reaction to price rises. With an official total of 80 dead and 600 wounded, the riots were finally put down. A nationwide round-up followed, and about 2,000 people with a wide range of political sympathies were arrested.

The riots caused an estimated damage of $1 billion to the economy. But they enabled Sadat to argue more convincingly with his financial backers that their fiscal demands were not politically feasible.[40] Internally, in the aftermath of the riots, Sadat launched a major campaign to convince citizens of his determination to see food production improve, spending hard currency to maintain the level of food imports. In April 1978 and early 1980, seasonal shortages in foodstuffs were met by quick deliveries from government stores to prevent civil unrest. Despite the deficits, authorities continued to subsidize bread, rice, beans, sugar, tea, and edible oil. Imported tractors, fertilizers, and pesticides were also subsidized. Conscious of declining support for the regime because of economic and political discontent, Sadat ignored domestic and foreign economists who had counseled more financial rigor and in 1980 ordered increased wages for workers and public employees, better prices to farmers for their crops, and, for some food items, even higher subsidies. Egypt meanwhile continued to defy the IMF's unrelenting demands for stringent economic reforms as a condition for new loans.

The fears that reform measures could be easily exploited by enemies of the regime, leading to violence on the scale of 1977 or worse, have also dictated the policies of Hosni Mubarak since he assumed the presidency. During his first months in office, Mubarak promised a comprehensive economic review, especially focused on subsidies and pricing policies. He stressed Egypt's urgent need to accept greater discipline and adopt more realistic policies. The issue of greater flexibility in U.S. aid was raised in the context of a more active policy dialogue with U.S. aid officials. Within nine months, however, the pronouncements of the government sounded more familiar with their emphasis on stability and continuity. With mixed advice given at a well-publicized February 1982 economic conference, and the warning of influential political advisors, President Mubarak reasserted Egypt's commitment to subsidize the prices of essential commodities and services in order to protect the country's masses. No radical overhauls of the system were contemplated, and any solutions would necessarily be gradual ones. It is to an examination of the options open to Mubarak, their economic costs, and perceived political feasibility that we now turn. As we will see, the government, although predictably hesitant to make adjustments, has not been entirely inactive.

Options and Risks in Changing Policies

The sense of urgency and potential for economic policy change in Egypt are naturally influenced by global and domestic economic conditions. World food prices, especially for food grains, global inflationary pressures and interest rates have all helped to set the parameters in which adjustments in policy can occur. Reforms also became more or less feasible and warranted as the country moved from the deep foreign exchange crisis of the mid-1970s through years of increased national income from external sources to the more recent mounting current account and budgetary deficits. The economic expansion realized during the latter part of the 1970s and early 1980s, based on oil revenues, remittances from Egyptian workers, canal tolls, tourism as well as massive Western aid and, until 1977, Arab aid, allowed the implementation of many of Sadat's *Infitah* policies. These exogenous factors in the economy, many a dividend of peace with Israel, made it easier for the government to extend its liberal reforms into such areas as foreign trade, sectoral investments, and banking and financial structures. At the same time, the positive resource flows also afforded Egypt the luxury of postponing other, more politically sensitive changes. Not only have few significant decisions been made in dealing with the underpricing of basic commodities and public services, pricing controls and distortions, but very little has occurred to confront the basic problems in public sector enterprise management, regulations, and employment.[41]

All the same, there are presently few among Egypt's policy leaders who would dissent with the view that pricing and subsidies policies must be, above all, substantially modified. With precipitous changes ruled out as socially and politically unsustainable, there is wide agreement that the means should be found to offset at least partially the impact of any adjustments. Most Egyptian economists concede that a shift is desirable from implicit subsidies and hidden taxes (as on exports through the exchange rate) to more explicit policies that make prices easier to measure and correct. Ideally, reform is seen as requiring a comprehensive package that contains, aside from price and subsidy reforms, changes in domestic taxation and an income policy and also addresses basic needs. The consensus largely breaks down and differences sharpen with Egypt's foreign advisors and creditors about the timing and phasing-in of the changes and the choice of instruments to effect the reforms.

Government expenditures for subsidies can be reduced in an across-the-board or selective manner, by limiting the number of commodities covered, or through better rationalization of distribution. Rather than a dramatic announcement of specific cuts and resulting price increases, the setting of a ceiling on the growth of subsidy costs over time is probably a less contentious approach. Savings can no doubt be found in a more efficient system that cuts waste and handling costs and seeks improvements in management and technology. Using food stamps and other means to restrict who participates or what may be subsidized may make it possible to improve the targeting. Forms of rationing or quotas can, if so designed, better ensure that the population's food requirements are met at prices more commensurate with their ability to pay. Whatever price increases occur, it may also be necessary to hold certain commodities to artificially low prices for an indefinite period, most notably the *balady* bread that is critical to the diets of lower income people and generally symbolic of the government's welfare concerns.

Income transfers as compensation for subsidies no longer provided through the price system are considered the most logical way to overcome the expected, pronounced decline in living standards. Were subsidies dropped entirely, it was estimated, for example, that prices would rise up to 470 percent and 760 percent respectively for wheat and frozen beef and 170 percent for flour and lentils.[42] Given the relative inelasticity of demand for most basic foodstuffs, quantities consumed and imported would be highly insensitive to increases in price, and the lower- and middle-income groups would feel the impact strongly.[43] To lighten the added burdens of change, carefully monitored wage and salary adjustments for public employees and increases in minimum wage rates are usually proposed. As further compensation, some insist on the partial reallocation of subsidies in the budget for low-rent housing, health services, and education. Private sector earning would also have to be permitted to rise. Where subsidized commodities serve as intermediate inputs in the production process, as in agriculture, higher, offsetting prices to farmers are probably indispensable.

International aid benefactors and creditors could play a critical role in helping Egypt to get through a transitional period to a more appropriate set of prices in a liberalized economy. In particular, the U.S. P.L. 480 sales and CIP can provide a cushion against the inevitable hardships of reform. The net addition of foreign aid to the government's financial resources can also facilitate efforts to furnish real income equivalents to low-income groups. Concessional commodities can go directly to support government programs as, for example, an in-kind form of wage increase to the private sector to offset price rises. In one scheme it is suggested that P.L. 480 shipments be used for a school lunch and food take-home program intended to raise the school attendance rate. One of the program's objectives would be to bring young, unskilled people out of the urban workforce where they are in oversupply, helping thereby to raise wages of those left employed. A more important long-range goal is to improve the country's human capital base by teaching the skills needed to better compete in a modern, industrial society. Such investment in lower income groups should increase their earnings potential. The food provided would, of course, have to be sufficient to compensate for the sacrifice in family income incurred by staying in school and participating in a training program, something the United States could help to guarantee.[44] But this kind of reliance on P.L. 480 and other aid programs has obvious drawbacks. Commodities released into the marketplace may have the familiar disincentive impact on local production. Moreover, unless dependence on the commodity aid programs is phased out in favor of domestic fiscal services during a period of a few years, Egypt's efforts to get its prices right may trade away still more of its economic independence.

Price adjustments and an income transfers strategy are not without other possible problems. Reforms that allow the prices of subsidized goods to rise relative to nonsubsidized items may have unforeseen consequences. The changes could establish a new set of comparative advantages for trade that would make Egypt's industries, at least for some time, less competitive against imports and in export markets.[45] Also, increases in nominal wages, boosting the comparative costs of production of goods and services in the public and private sectors, may work to the competitive disadvantage of local production. These outcomes would of course arrive at exactly the opposite point anticipated by those who advocate reforms: that by having prices reach their true domestic scarcity level and reflect their international opportunity costs they will correctly signal investment and enable Egypt to find its comparative advantages in world markets.

The Mubarak government confronts other uncertainties and constraints. Food stamps to offset the losses to lower income groups are unlikely to be introduced, if only because their administration may be impossible. For that matter, any income transfer approach as a substitute for food subsidies will be difficult because it must establish categories of wages both to be raised and to be ignored. A Ministry of Planning study, in the framework of the 1978–1982 Development Plan, had concluded that L.E. 624.4 million should be distributed yearly through increased wages and grants to poorer paid government employees, agricultural laborers, small landholders, and social solidarity beneficiaries, that is, those with average yearly incomes below L.E. 500.[46] Although good economic arguments exist to question whether wage increases are an effective, equitable alternative to food subsidization, the government's failure to date to approve a compensatory wage scheme is obviously out of concern for its reception politically by the nearly 8 million Egyptians, the somewhat better paid public employees and those in private sector employment who stand to lose valued income-equivalents without the present subsidy system.

Even those farmers who help to make the urban food subsidies feasible and should logically support its removal are not a reliable constituency for change. Farm owners cultivating twenty feddans (approximately twenty-one acres) or more are, after all, the major beneficiaries of the government's agricultural input subsidies. Although most of these producers would welcome a lifting of restrictions against private exports, they are not as concerned as smaller farmers about the low, fixed prices paid by the government for a portion of their output. Egypt's middle and larger farm owners can usually sell crops at higher prices because their larger holdings mean they have extra capacity to grow crops over and above the quotas or can dispense with government assistance in planting higher value, uncontrolled crops. Smaller farmers lack this flexibility and more often are obliged to plant controlled crops and to fulfill their quotas to the government at the announced low, fixed prices.[47]

Even if Egypt's small farmers were to become more conscious of their economic interest, they still lack the organization and skills to pressure the government to raise procurement prices or to end urban subsidies.

The bureaucracy is a strategically located obstacle to policy change. It is understandably not too keen on destroying a subsidies distribution system that enhances its power, influence, and prestige. Not unlike many other large and unwieldly bureaucracies, the Egyptian one is suspicious of any policy modifications that promise to streamline or dismantle an administrative apparatus, especially when this could lead to a sharp reduction in government jobs. Because almost the entire bureaucracy is recruited from the urban population, subsidy reform is bound to have an adverse impact on the buying power of a class that has long been critical of *Infitah*-inspired policies.

Egypt presents, then, what has been called a "class standoff." The politically dominant upper and upper middle classes, consisting of larger contractors, urban businessmen, senior and high ranking bureaucrats, and farmers with larger holdings are not in a position to force the lower classes to bear all of the burden for the country's economic problems and undertake alone the suffering that a readjustment of policies would entail. At the same time, the urban poor, small farmers, and landless laborers are not able politically to force those economically better off to change the system of taxation and subsidies in a fashion that would distribute the burdens and negative effects of policy adjustments among different classes according to their ability to pay. The result is a semi-paralysis of decisionmaking.[48]

In its dilemma, the government has moved, albeit very tentatively, toward adjustments in a number of policy areas. The regime's actions are uneven; although it has begun to tackle some issues, Mubarak's government shows little inclination to touch others and, in some instances, has retrenched on liberalizations. Public industry is comforted with assurances of no new encroachments from the private sector, and new legislation in 1983 gave state sector companies greater freedom to determine levels of employment and to pay incentive wages. Yet Mubarak remains determined to encourage still reluctant, fearful private invest-ment. He suggests no alternative to *Infitah's* dogma that external capital is essential for the country's economic growth and development. Current policy tends to follow the conventional wisdom of liberal economists that economic stabilization requires that domestically produced goods be freed up for export as expenditures are cut on imports. Aside from the import bans on many luxury food items implemented in 1982, changes also occurred in interest and exchange rates and export promotion during 1983 and 1984, policies that were, for the most part, welcomed by Egypt's international creditor community.

The pace of change also picked up after 1982 in price and subsidy policies. For the most part, the regime has undertaken an incremental, carefully tailored approach. The quality of the least expensive bread in Egyptian shops was reduced in order to encourage consumers to shift to a somewhat less subsidized, higher quality loaf. Price controls were lifted on some agricultural products, including grapes and oranges. Some price controlled items such as car batteries were phased out in favor of supposedly "improved" versions available at higher prices. A premium gasoline was introduced along with higher fares on new buses. In real terms, most changes are small and limited mainly to goods and services purchased by middle and upper income groups, thus minimizing adverse mass reactions. Higher natural gas prices were charged as new underground lines were installed in some of Cairo's better-off neighborhoods. Water tariffs were also raised for some customers. As noted earlier, the first increases in electricity rates for industrial users since 1976 were announced in 1983. Official prices paid for domestic production of key crops were meanwhile raised 5 to 20 percent in 1983—at the urging of AID and other creditors. For the most part, the government's approach through the state media and selected, more painless price increases has been to sensitize and educate the public to the need to face the subsidies problem. Leaders hope to gain popular toleration, if not approval, for additional price hikes.

A lone deviation from this approach and test of the government's will and capacity to make tougher adjustments to remedy consumption-oriented policies came in September 1984. Prices were quietly but steeply raised for cigarettes, macaroni, cooking fat, and several other subsidized items. One cent bread disappeared from markets in Cairo, Alexandria, and other cities. The changes were awkwardly timed as they coincided with an increase of 11 to 15 percent in deductions from government workers' pay for social insurance.[49] Workers at a textile plant in the northern industrial city of Kafr El Dawar refused to accept their salary packets and three days later staged a protest march. In the course of civil disorders, three people were reported killed by riot police and twenty-six injured.[50]

President Mubarak wasted no time in retreating, at least partially. He singled out the two food items that most directly impacted on the masses, pasta and cooking fat, and ordered their return to 1983 levels; increases in cigarettes, flour, and sugar prices were allowed to stand, however. Mubarak also told his ministries to make certain that the least expensive bread was available in lower income neighborhoods and that loaves be restored to their larger size. Additionally, he called for a freeze on prices for goods manufactured by public sector companies, stricter monitoring of price controls, and more efficient distribution of commodities.[51]

The government obviously had no intention of letting the disturbances about price increases spark troubles in the larger cities. Not only was the trauma of 1977 deep in the national psyche, but officials took heed from the January 1984 riots that had shaken the regimes in Tunisia and Morocco after real and presumed government cuts in subsidies.[52] Still, policymakers took only one step back after two steps forward. They seemed poised to begin again the slow, calculated process that was expected to move Egypt further toward free market prices and costs, especially for oil and electricity.

The IMF continues to press Egypt to reduce its budget deficit as well as more realistically tackle its foreign debt, and judges the government's economic reforms to date as too gradual. The case for budgetary austerity through cutting subsidies strengthened in late 1985 with a wave of terrorism touching Egypt that assured a sharp drop in the government's projected income from tourism as a result of canceled bookings. Even so, the future of reform initiatives remains in doubt as the 1985 coup in neighboring Sudan, following demonstrations protesting food price increases mandated by the IMF, the United States, and other creditors is bound to leave a deep impression on Mubarak. Whether the regime possesses the requisite political skills and power to mollify or, if necessary, override popular emotions also remains questionable. Its errors in handling the September 1984 price changes and missed opportunities in the previous May's parliamentary elections leave reason for skepticism.[53]

The same domestic economic policies that have sought to give no sector cause for serious complaint also result in the feeling among many that the government is drifting. Although Sadat may have been implusive, Mubarak seems often indecisive on a wide set of issues. His loss of luster has occurred even among those who generally agree with his policies. It is true that both Nasser and Sadat failed to act decisively at the outset in directions that would ultimately bring them stature in Egyptian eyes. But although some Egyptians detect in Mubarak an expanding ego to meet what is thought to be Egypt's natural desire for pharonic leadership, Mubarak is not a gambler, not an adventurer. Most important, although his predecessors were able to build a reputation at home by trading on their actions and acceptance outside their country, it is Mubarak's misfortune that today's resource-poor Egypt denies him the opportunities to undertake policies that could enhance his popular standing at home. Even if his performance internationally has been on the whole steady and sagacious, it is not bold or dramatic. Mubarak seems destined to be judged by what happens to Egypt's economy, and this is most likely a no-win situation. The long-range dismal outlook for the economy, given its basic, insolvable problems, leaves it likely that the president's popularity will continue to fade and his hold on power slip away.

Legitimacy and Change

The problem of legitimacy is, in a fundamental way, a prime obstacle in the pursuit of economic policy reforms by the last two regimes. There exists, in short, little sense of government as competent and caring, dedicated to serving the interests of all Egyptians. As such, there is presently virtually no toleration for policies that, whatever their supposed rationality, promise most people a reduced standard of living, at least in the short term. Much of this is understandable in view of Egypt's extended period of consumer deprivation prior to the mid-1970s and the number of people who still live uncomfortably close to the margin of physical survival. Policies that promise some necessary hardships are also difficult to accept when Sadat's promises of prosperity for all are still so fresh. But, in large measure, the popular alienation and suspicion in recent years grow out of feelings of powerlessness created by the absence of institutionalized and meaningful participation in policymaking. Nasser had symbolic satisfactions to offer the Egyptian people in the form of national pride, egalitarian idealism, and a sense of mission; in comparison, the Mubarak regime has little with which to distract the masses. At most it tries to buy them off with subsidies and fixed prices. Because the government lacks legitimate mechanisms either to communicate with or be answerable to the masses, it is obliged to operate out of instinct, often without either an appreciation of the real limits of its discretion in seeking policy reform or the means by which to lower the political risks in change.

A political leadership capable of mobilizing the population, either through charisma or ideology, can often get a bureaucracy and societal groups to forego their separate interests and accept sacrifices. But a bureaucratic regime of the type now found in Egypt is able to maintain itself in power by one of two means, either by exercising excessive repression or by giving concessions and thus buying time. Needless to say, both policies are dangerous, the former in the short run, and the latter in the longer run. The government cannot, as we have seen, go on following concessionary and economically self-defeating policies in order to buy time. The regime also lacks the mechanisms for large-scale, brutal repression and military enforced discipline. Moreover, after a period of relative consumerism and some political relaxation, Egypt's still authoritarian regime would find it difficult to return to many of

152   Aid and Policy Reform

the tight controls exercised earlier. It is also doubtful that the commitment to Open Door policies could survive a repression that would no doubt scare off foreign investors from a less stable Egypt. Pricing and subsidies reforms forced on the society would, as it curtailed consumption sharply, cut back on the necessary remittances from Egyptians working abroad. Some would argue that fuller economic liberalization and more political liberalization have to go hand in hand. In any event, meaningful policy changes probably require the kind of political courage born of a sense of regime security that has not been visible for some time.

Even if the odds now run against major reforms, many Egyptians sense that their economy is in a mess and sympathize in principle with efforts to correct the pricing and subsidies system. A two-pronged strategy that, on the one hand, seeks to raise public awareness of the consequences of continued inaction and, on the other, permits an active political process could result in conditions more favorable for far-reaching, even some self-sacrificing, changes. The goals are obviously to build support for a government willing to undertake risks and for a consensus on plausible and palatable solutions. It is difficult to conceive of this consensus occurring without the media being directed (or freed) to stimulate a national debate on the subject at the same time that elections are held for a more representative national assembly and most restrictions on political parties are removed. For all the economic liberties created, the climate for political pluralism has improved very slowly, and democratization is limited, uneven, and inconsistent. A mandate for further economic changes will no doubt require political coalition-building by politicians influential with their constituencies. Sharing the task with more democratic institutions poses obvious dangers for the regime. The possibility also exists that a more representative government might leave Egypt's leadership more constrained in pursuing pro-Western policies. But the failure to reverse the disturbing trends in the economy as Egypt's international dependence grows may even more certainly threaten the survival of the Mubarak government and, with it, the policies at home and abroad that have been in place since 1974.

Notes

1. Information in this chapter appeared in an earlier form in Marvin G. Weinbaum and Rashid Naim, "Domestic and International Politics in Egypt's Policy Reforms," *Journal of Arab Affairs*, Vol. 3, no. 2 (Fall 1984): 157–188. The material has been revised and updated.

2. For a full description of the structure of the food subsidy and distribution system see Harold Alderman, Joachim von Braun, and Sadr Ahmed Sakr, *Egypt's Food Subsidy and Rationing System: A Description*, Research Report no. 34

(Washington, D.C.: International Food Policy Research Institute, October 1982); pp. 19–35.

3. *MEED*, October 5, 1984. Also, *The New York Times*, October 5, 1984. The level of expenditures was similar to 1982-83 but 22 percent higher than 1983-84 when it has been held at $2 billion, due largely to lower world commodity prices.

4. U.S. Embassy, Cairo, "Economic Trends Report: Egypt" April 15, 1985, pp. 22–23. Also, David Ottoway, "Egypt Struggles to Revamp Economy," *The Washington Post*, January 28, 1985.

There are still other disguised or veiled subsidies in the economy. Through not given specific value, they are found in such areas as inflated wages in the government budget, excessive public sector employment, and tax exemptions for various groups.

5. Grant M. Scobie, *Food Subsidies in Egypt: Their Impact on Foreign Exchange and Trade*, Research Report no. 40 (Washington, D.C.: International Food Policy Research Institute, August 1983), p. 3.

6. *Middle East News, Economic Weekly*, October 1, 1982, p. 15.

For the most part in this chapter, no attempt has been made to express Egyptian pounds in their equivalent U.S. dollars. Aside from a gradual devaluation of the pound, the effective rate of exchange, especially in recent years, has fluctuated sharply and a conversion from pounds to dollars could be confusing and misleading.

7. Michael Hudson, *Arab Politics: The Search for Legitimacy* (New Haven, Conn.: Yale University Press, 1977), p. 238.

8. Ibid., pp. 239–241.

9. Alderman, *Egypt's Food Subsidy*, p. 13.

10. *Middle East News, Economic Weekly*, October 1, 1982, p. 16.

11. Alderman, *Egypt's Food Subsidy*, p. 14.

12. Scobie, *Food Subsidies in Egypt*, p. 1.

13. Alderman, *Egypt's Food Subsidy*, p. 16.

14. U.S. Agency for International Development, Cairo, "Egypt's Food and Energy Subsidies in 1979," 1981, p. 13.

15. Scobie, *Food Subsidies in Egypt*, p. 1.

16. *The New York Times*, November 16, 1981. In fact, there are increasing worries among nutritionists in Egypt about problems of obesity and diabetes. Anne M. Thompson, "Egypt, Food Security and Food Aid," *Food Policy*, Vol. 8, no. 3 (August 1983): 183.

17. "Egypt's Food and Energy Subsidies in 1979," p. 3A. These findings are analyzed in U.S. Agency for International Development, Cairo, "Egypt: Macro-Economic Performance, Problems and Prospects," February 15, 1981, pp. 16–21.

Subsidized food reaches the population through an extensive retail cooperative system. Ration card holders can buy fixed quantities of rationed items and almost unlimited quantities of price controlled items. In this way most families are able to afford such food staples as bread, rice, and sugar, and, at least occasionally, chicken, beef, and fish.

18. U.S. General Accounting Office, "The U.S. Economic Assistance Program for Egypt Poses a Management Challenge for AID," a report to the administrator, Agency for International Development, July 31, 1985, p. 21.

19. Alderman, *Egypt's Food Subsidy*, p. 42.

20. U.S. Agency for International Development, "Egypt's Food and Energy Subsidies," p. 5.

21. The assumption of the AID study that no part of the direct food subsidy went to rural areas may be hard to defend. Subsidized basic commodities such as sugar, tea, oils, and fats do reach the countryside. It is estimated, in fact, that about 15 percent of the food subsidy went outside the urban areas in the early 1980s. *Middle East News, Economic Weekly*, October 22, 1982, p. 9. Also, Alderman, *Egypt's Food Subsidy*, p. 48, finds in one rural governate, about one-third of the calories consumed came from subsidized commodities, most from cereal products. The report notes that the benefits are greater for richer farmers who are more likely to buy than make their own bread. As a result, the absolute value of the income gains from subsidies estimated for the urban areas in the AID study is probably too high.

22. *MEED*, July 1983, Special Report, p. 27. *The Wall Street Journal*, September 20, 1983.

23. *The Wall Street Journal*, September 20, 1983.

24. Normally, raising energy prices (by lowering subsidies) will have an inflationary impact. But over time inflation should be lower because the smaller budget deficits reduce excess demand and thereby ease inflationary pressures. See World Bank, "Arab Republic of Egypt: Current Economic Situation and Growth Prospects," Report no. 4498-EGT, October 5, 1983, p. v. Also, the gains for middle class groups from controlled prices can meanwhile be wiped out as retailers, such as bakers, raise prices on unsubsidized, higher value items.

25. See Marvin G. Weinbaum, *Food, Development, and Politics in the Middle East* (Boulder, Co.: Westview Press, 1982), pp. 23–36.

26. U.S. House of Representatives, Committee on Foreign Affairs, "Economic Support Fund Programs in the Middle East," report of a staff study, April 1979, p. 26.

27. U.S. Embassy, Cairo, "Annual Agricultural Situation Report—1983," February 28, 1984, p. 4.

28. The Egyptian government makes compulsory the delivery of sugar cane, cotton, and soybeans at a fixed procurement price. Other crops, including wheat, rice, lentils, and beans are subject to the mandatory procurement for only a portion of the crop. Any production above the quotas may be sold on the open market. The enforcement of the government's quota delivery obligations will vary with the crop and the year. Ibid., p. 8.

29. *The Wall Street Journal*, August 2, 1983.

30. *MEED*, September 21, 1984, p. 6.

31. The Egyptian farmer gets about one-half of what Egypt is paying to U.S. farmers for producing a ton of wheat for local consumption. Donald S. Brown, *Economic Development in Egypt—An American's Perspective* (Cairo: U.S. International Communications Agency, March 1982), p. 27.

32. World Bank, "Current Economic Situation and Growth Prospects, Arab Republic of Egypt," Report no. 4498-EGT, October 5, 1983, p. v.

33. U.S. Agency for International Development, "AID Policy Paper: Food and Agricultural Development," May 1982, pp. 7, 8.

34. Egypt's largest commercial supplier of food is France, and the European Community together contributes in most years about one-third of Egypt's food imports. Australia ordinarily serves as Egypt's major source of commercially sold wheat.

35. U.S. General Accounting Office, "The U.S. Economic Assistance Program Poses a Management Challenge for AID," p. 10.

36. Ibid., p. 20.

37. U.S. Agency for International Development, "Country Development Strategy Statement, FY 1984, Annex D: Policy Issues Facing Egypt," February 1982, p. 24.

38. Ibid., "Annex: Industry Sector Strategy for AID," p. 24.

39. Alderman, *Egypt's Food Subsidy*, p. 59.

40. Weinbaum, *Food, Development, and Politics in the Middle East*, pp. 161–162.

41. The progress and prospects for policy change in all areas of the economy are surveyed in U.S. Agency for International Development, "Country Development Strategy Statement, FY 1985, Annex D, Selected GOE Policy Changes (1974–1982) and Implications for the Future," Washington, D.C., February 1983, especially pp. 27–31.

42. This is in terms of 1979 prices. *Middle East News, Economic Weekly*, October 29, 1982, p. 18.

43. The Scobie study found that a 10 percent cut in real per capita subsidies resulted in reducing the volume of food imports by only 4 percent. It concluded furthermore that the government could better manage to reduce the costs of importing wheat by limiting access to the subsidized product than by reducing the per unit subsidy and letting prices rise. Scobie, *Food Subsidies in Egypt*, p. 2.

44. Many of these options and obstacles are discussed in G. Edward Schuh, "Integration in Programming and Implementing Development is More than Projects," a paper delivered at a conference on the Economic Challenges of Peace, Alexandria, Egypt, July 7–16, 1980, pp. 16–20.

45. This is cogently argued in U.S. Agency for International Development, "Egypt: Macro Economic Performance, Problems and Prospects," p. 20.

46. *Middle East News, Economic Weekly*, November 5, 1982, p. 20.

47. *Middle East Annual Review 1977*, p. 162.

48. For a discussion see Alan Richards, "Ten Years of Infitah: Class, Rent, and Policy Stasis in Egypt," *Journal of Development Studies*, Vol. 20, no. 4 (July 1984): 323–338. This thesis is elaborated in John Waterbury, *The Egypt of Nasser and Sadat: The Political Economy of Two Regimes* (Princeton, N.J.: Princeton University Press, 1983). Also see Derek Hopwood, *Egypt: Politics and Society, 1945–1981* (London: George Allen and Unwin, 1982).

49. *The New York Times*, October 4, 1984. *The Washington Post*, January 4, 1985.

50. *Middle East Economic Digest,* October 5, 1984, p. 7.

51. *Middle East News, Economic Weekly,* October 5, 1984, p. 24.

52. For a discussion see Marvin G. Weinbaum, "Food Security and Agricultural Development Policies in the Middle East," *Policy Studies Review,* Vol. 4, no. 2 (November 1984): 348–349.

53. The elections to the 448 seat Parliament were more open and honest than any under the Egyptian Republic and compare very well with others in the Arab Middle East. Still, much of the legitimacy of the results, where the ruling National Democratic party of President Mubarak won 87 percent of the seats, was tarnished by a government decision that set a high, 8 percent of the vote, minimum for representation. This eliminated all but one opposition party, the New Wafd, which took 57 seats.

7

Aid in the Future of U.S.-Egyptian Relations

After more than a decade of renewed U.S.-Egyptian political and economic ties, significant strains have appeared in the relationship. Neither country has found its expectations fully realized, and each is increasingly disappointed with the other's policies. Officials in Washington continue to express doubts about Egypt's capacity and willingness to absorb aid effectively and are uneasy about how far the Mubarak government might go to end Egypt's estrangement from the Arab world and try to recapture former influence. For its part, Egypt's leadership faces mounting criticism from within and without for the believed constraints on foreign and domestic policies imposed by the U.S. connection. Despite the massive capital, commodity, and technical transfers, Egypt's economic self-reliance appears to be a receding goal. For all the constancy of U.S. aid since 1975, its origins and motives also raise questions for some Egyptians of U.S. reliability. Aid that is justified more on political than economic or development grounds is liable to fade quickly should U.S. policymakers ever lose interest in Egypt or come to doubt its friendship.[1] At the same time, growing numbers of Egyptians appear willing to forego U.S. economic support if that is the necessary price to end perceived U.S. affronts to Egypt's pride and dignity.

Public Attitudes

A resurgent Egyptian nationalism and overall decline in U.S. standing in the Middle East account in large part for the erosion of public approval of U.S. aid activities in Egypt. Perhaps inevitably, a country that had for nearly two decades led the Arab states and championed the causes of pan-Arabism and Third World non-alignment would again seek to play a more independent, assertive role in regional and world affairs. Anwar Sadat's formula for restoration of Egypt's economic health and political/territorial objectives relied heavily on U.S. financing and leverage with Israel. The peace treaty with Israel that left Egypt isolated from much of the Arab world was bound to sour with Prime Minister Menahem Begin's terms for Palestinian autonomy and Israel's West Bank settlement policies. Demands for more balance in Egypt's international relations and concerns about losing political and economic autonomy, continuously voiced in opposition circles during the years, acquired a popular resonance by the early 1980s.

The Lebanon invasion, the siege of Beirut, and the massacres in the Palestinian camps greatly accelerated this process. They stimulated an already latent sense of guilt among many Egyptians that they had, in effect, deserted the Arab cause and, by pacifying their southern frontier with Israel, left the Jerusalem government free to undertake military aggression elsewhere. The transformation of public opinion was accompanied by deepening frustrations within the Mubarak regime about its lack of influence over U.S. policy. Mubarak repeatedly failed in his effort to get the Reagan administration to restrain Israeli forces in Lebanon or to win U.S. backing for proposals for the mutual and simultaneous recognition between Israel and the Palestine Liberation Organization. Government officials in Cairo considered Washington insensitive to the delicate position of Egypt and other pro-Western Arab states now that events had played into the hands of anti-U.S. Islamic fundamentalists and the rejectionists, domestic and regionwide, who had always contended that a peace with Israel was impossible. Egyptian officials were annoyed that the U.S. administration seemed to ignore the fact that Egypt, almost alone in the region, had unequivocally backed Reagan's September 1982 peace initiative. Confidence in the U.S. was shaken with the announced U.S. strategic cooperation accord with Israel late in 1983, and the (Egyptian-opposed) hasty departure of U.S. Marines from Beirut. Mubarak also denounced the U.S.-supported, short-lived Israeli-Lebanese pact. In October 1985, Israel's air strike on PLO headquarters in Tunis, initially condoned by the Reagan administration, and the humiliation felt when U.S. jets forced down an Egyptian plane to capture Palestinian terrorists, left the Mubarak government trying to defuse public outrage by, for a time, orchestrating the anti-U.S. rhetoric. In general, these events reinforced a view that close U.S. ties carried political risks that had to be weighed more carefully in the relationship.

If the attitudes of most Egyptians have become, at best, ambivalent toward the United States, the change is in no small way also related to the popular impression that U.S. aid has done little to improve the life of the average person. Very few Egyptians, including the better informed, have an accurate sense of where the U.S. investment has gone. The most articulate often assert that U.S.-financed commodities and development projects have at most benefited an affluent few and are responsible for a widening economic gap in Egyptian society.

The absence of high visibility for U.S. aid efforts was in part deliberate. Beginning in the mid-1970s, U.S. officials were anxious to maintain a relatively low profile for the program. They were concerned that everything be done to avoid anticipated charges of aid imperialism that could offer ammunition to the enemies of President Sadat. Any concerted effort, for example, to dramatize or seek expressions of gratitude for U.S. wheat could only stress the country's economic vulnerability.[2] AID professionals argued, moreover, that more could be accomplished developmentally with a broad investment portfolio that eschewed major, in part symbolic, undertakings of the kind that characterized Soviet aid and was manifest in the Aswan High Dam and the steel mills constructed at Helwan. This conscious decision by U.S. officials to shun aid investment in "Soviet-style monuments" dictated against any conspicuous demonstrations of U.S. largesse. It ensured that the impact of U.S. assistance would be registered indirectly and surely less visibly. Many U.S.-financed infrastructural investments have been, to be sure, large in scale and expensive. But few of the slow progressing projects succeeded in capturing the attention or, more important, the imagination of the Egyptian public. Most Egyptians fail to associate more dependable electricity or increased availability of bread at lower prices with U.S. financing. Increased generating capacity that provides in aggregate as much electric power as was created by the Aswan High Dam is typical of incremental improvements through U.S. aid whose economic impact is significant but whose popular recognition is minimal. Cooperative ventures with other Western donors countries and international aid agencies also dilute in the public mind the U.S. contribution to development and immediate consumption.

The broad, often seemingly opportunistic, U.S. aid approach raises suspicions. The very pervasiveness of the assistance, touching virtually every facet of Egyptian life, rather than being accepted as evidence of the extent of U.S. development concerns, is often taken as proof of an unhealthy influence over the country's policymakers and a threat to Egypt's economic independence. Curiously, many of these same people who see undue influence are also among those who discount the significance of the U.S. effort for Egypt. The Reagan administration's championing of an increased private sector role in foreign aid often reinforces the impression that the United States lacks interest in the common man and largely precludes support for the very projects that could possibly alter that impression.

It is difficult for many Egyptians to separate the U.S. program, as noted in Chapter Two, from the U.S.-encouraged economic policies of

President Sadat and the disappointments, suspicions, and animosities they left behind. Aid policies that were supposed to improve Sadat's standing with key supportive elements instead now bring to mind get-rich-quick schemes and corrupt elites. Some critics tie the aid to what they perceive as a broader social disintegration. The Mubarak regime's willingness to prosecute a select few who had accumulated immense personal wealth and to permit some reassessment of previous economic policies also left the U.S. role more exposed.

There began in fall 1982 a series of newspaper and magazine articles, tolerated by the authorities for a time, that attacked the U.S. aid effort on several accounts. The AID mission in Egypt was accused of trying to penetrate every sector of the society, of permeating "the whole structure of Egyptian life."[3] This alleged plan was conceived to make Egypt fit the U.S. image and serve the interests of U.S. capitalism.[4] To its most severe critics, foreign aid was characterized as a new colonialism, foisted on Egypt through economic dependencies and exploitation by foreign firms. The U.S. programs in Egypt were portrayed as explicitly designed to promote private sector expansion in what was, in effect, an assault on social justice. AID personnel supposedly followed closely the activities of Egypt's government agencies and, taking the form of a "shadow government," were able to influence policies and obtain information that, even if not directly intended to harm Egypt, had compromised its national security.[5]

U.S.-sponsored research, whether conducted by U.S. experts or con-tracted to Egyptians, came under particular attack as intelligence gath-ering. In articles that suggested a xenophobic mood reminiscent of the Nasser years, Egyptians were warned to be careful of foreigners asking questions of those in the bureaucracy. A leading jurist called for a jail term for officials disclosing any information relating to national planning, domestic food consumption, or international trade.[6] Complaints were raised that Egyptians had little control over how information obtained was used and that the collected data is often unavailable in Egypt.[7] Even Egyptians studying in the United States were alleged to be denied technological information that could be obtained by Israeli students. The motives behind various ongoing programs were questioned. One op-position party newspaper explained U.S. interest in population and family planning as part of a Zionist conspiracy aimed at "controlling the birth of Egyptians in the interests of Israel."[8] Other, only somewhat less bitter detractors, have argued that the U.S. preoccupation with population growth provides a convenient explanation when programs do not work. Approaches to population control are also conceived as a technical strategy that avoids getting to underlying causes in the social, economic, and political structure of the country. In general, the clearer

U.S. officials are in stating development objectives and the need for Egyptian policy adjustments, the more the United States is accused of trying to dictate to the Cairo government.

An outspoken critic, Saad Ibrahim, has written that Egypt never fully threw off its earlier feelings of inferiority with foreigners. The dependency of Egypt, he argues, is a psychological as well as an economic condition. Ibrahim complains that Egypt's political leadership hesitates to take decisions that would anger the United States (e.g., in dealing with Israel) for fear that the country would be cut off from assistance, that "the Americans will starve us."[9] His view well reflects the hostility to U.S. policies, though not necessarily to U.S. citizens, that pervades much of the educated and intellectual community in Cairo. Most from this community are not ideologically well disposed to U.S. aid and object to the price of Egypt's integration into the West's military, political, and market systems. Although conceding that the Russians gave technologically less sophisticated equipment to Egypt, these Egyptians are increasingly heard to suggest that the less expensive equipment during the Nasser years limited the financial burden and allowed for technologies more appropriate for the country's state of development. As is pointed out in Chapter Two, the salaried middle class has suffered economically in the liberalized economy in which government salaries grew very slowly as inflation surged. This educated group failed to keep pace with gains by Egyptians in the trades, or even rural and urban workers, especially those in private sector industry. Of no less importance, journalists and educators identify with and normally maintain personal contacts with the larger Arabic-speaking world. It is here that they find lucrative outlets for writing, lecturing, and teaching, and where their aspirations for a proud, influential Egypt still lie.

The U.S. Profile

The challenge for AID, at least until the early 1980s, was to be able to convey the impression of serving as economic benefactor without taking from the Egyptian government credit for any progress. The interests of both governments called for an aid approach that would look subordinate as well as distinctive and constructive. The prevailing view among officials in Cairo and Washington more recently is that the United States must act quickly to give the Egyptian public a clearer understanding of the U.S. aid program. Concern is expressed that the low profile has led to an ignorance of U.S. activities that, in turn, creates unfounded suspicions. It is now felt that without greater evidence that the program's impact is directly attributable to the United States, domestic support for U.S. economic aid may sink so low that an Egyptian government might expediently bow to domestic pressures by sacrificing rational economic development and political cooperation with the United States. The replacement of Donald Brown as AID director in Cairo in 1983 accentuated the change in course. Under Michael Stone, the analytic and managerial aspects of the directorship became secondary to clarifying and publicizing AID's activities and objectives. Stone freely gave interviews to the local press and welcomed speaking engagements before Egyptian audiences. He brought to the Cairo mission a specialist in public relations and produced a slick annual report in English and Arabic.

Stone and others believed that at least some of the exposure problem could be self-correcting. A number of larger infrastructural projects were nearing or had reached completion and were expected to provide more physical evidence of the U.S. contribution to Egypt's economy. For the future, the director and others became convinced that the AID mission could improve its image by concentrating on fewer, higher visibility ventures. Egyptian proposals for projects that AID had previously refused to entertain as splashy and of dubious economic value were taken under consideration in 1983 and 1984. The mission reevaluated an idea to help finance a 500-mile-long road to be built from Cairo to Aswan and agreed to back a feasibility study for a ring road around Cairo expected to cost between $250 and $500 million. AID still refused to touch public housing, although the single venture of AID into the sector, a housing project in Helwan, remains locally popular. Nor would the United States soon reverse itself on land reclamation just to please the government, even though the idea of new lands continues to inspire most Egyptians. But with an eye on winning friends, the AID mission has been more conciliatory in announcing its willingness to support reclamation projects if proven economically feasible.[10]

Ready identification of the United States with a highly visible program has been found to be no guarantee of enhancing its image. Probably the best illustration is the financing in the late 1970s of 1,800 Ward buses from the United States, each conspicuously marked with the clasped-hands AID logo. In a short time, these school-frame buses on truck chasses were labeled the VOA, Voice of America, not for the worldwide radio service but for the noise they created. The often defective buses compared unfavorably with older ones from Iran (West German design) and from England, both better suited for overloading and traffic in a highly congested city. It made little difference to the public that their own government had to share blame for the error. Egyptian officials had set the specifications of the buses, including a weak muffler that was supposed to improve gas consumption. The Egyptians had also not objected to AID procedures designed to contract for the least expensive bus, in this case some one-third the cost of standard buses.[11] Even though the Ward buses were filling an immediate need in Egypt's urban transportation system, they remained an object of ridicule.

Curiously, the one set of programs that in recent years has attracted the most favorable publicity for AID is also the least focused—support for decentralization and local participation in development decisions. With this funding, mainly for small public works projects in the countryside, AID is believed to have made a strong impression in many villages. Although, as described in Chapter Four, the mission plays no direct role in the disbursement of money, which is administered at the provincial governate level or below, the affected peasant cannot help but notice the AID emblem on new pieces of equipment and materials. Members of village councils are believed to be aware that the credits are being provided by the United States for projects, ones that they themselves have selected. However, the pervasive program raises fears among some in the Egyptian bureaucracy of U.S. meddling at the grass roots.

The AID mission's attempt to raise the public's consciousness poses other drawbacks. New programs that seem to cater too much to popular tastes in order to increase the visibility of U.S. aid are open to attack as sacrificing feasibility for symbols of good relations between the two countries.[12] Director Stone's strong promotional pitch in the public forum revealed a blunt, at times patronizing, style, and his candor was frequently misconstrued by Egyptian audiences. In one lecture in early 1984, he observed that it was general knowledge that aid to Egypt is misused, especially food assistance. He was subsequently denounced as trying to interfere in the country's domestic policymaking and for questioning Egypt's understanding of its own needs.[13] The widespread press criticism and pressures from within Egyptian government circles to have Washington replace Stone helped to convince most officials in the AID mission that a more subtle, gradual approach is required, and, to the extent possible, the Egyptian government must help in advertising the U.S. aid effort.

In development terms alone, the inability of the United States to win the hearts and minds of ordinary Egyptians might be a subordinate matter. So long as the aid program allocates resources in an effective manner and the long term impact of the assistance is positive, the public's gratitude, although welcomed, is not critical. Assistance that succeeds in improving the overall economic stability and enables the Egyptian government to continue following a consistent course in foreign policy would at the same time satisfy U.S. political objectives. Here is the rub, however. Cooperative policies with the United States probably cannot be sustained without popular acceptance of broader U.S. ties.

At least until Israel's actions in Lebanon, generally favorable attitudes toward the United States prevailed, even where the U.S. aid program was impugned. Should mass opinion remain entirely hostile after the events of fall 1985, it would not be enough to retain the understanding of the governing circles. The regime's survival would dictate that it try to divorce itself from Washington-sponsored strategic plans for the regime and pressure the leadership to look for substitutes for U.S. economic aid.

No doubt, the criticism of AID and its far-flung operation in Egypt is based much of the time on superficial observation and faulty information. Charges are often constructed on anecdotal evidence. Some attacks are petty, not a few of them from individuals bitter after failing to win contracts, loans, or employment with a U.S.-funded project. U.S. aid often becomes a convenient "whipping boy" for anger directed at the United States for its alleged one-sided policies in the region. Objections that are essentially ideological impute the worst motives and may deliberately distort the facts. High public officials frequently express opinions that reflect a lack of even general familiarity with the aid program.[14] Because more is expected of the United States in the public mind, that is, it is supposed to have the best technologies and the highest capability to solve Egypt's problems, people often feel cheated or deceived when nothing happens after an aid agreement is signed or when U.S. equipment and expertise turn out to be faulty. The United States may be blamed as well for its failures to act: Egypt's disappointments with new lands projects could have been avoided if only U.S. planners had established reclamation as their own development priority. The media rarely give credit to foreign aid in those areas where Egyptian life has conceivably been improved by virtue of U.S. or other assistance. Yet this lack of information and sometimes deliberate denigration of aid, it must be conceded, are important pieces of data. Accurate or not, prevailing views of U.S. aid mark the declining good will that the United States has in the past been able to draw upon in the general population. These attitudes have some bearing on the government's need to seek modifications in the aid relationship.

Bilateral Dialogue

Demands for greater flexibility in and control over U.S. economic aid by Egyptian authorities had been expressed from time to time during the Sadat era but never pressed very hard. However, with Mubarak's first visit to Washington as president in February 1982, it became clear that the assistance program would assume a high priority in the dialogue with the Reagan administration. Mubarak and his advisors couched their arguments for change in terms of Egypt's right to use U.S. grants, especially those for development projects, in a way that would better allow resources to be distributed according to "the conditions of Egypt's social and economic development, and its priorities and goals."[15] Washington agreed in principle with this view in a Memorandum of Understanding following the discussions. Other, less formal requests were also given at least a sympathetic hearing, including Egypt's call for more local procurements in development projects and increased participation of Egyptian consultants in project planning and implementation.

AID officials concluded in subsequent discussions that the Egyptians had, in fact, no alternative agenda or concrete ideas for how they would pursue development. What the new regime did have was a determination to assert its full partnership in the aid process and a belief that with increased discretionary authority over funds it could increase the monetary returns for Egypt. Ideally, the Cairo government desires to have the economic aid in a lump sum, unlinked to projects, on a similar footing with the way Israel receives its economic support from the United States. Egyptian officials observe with some envy that no AID mission exists in Tel Aviv, and funds go essentially to underwrite the Israeli economy. The United States sets few conditions on where the cash transfers are placed, allowing for budgetary support that eases costs of a consumer subsidy program as well as development projects. Thus, as Egypt is instructed on how it should use its economic aid, Israel is told only how it may not spend the money, i.e., for military purposes and expenditures beyond its pre-1967 frontier. Although Mubarak and his advisors have been insistent on a continued rough balance in economic assistance, they have never fully expected to receive Israel's largely "blank check" in the use of funds. Egyptian negotiators are willing to settle for eliminating restrictions on already obligated funds and allowing Egypt to more quickly and fully capture the authorized aid dollars. Aid dollars set aside for projects that were having difficulty being absorbed or that were otherwise questionable would be reobligated and, essentially at the Egyptian government's discretion, applied to other projects, restricted only in that they be in the same economic sector and justifiable. Additionally, Mubarak sought to have all new project monies obligated on an incremental budgeting basis. The practice of obligating the expected full costs in advance had led to the enormous backlog of unspent but committed funds—more than $2.4 billion at the beginning of FY 1985.

The Egyptians saw obvious advantages in deobligation authority and the release of previously earmarked funds. As matters stood, if a project had been allocated $25 million and only $20 million were spent, the differences would revert to the U.S. Treasury. In one program designed to provide $31 million in medium-term credit to private sector Egyptian companies, the bureaucracy in Cairo had never managed to disburse most of the funds. Given new authority, it was estimated that at least $20 million could be released for use elsewhere in the industrial sector.[16] A respected Egyptian economist estimates the magnitude of the annual loss to Egypt as a result of U.S. unwillingness to use incremental budgeting to be in the vicinity of $200 million.[17] Whatever the actual amount, funds held by the United States ordinarily depreciate in purchasing power and do not draw interest for Egypt. Very probably, if left to make more of its own investment decisions, Egypt would feel less handicapped in channeling resources toward public enterprises. With sectoral grants, the government could, without making basic changes in direction, assure that increased allocations went, for example, for basic school education and housing.

Politically sensitive U.S. officials have not been entirely unsympathetic to Egyptian complaints. The transfer of some appropriations and a limited sectoral approach in lieu of a predominantly project orientation could soften some criticism of the United States (see Chapter Four). More extensive use of local consulting firms might also alleviate feelings of technical inferiority created by current practices. Although few U.S. officials considered Egypt ready for a total cash transfer, the current Five Year Development Plan at least puts Egypt in a better position to rationalize its development activities. Significantly, Egypt refrained from asking directly for the kind of discretion that would allow a diversion of funds to help finance those expenditures most frowned upon by U.S. officials—consumer food and energy subsidies. To the contrary, increased flexibility in aid to Egypt, it was hoped, might encourage concessions from the government or otherwise support them in undertaking tough domestic economic reforms.[18]

Serious questions are raised, all the same, about the wisdom of fundamentally altering the mode of funding to Egypt. The advantage of full aid appropriations in advance means that a project or program can be assured that the money will be there through completion. To rely on incremental appropriations means taking a chance, albeit not a high risk, that future U.S. legislators may, for example, leave a power plant's construction or a dam renovation unfinished. Lacking a long-term U.S. dollar commitment, U.S. contractors essential to a project may not be anxious to sign an agreement because they could not be guaranteed funds through the end of the project. Some skeptical U.S. officials point out that the initial windfall of funds in deobligation would undoubtedly make possible many new programs in the first year. Subsequently, however, U.S. allocations would have to go mainly to meet these obligations, permitting few new programs each year and resulting, in the end, in a less flexible program. AID officials point to the pliancy or liquidity already available in the aid program in the form of quick disbursing P.L. 480 and Commodity Import Program funds, which together make up more than one-half of the total economic assistance package to Egypt. As for the pipeline, AID spokesmen are pleased to show that by 1983, dispersals had pulled ahead of new allocations and that the total amount of unspent money, though still high, has continued to decline. U.S. officials suggest that aid to Egypt might someday be handled entirely though allocations to Egyptian investment banks or in outright cash grants to the regime. Yet they are quick to point out that local institutions have a long way to go before they can provide an acceptable, effective alternative to the current process. Behind the present reluctance to give the Cairo government unrestricted use of aid funds is of course the conviction that whatever its promises, Cairo would eventually apply the funds to finance its ever more expensive consumer subsidy programs.

Doubts about speeding up the aid process and turning over greater authority to the Egyptians are most often expressed by development professionals in Washington. They have resisted attempts to move faster on projects by shortening the usually time-consuming feasibility studies. These officials also question the ability of the Egyptian bureaucracy to reach agreements on development programs, to implement programs any more quickly, or to reach objective assessments based on cost-efficiency criteria. AID officials concede that more flexibility, allowing the government to shift around funds and recover appropriated money, may be an understandable demand in view of AID's drawn-out procedural requirements. They suspect, however, that the Egyptian government wants control more than flexibility, the kind of authority that would permit it to look anywhere, using U.S. funds, for contractors and commodities, and to secure the removal of all restrictions on where the aid dollars can be spent. Permission to use U.S. financing to import commodities from less expensive non-U.S. suppliers stands no chance of being granted because of U.S. law and the political realities in Washington. AID officials are certain that such changes would soon jeopardize political support for aid to Egypt in the U.S. Congress.

Under the Foreign Assistance Act, the use of funds for purposes other than those specifically authorized is prohibited without congressional approval. The Reagan administration asked Congress in early 1983 to unfreeze aid accounts totaling more than $100 million on thirteen project loans and grants and on eight CIP agreements; Congress approved the request in late July. However, the legislation ran out at the end of the fiscal year, two months later, and most of the released funds turned up not as the Egyptians had sought as intrasectoral transfers, but reallocated in the commodity program. Congress was again asked in a fiscal 1984 supplemental appropriations bill for aid to Egypt to approve a roughly similar amount and with it the authority to deobligate and then reobligate project funds. The proposal was caught up for a time in a congressional standoff after drawing criticism in both houses, including the alleged misuse of the development funds and claims that the proposed cash grant would be used by Egypt, if indirectly, to help pay for U.S. arms purchases.[19] The Mubarak government complained that the administration was not fighting hard enough for the legislation.[20] In retaliation, the Egyptian bureaucracy allegedly delayed agreement during 1984 on several programs proposed by the AID mission in Cairo. A $100 million cash transfer was finally included along with regular project funding in the fiscal 1985 congressional allocation for Egypt. Resistance to the cash transfers in several subcommittees was dropped when Egypt agreed to use an amount equivalent to the grant to support its health and housing sectors.[21]

Aid to Egypt has been subject of late to the kinds of scrutiny and criticism in congressional circles that reflect the greater competition for scarce dollar resources and doubts about the payoffs of U.S. foreign aid. Some in the Congress question whether the shrinking aid pie should be cut up so disproportionately, with Egypt and Israel receiving so large a share of U.S. economic assistance to the developing world. The death of Sadat deprived Egypt of its best spokesman for generous aid from Congress, and skepticism is expressed among legislators about Egypt's ability to avoid concessions in its readmission to Arab councils. Some conservative members of the Congress continue to question why the United States should support what they see as an essentially state-run economy. The charges of corruption and mismanagement in the aid program have also changed the views of several once supportive senators and congressmen.

The Mubarak government repeatedly reminds Washington that it is every bit as much a strategic ally as Israel and that it has earned U.S. support. Most of all, the regime is intent on signaling that neither Egypt's political cooperation nor its economic gratitude should be taken for granted. Although policymakers in Cairo expect to remain dependent on the United States, they also continue to demand a role in helping to set the terms and limits of that dependency. Mubarak had these thoughts no doubt in mind when he arrived in Washington in March 1985. He came asking for $1.6 billion in supplemental economic and military aid for fiscal 1985 and 1986 to carry Egypt through a difficult economic period.[22] Discussions with Mr. Reagan dealt primarily with Mubarak's efforts to get the United States committed to a more active role in mediating Middle East peace. Although rebuffed on a proposal for a meeting between U.S. representatives and a joint PLO and Jordanian delegation, the Egyptian president was rewarded with $500 million in additional aid for the rest of 1985 and the next fiscal year. Once more the assistance was tied to increased U.S. support for Israel, $1.5 billion more during the same time period. Importantly, the new funds promised Egypt were in the form of a grant with few conditions attached. As such they constituted a substantial concession by the United States in Egypt's continuing quest for a more unrestricted aid package. Whether Congress could be expected to be so accommodating to Egypt after October 1985 became problematic in light of U.S. lawmakers' anger with President Mubarak's handling of the *Achille Lauro* hijackers, in particular his efforts to avoid the appearance of cooperating with the U.S. and demand for an apology from Washington.

The Stakes

Under Hosni Mubarak there has been no rush toward a new set of political alignments or economic policies. Egypt's options had at first appeared to broaden under President Mubarak. Despite his vice presidency to Sadat, Mubarak was not held personally accountable by most Egyptians for foreign policy and economic decisions in the 1970s. Sadat's style was far too individualistic to allow others to share in either his policy successes or failures. Thus, the bridges that the former president had burned to much of the Arab World and Eastern Europe did not seem to circumscribe the new government's actions to the same degree. Without disavowing basic economic and foreign policies, Mubarak became freer to change the terms of previous agreements and to take advantage of opportunities for some diversification in Egypt's economic and military aid.

For all the government's promises to retain the best of Sadat's economic liberalization while restoring the desirable elements of Nasser's socialist economy, Mubarak has retained more continuity with the recent than the more distant past. Public sector industry feels less insecure than during the Sadat years when some feared a wholesale transfer of public industries to the private sector or, at least, that Egypt's sheltered and controlled public sector would be forced into a more competitive environment. But the Egyptian president has refrained from turning back the ideological clock to emphasize nationalizations and expropriations. Nor has he initiated any bold program that would newly redistribute incomes as a means of reversing the trends of the 1970s. As concluded in Chapter Two, *Infitah* remains very much alive in the government's hopes of attracting foreign investment. Economic liberalization can be disowned by the regime only at the possible price of scaring away still sought-after capital investments and much needed credits. More broadly,

Infitah is linked symbolically with the peace treaty with Israel and materially to Egypt's political as well as economic opening to the West.

Considerable skill is required, then, to allow complaints in the Egyptian press and elsewhere, on the one hand, about undue U.S. influence in domestic development policies and, on the other, to insist on the indispensability of high levels of U.S. support. Similarly, it has taken much agility for the Egyptian leadership to disassociate itself from the widely criticized U.S. diplomatic and military actions in the Middle East and still maintain and justify economic and political ties with Washington. If at times it seems wise to keep cooperation with the U.S. military discreet, there are other occasions when the regime, feeling threatened by the region's more radical states, is anxious to advertise its military connection. Whether in Afghanistan, Pakistan, or Iraq, there exist areas where U.S. and Egyptian strategic-security objectives clearly intersect, and Egypt has willingly, if quietly, served as a supplier or conduit for arms against common adversaries. U.S. military equipment and arms financing have also figured importantly in Egypt's effort to replace aging Soviet weapons. But, however pivotal the military links to the United States in Egypt's national security planning, strict limits are placed on a U.S. armed presence on Egyptian soil and U.S. access to Egyptian military facilities in deference to public feelings.

The United States, too, has had to reconcile its objectives with the political realities in Egypt. The country's designated role in U.S. plans for a negotiated peace in the region notwithstanding, Washington's foreign policymakers have had to concede Egypt's need to seek improved relations with other Arab states, most of whom still refuse to acknowledge Israel's existence or accept the proposition that the Soviet Union is the region's most immediate threat. Moreover, with reluctance, the Reagan administration has accepted that it is reasonable for Egypt to diversify its arms assistance through purchases from competitive European suppliers. Officials in the Department of State, if not the Congress, are largely resigned to Egypt's determination to reactivate its credentials as a nonaligned state, and they quickly adjusted to Mubarak's decision to resume diplomatic ties with the Soviets in July 1984.

Not infrequently, U.S. aid policies appear to undermine the very political objectives the United States seeks. Washington's efforts to assure economic growth for Egypt and constancy in its foreign policy have sometimes threatened the domestic political stability on which these policies rest. In the long run, the United States' smothering embrace of Anwar Sadat unwittingly acted to weaken the president's credibility with his own people. No doubt, the acclamation that Sadat received abroad heightened his arrogance in dealing with his domestic critics and encouraged his self-righteousness with the public. The large aid package in particular confronted Sadat with the formidable challenge of how to distribute these resources in ways that did not lose him the people's confidence. Although a major part of U.S. support has gone to reorient the Egyptian economy through programs favorable to the entrepreneurial class and the technically trained, that policy often overlooked Egypt's large salaried middle class and the urban poor, both of whom, along with the military, are capable of bringing down a government. U.S. military assistance has not to date come at the expense of economic aid. Still, the recent emphasis on U.S. arms sales intended to enhance Egypt's capacity to play a pro-Western international role has emboldened and unified opposition elements who question the wisdom of a strong military dependence.

AID's finesse in trying to retain a sense of partnership with the Cairo government while using aid to induce economic reforms will probably set much of the tone for U.S.-Egyptian relations in the near term. As seen in Chapter Five, U.S. advisors still debate how strongly to press the government into introducing far-reaching policy changes in view of likely public reaction and the precariousness of urban peace. Aid donors have an understandable interest in the prevailing policy environment. External assistance is very likely to be inefficiently absorbed in the absence of policy reforms on basic goods and fixed prices. Failure by the United States to discourage the government's stimulating monetary and fiscal policies could, in effect, make the United States an accomplice to a disastrous economic course and assure Egypt's indefinite status as a burden. The financial commitment to Egypt carries, after all, no projected termination date or a planned phase down. An economically prostrate Egypt, unable to make progress in coping with its own problems, is also less capable of working with the United States toward common political-strategic goals. But just as aid has rarely served to extract political concessions, pushing too hard on the Cairo government for revision of well-established economic policies can be counterproductive.[23] Popular resistance to change will surely increase if it appears that the regime is buckling under foreign pressures. It confirms the charge by opponents that the government is willing to sacrifice traditional social and economic commitments to the people. The fear that haunts many U.S. officials is that the United States might find itself tied to a financially dependent yet also politically resentful client state.[24]

The seemingly powerful weapon available to the United States—to withdraw aid as a means of assuring compliance on economic policy reforms—may not only fail (as an Egyptian government continues to subsidize consumption, whatever the budgetary sacrifices), but could engender a bitter anti-U.S. mood as it further cripples the local economy. As earlier discussions point out, the political decision that AID transfer each year large sums of money to Egypt removes the possibility that the promised support level will be lowered or tied to tough assessments about the Egypt's performance on projects or made contingent on the enactment of specific economic changes. For any sizable cuts in U.S. aid would be quickly exploited by opponents of the regime, both domestic and foreign, as proof of the unreliability of the United States and of the government's basic error in pursuing pro-Western policies. (Reactions are less predictable if U.S. foreign aid cuts affecting Egypt are part of larger across the board spending cuts forced on the Congress by the new deficit reduction law.) Egyptian leaders thus know that money authorized under the ESF program will be spent in one fashion or another. Should mutually agreeable projects not be found, the political context assures the Egyptians that the funds will be used in some form of commodity assistance—the most unfettered, direct kind of aid. Ironically, then, the most likely means of "punishing" the government is to move aid into a category of earmarked assistance that is, in fact, usually the preferred type. Conversely, a satisfactory performance by the Egyptians could be "rewarded" by continued support for programs that are not necessarily the government's highest priority, and that, in any event, bring a slower disbursement of funds. Under these conditions, the government has still less incentive to undertake tough reforms that are certain to be politically risky.

The Alternatives

To the question of whether U.S. aid during the decade has been a success or failure, there can be no simple answer. Any assessment depends on what aid efforts could hope to accomplish, were expected to accomplish, did in fact accomplish, and for whom. The answers are certainly likely to vary depending on what criteria are used. If measured by the United States in strictly political terms, the program has probably gotten its money's worth. The billions spent may be a reasonable price to pay for a peace between Egypt and Israel and a domestic order in Egypt that permits the high degree of continuity in Egypt's foreign policy. The physical evidence is sufficient that aid has made a sizable contribution to rehabilitating and stabilizing Egypt's economy. Commodity financing undoubtedly enabled the country to overcome its severe foreign exchange deficit early in the program. U.S. aid has been more than marginal in its timely injection of capital and technology and in helping to upgrade Egypt's capacity to recognize and analyze its development problems. Development projects, however slow to be implemented, have begun to strengthen several areas of the economy's infrastructure and have slowed the rapid deterioration of others. The life of the average Egyptian is probably better off for there having been a U.S. aid program. Health and educational facilities are surely improved over the pre-1974 period. Moreover, although the contribution of many forms of assistance are measurable, the benefits to Egypt of a process of institution building and the transfers of attitudes and skills may not be calculable even after a decade of aid.

Yet, as these chapters show, the massive U.S. program can hardly be labeled a success story if judged by the proportion of promised dollars actually disbursed, the projects completed, and the popular image of the U.S. role. Those who expected that U.S. assistance would by the mid-1980s have stimulated massive foreign investment in Egypt's industries are surely disappointed. Despite the aid, Egypt has been unable to construct the kind of productive and equitable economy that so many Egyptians and Americans had anticipated. The country is actually less self-reliant today in many critical sectors, especially food, and U.S. aid probably bears some of the responsibility. Most industries have failed to become competitive, whether in domestic or foreign markets. Some elements in the society have done poorly relative to others in the overall economic expansion that began in the late 1970s. As with the government-to-government aid transfers anywhere, financial and technological support enhances the status and power of existing elites. In helping to sustain elements of a dual economy, external aid has, even if unintentionally, had less to offer low-income segments of the economy tied to traditional activities and values. The registered gains have not altered basically the structural conditions that account for Egypt's large underemployed and unemployed urban population. The creation of employment opportunities for the country's masses was a basic objective of AID. A valid question is, then, could there have been appreciably better use of the aid funds during the decade, and were there preferable alternatives to U.S. economic assistance?

Most U.S. officials would admit that the United States has not always chosen the optimal development strategies for Egypt. They concede that there appears to be too little to show for the large dollar amounts invested in Egypt during the decade. In view of the political requirements that large sums of money be spent quickly and because of the shortage of viable projects in the early years, undoubtedly some undertakings were ill-conceived and funds wasted. Nevertheless, officials also contend that U.S. aid, together with other foreign assistance, was never by itself sufficient in scale to assure a productive and equitable economy. The significance of foreign aid for Egypt has not been as great as either its advocates or detractors have argued. Minimally, it could carry the country through a period of crisis and at its best could help stimulate more rational investment and development decisions by the Egyptians themselves. Although the United States, EEC countries, and Japan provide a large piece of the government's development budget, the enormity and complexity of the task in Egypt make it unlikely that aid programs can alone yield solutions. It is hardly possible for aid to make more than a dent in such problems as urban unemployment, low industrial productivity, and the rising birth rate. The handsome growth rate in the economy and rise in real income of many Egyptians after 1977 are traceable not so much to foreign aid as to the sharp increase in petroleum export revenues and workers' remittances.

Observers in and outside the aid program have pointed out that the project approach emphasized by the United States spreads aid funds too thinly for any development impact. The very size of the program, it is often conceded, has resulted in inefficiencies and scattered efforts. It also invited the paralyzing procedural requirements in the delivery of assistance that confounded the Egyptians as well as the AID mission in Cairo. These critics argue that incremental aid funding by sector should have been adopted from the outset. A smaller, more specialized AID mission could have sufficed and the necessary commodity program handled, like P.L. 480 grain agreements, by U.S. Embassy personnel. Far fewer, more carefully chosen U.S. contractors and experts might have been employed, and only a handful of top U.S. economists would have been sufficient to advise the Egyptians on sectoral or macrolevel decisions.

A highly modified U.S. approach that hands over to Egypt more responsibility for its own development does not of course guarantee enhanced stature and survivability for the regime. The strong probability that U.S.-financed but entirely Egyptian-managed programs would also fail to realize popular expectations might actually leave the government *more* exposed to criticism. Foreigners could not be held accountable for uncompleted projects or waste and corruption. Ironically, a hands-off policy by the United States would probably lead to accusations by some Egyptians that the United States, interested only in buying political support, had failed to met its full responsibilities for Egypt's development.

Egypt would appear to have limited options in substitution for U.S. supplied commodities, technical assistance, and private capital investments. Many Egyptians expect Arab countries to come to the rescue. Renewed official Arab economic aid could compensate for much of the value of U.S. nonmilitary grants and loans. If restored to its earlier form, Arab government assistance would assume the form of budgetary supports, untied to specific projects, allowing the Egyptian authorities to shop around internationally for goods and services. As mentioned, private Arab investment did not entirely disappear during the economic trade boycott of Egypt that followed the accords with Israel. It was far less, however, than in the mid-1970s when it accounted for more than one-half of all private foreign investments.[25] Arab economies have all along remained critical to Egypt, if only for the estimated $3 billion in foreign currency revenues that come from remittances by the more than 2 million Egyptians employed throughout the region. With improved relations, modest increases in trade with regional states are likely, though the commercial and concessional sales with Western Europe and Japan could be expected to take up more of the slack left by a U.S. departure from the aid scene. The Soviets and their European allies are, moreover, always in the wings, ready with countertrade deals to win a political foothold. Realistically, however, a reorientation that broke the U.S. aid connection would carry with it political choices and economic risks that the present Egyptian government seems unwilling to face.

Arab money comes, of course, with its own political strings attached. Egypt is not prepared at present to accept the price of this aid if it requires early, renewed confrontation with Israel and the costs of a military mobilization. Private Arab sources have proven fickle in the past and are often uninterested in those economic sectors accorded priority by the Egyptian government. Arab government aid may be neither reliable nor generous in periods of declining oil revenues and with OPEC in disarray, and during times when political distractions, such as the defense of Iraq, require massive financing. Indeed, the level of Arab financial support in the region has fallen off sharply since peaking in 1977. No sources of economic assistance can match the concessional terms and reliability and size of U.S. grain sales to Egypt and be expected to duplicate the level of U.S. development aid activities. It is difficult to conceive, moreover, of a rupture of relations with the United States, leaving behind unpaid debts and bad feelings, that would not also affect broader political and economic ties to Western governments and undermine the confidence of international creditors. The Mubarak government is in no rush to weaken its military ties with the West, surely not as long as it still perceives threats to Egypt's security from Soviet-armed Libya and Syria, and from a vengeful, volatile Iran. The Cairo government has instead asked for faster delivery of advanced U.S. military equipment and assurances of continued high levels of support. It may be more important than ever, with the strains in relations with the United States, that the Mubarak regime be able to demonstrate to a popular audience the payoffs from U.S. aid.

As for Soviet ties, no government or even major opposition group seriously contemplates embarking on a new communist bloc economic and military dependence as long as the bitterness of the pre-1972 period lingers. Nor is there reason to expect, in view of its past experiences, including Egypt's unpaid $11 billion debt, that the Soviets will be anxious to sink large sums of money into the country without promise of mutual economic benefits and greater political control.[26] A final option for Egypt, to try insulating itself from the international economy and striving for self-sufficiency, seems least probable. Any Egyptian government would find politically suicidal so sharp a constriction in domestic consumption. President Mubarak, in his cautious efforts to normalize relations with the Arab and communist countries, seeks not so much to replace the U.S. aid program as to supplement it.

A consensus holds that the United States, especially through its commodity assistance, holds a powerful lever for political influence over Egypt that will not succeed if applied too blatantly but that used more subtly can gain Egypt's sympathy and cooperation. Perhaps as a result, U.S. assistance to Egypt since 1975 has not been finely tuned to signal approval (or disapproval) of all Egypt's international policies. Clearly, the aid does not buy the United States a compliant ally at the UN. This is amply demonstrated by Egypt's voting in the General Assembly. In 1984, while U.S. Western allies were in agreement with the U.S. position approximately 80 percent of the time (and Israel sided with the United States nearly 90 percent of the votes), Egypt was at odds diplomatically with the United States in 87 percent of the votes (75% in 1983), a rate higher than the majority of Third World countries in the assembly.[27] Even so, Egypt was supportive in several key votes. By paying homage to the Camp David accords and following the letter if not the spirit of the peace treaty with Israel, Egypt is able to convey enough of its gratitude for U.S. aid to retain an essentially favorable public image in the United States and limit complaints among U.S. lawmakers.

Egypt does not, to be sure, occupy center stage in U.S. strategies for the region as it did in the late 1970s and while President Sadat lived. It was then certainly the fulcrum around which U.S. designs for a peace in the region revolved. But in the mid-1980s, most U.S. options for a general peace settlement seem to have run out, and, if any country in the region does, Jordan rather than Egypt appears to hold the important cards. Egypt's leaders at times show concern about this declining attention by Washington's foreign policymakers but also feel confident that they hold some bargaining chips and that strategic concerns will continue to keep U.S. aid flowing, with or without a peace process. The United States is seen as having an indefinite stake in Egypt's economic stability and military defense, if only to prevent the Soviets from regaining undue influence. (For much the same reason, the Mubarak regime may be willing to let the economy drift and avoid unpopular economic reforms in the belief that, in the end, the country's political allies will come to the rescue with financial assistance, even the hard-to-please IMF.) With

Israel's security always a top concern in the United States, Washington would seem to have enough motive to sustain its supportive role in Egypt as a means of holding chances of a new Egyptian-Israeli conflict low. Remaining opportunities for warming the "cold peace" between Cairo and Jerusalem may depend on the United States as an active catalyst. Curiously, the link since 1975 between U.S. aid to Egypt and Israel probably counts as much as anything to assure that programs for Egypt are able to hold their ground despite Washington's more skeptical view of foreign aid. The Israeli lobby in Washington not only offers no challenge to Egypt's privileged political status but Egypt no doubt benefits from the lobby's access to U.S. congressmen.

Israel's armed actions in Lebanon and the crises of late 1985 severely tested the limits of Egypt's cooperative relationship with the United States. However, the events also revealed a great deal about the Cairo government's commitment to inherited policies. In these difficult periods, Mubarak never directly threatened to end Egypt's political and economic alignment with the United States. Nor did he renounce the search for a peaceful settlement of issues with Israel. Any confrontation that he sought with Israel was political, never military. The Egyptian ambassador was recalled only after the refugee camp massacres left Mubarak with little choice in view of popular anger. Israel's diplomatic mission in Cairo remained in place, and shipments of the 40,000 barrels of oil per day that Eygpt sells to Israel were uninterrupted. When in September 1982, President Reagan announced his peace formula, Egypt welcomed the initiative and also insisted that both the U.S. approach and the later Fez Plan of the Arab states be consistent with the Camp David accords. In subsequent crises involving terrorism aimed at the United States and Israel, Mubarak urged the Reagan administration not to become so distracted with avenging these acts as to neglect resolution of the larger Middle East conflict.

Consistency is found as well in Mubarak's willingness to cooperate in U.S. strategic planning. Joint U.S.-Egyptian exercises are no longer conducted with the fanfare they received in the wake of the Sadat assassination. They were suspended in the aftermath of the Lebanon invasion but were resumed in 1983, and joint maneuvers with air, sea, and land units were again conducted in 1985. On a more regular basis, the U.S. military has access to Egyptian bases. The United States quietly uses Egyptian military airfields in the Cairo area and in the southern part of the country. Where Mubarak has balked, and Sadat had done the same, is in allowing the appearance that Egypt has abrogated responsibility for its defense planning. The war games with the United States are officially at Egypt's request, and an Egyptian spokesman emphasized in 1985 that U.S. troops would leave Egypt immediately the exercises.[28] Negotiations broke down in 1983 regarding U.S. financing of $525 million for upgrading the airbase at Ras Banas when the Egyptians refused an overt U.S. presence in connection with the prepositioning of equipment and rejected the control demanded by Washington. However, a scaled-down agreement was later negotiated. For along with the military exercises, Mubarak is prepared to go some distance, despite criticism from both his left and right domestic opposition, to avoid deeply offending the United States and thus assure continued large-scale military aid.

Conclusion

The "special relationship" between the United States and Egypt that has existed since 1974 remained largely intact through 1985 despite the increased strains. The U.S. economic aid program is the most important manifestation of that relationship and an on-going measure of its health. The two countries seem agreed that changes must occur in the aid process that has prevailed during the program's first decade. Uppermost is the need for U.S. efforts to become better identified with Egypt's own long-term aspirations and priorities. To sustain mutual respect and cooperation between the countries, the United States probably will have to agree to some middle ground between what the Israelis have in aid transfers and the project approach that has left many Egyptians impatient and resentful. Most likely the United States will have to give greater attention to Egypt's public enterprises, thereby overcoming ideological inhibitions in doing so. As an aid donor, the United States has the right to assure that its resources are not squandered and to promote economic policy reforms. But it cannot expect easy or early actions by the Egyptians and may have to approve partial and incomplete changes in the hope of deeper reforms later.

Egypt is too important a country politically and economically in the Middle East for it to have become as excessively dependent as it has been on foreign resources. Not all of the country's dependence is, as has been argued here, indefensible or economically irrational. Without U.S. and other aid from the West, Egypt could not have met its consumption requirements and also had available the needed investment for economic development. External financing and advice also have helped the government to better mobilize its resources and realize potentially higher rates of return on its investments. Even so, the large-scale foreign aid adversely affects production incentives in several sectors and underwrites ill-conceived economic policies. The United States and other foreign donors have also inhibited more self-generated processes of change that might have sacrificed fewer societal values and avoided the concentration of aid benefits in certain economic groups. Significantly, an aid program that fails to achieve a better mix of political expectations and careful assessments of economic needs and capabilities exposes the Egyptian government to criticism, domestic and foreign.

No regime can expect domestic acceptance for very long with popular and elite perceptions that outsiders are interfering in the country's internal affairs and deciding its future. Ajami describes an historical pattern in Egypt that begins with a dialogue with the West and ends in an "embrace and surrender." He observes that the legitimacy of the modernizers and liberal nationalism vanishes and its adherents are exposed as collaborators.[29] U.S. assistance strikes increasing numbers of Egyptians as just such a detraction from their leaders' authenticity and a diminishment of the nation's Islamic and Arab heritage. A real danger exists in the exploitation of cooled U.S. relations by Egypt's opposition parties and militant fundamentalists trying to fan anti-U.S. sentiment as a means of reversing the Mubarak government's policies. Even if the continuity with the United States that has been a prime feature of the Mubarak regime is not immediately threatened, it has become harder to sustain. Those countries such as the United States that have a high stake in the regime's survival may have to take greater cognizance of the constraints on the present Egyptian policymakers even as they may try to bolster the leadership's courage and ability to pursue its own liberal economic convictions. It is probably necessary to support the Egyptian government in drawing up workable counterstrategies to dependence that will increase self-reliance in certain economic spheres. These changes can be in the long-term interest of Egypt's economic partners and political friends; for otherwise, the country is likely to become a serious financial liability and, because of increased instability at home, an inactive or unreliable actor in the region.

Notes

1. Some portions of this chapter appear in a revised form in Marvin G. Weinbaum, "The Prospects for Economic and Political Cooperation in U.S. Egyptian Relations," *Journal of South Asian and Middle Eastern Studies*, Vol. 9, no. 1 (Fall 1985): 3–25.

2. One Egyptian scholar argues that some of AID's problems stem from its title in Arabic in which the word *maowna* meaning charity is used. He suggests instead the use of the words *tamwil* or *musaadat* meaning finance or assistance in English since charity is perceived by Arabic speakers to be demeaning to the recipient. Dr. Ibrahim El Eisawi, a professor at the Institute of National Planning, Cairo, at a seminar on "Assessment of USAID Programs in Egypt," March 15, 1983.

3. Saad Eddin Ibrahim, "A Description of Egypt: The American Style," *Al-Ahram Al-Iqtisadi* (Cairo), October 11, 1982.

4. Interview with Dr. Alphone Asis, Institute for National Planning, *Al-Ahram Al-Iqtisadi*, October 11, 1982.

5. Ibrahim, *Al-Ahram Al-Iqtisadi*.

6. Interview with Judge Zakaria Abdel Aziz, *Al-Ahram Al-Iqtisadi*, November 8, 1982.

7. *Al-Ahram Al-Iqtisadi*, October 18 and November 1, 1982. Also, *Akhbar El-Yom*, October 1, 1983.

8. *Al-Ahrar*, Cairo, February 14, 1983.

9. Ibrahim, *Al-Ahram Al-Iqtisadi*.

10. *Al-Gomhouria*, September 20, 1963.

11. Donald S. Brown, *Economic Development in Egypt—An American's Perspective* (Cairo: U.S. International Communications Agency, March 1982), pp. 23–24.

12. Heba Ahmad Handoussa, "Conflicting Objectives in the Egyptian-American Aid Relationship," Earl Sullivan, ed., *Impact of Development Assistance on Egypt*, Cairo Papers in Social Science 7. Monograph no. 3 (September 1984), p. 88.

13. *Al-Ahram Al-Iqtisadi*, February 24, 1984.

14. During a public appearance in May 1984, President Mubarak revealed that he had no idea that AID was involved in funding for the construction of public schools and had already helped to build 125 schools in Egypt.

15. *Al-Ahram*, January 17, 1982.

16. Muriel Allen, *The Journal of Commerce*, September 2, 1983.

17. Handoussa, "Conflicting Objectives," p. 87.

18. U.S. Agency for International Development, "Congressional Presentation, FY 1984, Egypt, Annex IV; Near East," March 1983, p. 24.

19. These charges were aired by Jack Anderson in *The Washington Post*, February 3, 1984.

20. *MEED*, October 7, 1983, p. 3.

21. U.S. General Accounting Office, "The U.S. Economic Assistance Program for Egypt Poses a Management Challenge for AID," a report to the administrator, Agency for International Development, July 31, 1985, p. 40.

22. The Mubarak government transmitted to Washington in early 1985 a confidential document portraying Egypt as a "strategic asset" and requesting additional U.S. aid. It was in fact written by U.S. citizens under contract to the Egyptian government. *The New York Times*, January 16, 1985. In December 1982, when there were some fears that the United States was planning to reduce its financial commitment to Egypt, the American Chamber of Commerce in Egypt cabled President Reagan to support funding for Egypt.

23. Undisguised efforts to use food aid as a blunt instrument of U.S. foreign policy in Egypt are described in Marvin G. Weinbaum, *Food, Development, and Politics in the Middle East* (Boulder, Colo.: Westview Press, 1982), pp. 123–124.

24. Ellen B. Laipson, "Egypt and the United States" (Washington, D.C.: Congressional Research Service, Library of Congress, June 4, 1981).

25. Victor Lavy, "The Economic Embargo of Egypt by Arab States: Myth and Reality," *The Middle East Journal*, Vol. 38, no. 3 (Summer 1984): 432. Lavy

puts private Arab investments in 1982 at only 16 percent of foreign investments in Egypt.

26. Mohammed Heikal, *Autumn of Fury: The Assassination of Sadat* (London: Andre Deutsch, 1983), p. 152.

27. Based on a State Department, congressionally ordered study, Robert W. Kasten, Jr., "Our Alleged UN Friends," *The New York Times*, June 17, 1985. Also, *Time*, March 26, 1984, p. 27.

28. *The New York Times*, July 31, 1985.

29. Fouad Ajami, *The Arab Predicament* (New York: Cambridge University Press, 1982), p. 116.

Selected Bibliography

Abdalla, Nazem. "Egypt's Absorptive Capacity."*International Journal of Middle East Studies* 16, no. 2 (May 1984):177–198.

Abdel-Khalek, Gouda. "Looking Outside or Turning Northwest? On the Meaning and External Dimensions of Egypt's Infitah." *Social Problems* 28, no. 4 (April 1981):394–409.

Abdel-Khalek, Gouda and Tigner, Robert L., eds. *The Political Economy of Income Distribution in Egypt.* New York: Holmes and Meier, 1982.

Ajami, Fouad. *The Arab Predicament.* New York: Cambridge University Press, 1982.

Alderman, Harold, von Braun, Joachim, and Sakr, Sadr Ahmed. "Egypt's Food Subsidy and Rationing System: A Description." Research Report no. 34. Washington, D.C.: International Food Policy Research Institute, October 1982.

Amin, Galal Ahmad. "External Factors in the Reorientation of Egypt's Economic Policy." *In Rich and Poor States in the Middle East,* edited by Malcolm H. Kerr and El Sayed Yassin, pp. 285–315. Boulder, Colorado: Westview Press, 1982.

Arab Republic of Egypt, Central Agency for Public Mobilization and Statistics. "Status of the Open Door Economy in the A.R.E. Up to December 21, 1981." Edited by Shafick S. Hassan, February 1982.

Arab Republic of Egypt, Ministry of Agriculture and the USAID. "Strategies for Accelerating Agricultural Development: A Report for the Presidential Mission on Agricultural Development." July 1982.

Arab Republic of Egypt. *Egypt's Five Year Plan, 1982/83–1986/87.* December 1982, Part 1.

Aswan Aid Donors. *Egypt: Economic Update 1981.* Cairo: Fiani and Partners, 1981.

Aulas, Marie-Christine. "Sadat's Egypt: A Balance Sheet." *MERIP Reports,* no. 107 (July-August 1982):6–18.

Ayubi, Nazih N. M. *Bureaucracy and Politics in Contemporary Egypt.* London: Ithaca Press, 1980.

Badeau, John S. *The Middle East Remembered.* Washington, D.C.: The Middle East Institute, 1983.

Bednar, James F. "Stopgap: U.S. Assistance is Buying Time for Development." *Agenda* 5, no. 2 (March 1981):11–14.

Brown, Donald S. "Egypt and the United States: Collaborators in Economic Development." *The Middle East Journal* 35, no. 1 (Winter 1981):3–14.

Brown, Donald S. *Economic Development in Egypt—An American's Perspective.* Cairo: U.S. International Communications Agency, March 1982.

Bruton, Henry. "Egypt's Development in the 1970's." *Economic Development and Cultural Change* 31, no. 4 (July 1983):679–703.

Burns, William J. *Economic Aid and American Policy Toward Egypt, 1955–1981.* Albany: State University of New York Press, 1985.

Caporaso, J. A. "Dependence, Dependency, and Power in the Global System." *International Organization* 32:13–44.

Chilcote, Ronald H. *Theories of Development and Underdevelopment.* Boulder, Colorado: Westview Press, 1984.

Cooper, Mark N. "State Capitalism, Class Structure, and Social Transformation in the Third World: The Case of Egypt." *International Journal of Middle East Studies* 15, no. 4 (November 1983):451–469.

Duvall, R. D. "Dependence and Dependencia Theory: Notes Toward Precision of Concept and Argument," *International Organization* 32, no. 1 (Winter 1978): 51–78.

Heikal, Mohamed. *Autumn of Fury: The Assassination of Sadat.* London: Andre Deutsch, 1984.

Hinnebusch, Raymond A. "From Nasser to Sadat: Elite Transformation in Egypt." *Journal of South Asian and Middle Eastern Studies* 8, no. 1 (Fall 1983):24–49.

Hopwood, Derek. *Egypt: Politics and Society, 1945–1981.* London: George Allen and Unwin, 1982.

Horton, Alan W. "Egypt Revisited." *American University Field Staff Reports*, no. 23, African Series, 1981.

Hudson, Michael. *Arab Politics: The Search for Legitimacy.* New Haven, Connecticut: Yale University Press, 1977.

Ibrahim, Saad Eddin. "Superpowers in the Arab World." *The Washington Quarterly* (Summer 1981):81–96.

Kinley, David, Levinson, Arnold, and Lappe, Frances Moore. "The Myth of Humanitarian Aid." *The Nation,* July 11–18, 1981:42.

Laipson, Ellen B. "Egypt and the United States." Washington, D.C.: Congressional Research Service, The Library of Congress, June 4, 1981.

Lavy, Victor. "The Economic Embargo of Egypt by Arab States: Myth and Reality." *The Middle East Journal* 38, no. 1 (Summer 1984):419–432.

Lewin, Ernst A. "Foreign Aid: Paying the Pittance." *Washington Quarterly* (Winter 1981):189–195.

Lubar, Robert. "Reaganizing the Third World." *Fortune* (November 6, 1981):81–90.

Marden, Keith, and Roe, Alan. "The Political Economy of Foreign Aid." In *Foreign Aid and Third World Development,* edited by Pradip K. Ghosh. Westport, Connecticut: Greenwood Press, 1984.

McPherson, Peter. "Statement by the Administrator of the Agency for International Development: Background Briefing on the AID Budget," February 1, 1984.

McPherson, Peter. "Administrator's Message to Employees of the Agency for International Development: State of the Agency," March 2, 1984.

Morss, Elliott R. and Victoria A. *U.S. Foreign Aid: An Assessment of New and Traditional Development Strategies.* Boulder, Colorado: Westview Press, 1982.

Moustapha, Mohamed Samir. "American Food Aid and Its Impact on the Egyptian Economy." Memo no. 1328, Arab Republic of Egypt, The Institute of National Planning.

Owen, Roger. "Sadat's Legacy, Mubarak's Dilemma." *MERIP Reports*, no. 117 (September 18, 1983):12–18.

Parker, John B. and Coyle, James R. "Urbanization and Agricultural Policy in Egypt." *Foreign Agricultural Report*, no. 169 (September 1981):1–47.

Paul, Jim. "Foreign Investment in Egypt." *MERIP Reports*, no. 107 (July-August 1982):17.

Richards, Alan. "Egypt's Agriculture in Trouble." *MERIP Reports*, no. 84 (January 1980):3–13.

Richards, Alan. "Ten Years of Infitah: Class, Rent, and Policy Stasis in Egypt." *Journal of Development Studies* 20, no. 4 (July 1984):323–338.

Reed, Stanley. "Dateline Cairo: Shaken Pillar." *Foreign Policy*, no. 45 (Winter 1981-82):175–185.

Schuh, G. Edward. "Integration in Programming and Implementing Development is More than Projects." A paper delivered at the Conference on the Economic Challenges of Peace. Alexandria, Egypt, July 7–16, 1980.

Scobie, Grant M. *Food Subsidies in Egypt: Their Impact on Foreign Exchange and Trade.* Washington, D.C.: International Food Policy Research Institute, Research Report no. 40, August 1983.

Sommers, William. "Rescuing AID." *Foreign Service Journal* 59, no. 5 (May 1982):15–21.

Spero, Joan E. *The Politics of International Economic Relations,* 2nd Edition. New York: St. Martin's Press, 1981.

Springborg, Robert. "Patrimonialism and Policy Making in Egypt: Nasser and Sadat and the Tenure Policy for Reclaimed Lands." *Middle Eastern Studies* 15, no. 1 (January 1979):49–69.

Stork, Joe. "Egypt's Debt Problem." *MERIP Reports,* no. 107 (July-August 1982):12–13.

Sullivan, Earl L., ed. *Impact of Development Assistance on Egypt.* Cairo Papers in Social Science 7, Monograph no. 3 (September 1984).

Thompson, Anne M. "Egypt, Food Security and Food Aid." *Food Policy* 8, no. 3 (August 1983):178–186.

Tolchin, Martin. "The Role of 'Barnacles' in Foreign Aid." In *The New York Times,* July 5, 1983.

U.S. Agency for International Development. "Egypt: Country Development Strategy Statement, FY 1983." Washington, D.C., January 1981.

U.S. Agency for International Development. "Country Development Strategy Statement, FY 1984, Annex: Benefits of Growth." Washington, D.C., February 1982.

U.S. Agency for International Development. "Congressional Presentation, FY 1984, Egypt, Annex IV: Near East," April 1982.

U.S. Agency for International Development. "Congressional Presentation, FY 1986." Washington, D.C.: April 1985.

U.S. Agency for International Development, Bureau for Program and Policy Coordination. "AID Policy Paper: Food and Agricultural Development," May 1982.

U.S. Agency for International Development, Cairo. "The Decentralization of Local Government in Egypt; A Special Assessment for USAID." Office of Local Administration and Development, Development Resources and Program Support, January 1983.

U.S. Agency for International Development. "Country Development Strategy Statement, FY 1985." Washington, D.C., April 1983.

U.S. Agency for International Development. "Change." Cairo: Arab World Printing House, 1983.

U.S. Agency for International Development, Cairo. "Mid-Term Evaluation of the Decentralization Support Fund." Office of Local Administration and Development, February 1983.

U.S. Agency for International Development, Cairo. "Status Report of United States Economic Assistance to Egypt as of January 1, 1984."

U.S. Agency for International Development. *Ten Years of Progress, USAID in Egypt.* Cairo: Arab World Printing House, 1984.

U.S. Agency for International Development, Cairo. "The Government of Egypt's and USAID's Decentralization Sector Support: Its Accomplishments and Expenditures." Offices of Local Administration and Development and Urban Administration and Development, April 1984.

U.S. Agency for International Development. "Country Development Strategy Statement, FY 1986," April 1984.

U.S. Agency for International Development, Cairo. "Decentralization Sector Review Analysis, Sector II PID." Office of Local Administration and Development, May 1984.

U.S. Agency for International Development, Cairo. "Rural and Urban Development: The Decentralization Program." Office of Local Administration and Development, February 1984.

U.S. Agency for International Development. "Near East Reviews, Staff Utilization Report for Egypt," September 12, 1984.

U.S. Department of Agriculture. "Fact File." *Foreign Agriculture* (February 1984):13.

U.S. Department of Agriculture. "Egyptian Agriculture and the U.S. Assistance Program." Office of International Cooperation and Development, Technical Assistance Report, no. 2, June 1979.

U.S. Embassy, Cairo, "Economic Trends Report: Egypt." April 17, 1984.

U.S. Embassy, Cairo, "Economic Trends Report: Egypt." April 15, 1985.

U.S. General Accounting Office. "Report on Egypt's Capacity to Absorb and Use Economic Assistance Effectively." Washington, D.C., September 15, 1977.

U.S. General Accounting Office. "Report to the Congress: U.S. Assistance to Egyptian Agriculture: Slow Progress After Five Years," March 16, 1981.

U.S. General Accounting Office. "Report to the Chairman of the Committee on Foreign Affairs, House of Representatives, on Private Sector Involvement in the Agency for International Development's Programs," August 26, 1983.

U.S. General Accounting Office. "The U.S. Economic Assistance Program for Egypt Poses a Management Challenge for AID." Report to the Administrator of the Agency for International Development, July 31, 1985.

U.S. House of Representatives, Committee on Foreign Affairs. "Economic Support Fund Programs in the Middle East." Report of a Staff Study, April 1979.

Waterbury, John. "The Implications for U.S.-Egyptian Relations of Egypt's Turn to the West." A paper delivered at a Conference on "Politics and Strategies of USAID in Egypt," at the Middle East Center, University of Pennsylvania, January 18–20, 1978.

Waterbury, John. *The Egypt of Nasser and Sadat: The Political Economy of Two Regimes.* Princeton, New Jersey: Princeton University Press, 1983.

Weinbaum, Marvin G. *Food, Development, and Politics in the Middle East.* Boulder, Colorado: Westview Press, 1982.

Weinbaum, Marvin G. "Politics and Development in Foreign Aid: U.S. Economic Assistance to Egypt, 1975–1982. *The Middle East Journal* 37, no. 4 (Autumn 1983):636–655.

Weinbaum, Marvin G., Naim, Rashid. "Domestic and International Politics in Egypt's Policy Reform." *Journal of Arab Affairs* 3, no. 2 (Fall 1984):157–188.

Weinbaum, Marvin G. "Food Security and Agricultural Development Policies in the Middle East." *Policy Studies Review* 4, no. 2 (November 1984):341–350.

Weinbaum, Marvin G. "Egypt's *Infitah* and the Politics of U.S. Economic Assistance." *Middle Eastern Studies* 21, no. 2 (April 1985):206–222.

Weinbaum, Marvin G. "The Prospects for Economic and Political Cooperation in U.S.-Egyptian Relations." *Journal of South Asian and Middle Eastern Studies*, 9, no. 1 (Fall 1985):3–25.

Weinbaum, Marvin G. "Dependent Development and U.S. Economic Assistance in Egypt." *International Journal of Middle East Studies* 19, no. 2 (May 1986).

Whitaker, Jennifer Seymour. "They Don't Miss Sadat." *Atlantic Monthly* (January 1982):16–18 and 22–23.

White, John A. *The Politics of Foreign Aid.* New York: St. Martin's Press, 1974.

World Bank. *World Development Report 1980.* New York: Oxford University Press, 1980.

World Bank. "Arab Republic of Egypt's Domestic Resources Mobilization and Growth Prospects for the 1980s." Report no. 3123-EGT, December 10, 1980.

World Bank. "Arab Republic of Egypt: Current Economic Situation and Growth Prospects." Report no. 4498-EGT, October 5, 1983.

World Bank. *World Bank Tables.* Washington, D.C.: Johns Hopkins University Press, 1980.

Yassin Sayeed, Palmer, Monte, and Laila, Ali. "Innovation and Development: The Case of the Egyptian Bureaucracy." A paper presented at the Annual Meeting of the Middle East Studies Association, Chicago, November 1983.

Index